THE MAGYARS
Their Life and Civilisation

To John Steane!

To thank all your kindness, patience
and support.

Love: Réka and Gábor
Virágos

Pécs, 2003. 05. 03.

GYULA LÁSZLÓ

THE MAGYARS

Their Life and Civilisation

CORVINA

Published in 1999 by Corvina Books Ltd.
1051 Budapest V., Vörösmarty tér 1, Hungary

First published in Hungarian as *A honfoglaló magyarok*, Corvina, 1996

Translated by Timothy Wilkinson

This book has been published with support from the Hungarian Ministry of Cultural Heritage
and the Frankfurt '99 Kht.

ISBN 963 13 4807 5

Design by Éva Illyés

CONTENTS

PREFACE   6

THE CARPATHIAN BASIN
IN THE CONQUEST PERIOD   7

THE CONQUERORS: ÁRPÁD'S MAGYARS   10

WRITTEN SOURCES ON THE CONQUEST   17

MAGYAR VILLAGES OF THE CONQUEST ERA   23

BURIAL CUSTOMS   28

FEATURES OF CLAN ORGANIZATION   34

AGRICULTURE, ANIMAL HUSBANDRY   37

HUNTING, FISHING   40

CRAFTS   42

DRESS   53

WARFARE   56

THE CYCLE OF LIFE   58

RELIGION, BELIEFS, AND CULTURE   61

EPILOGUE   68

NOTES   69

LIST OF ILLUSTRATIONS   71

**A READER ON THE MAGYARS
OF CONQUEST-PERIOD HUNGARY**

I. CHRONICLES AND SOURCES   77

II. ANCESTRAL HOME, ANCESTRAL CULTURE   92

PREFACE

Yet another book about the Magyar conquest of Hungary? Is it really needed given the many excellent essays and books on the subject that have appeared over the last few decades – not least the splendid material provided by György Györffy in the Hungarian Academy of Science's *History of Hungary?*[1]

Usually a book justifies itself by presenting previously unpublished data. But can that be said of this volume? In my humble view, the answer is 'Yes'. The works which have been available to date have been concerned mainly with the chronology of events, or sought their causes, or surveyed the archaeological relics. Yet, except for a short monograph by István Dienes[2] and my own *Life of the Conquest-period Magyar People,* relatively little attention has been given to the conquerors themselves, their everyday life, their occupations, and their intellectual interests. It is those aspects that are the main subject of my present offering.

How, the reader may ask, can we be certain about things which have surely been lost in the mists of time? Is this book not just another excuse to evoke those dazzling images of the past so beloved of Romantic dilettantes? Emphatically not! In what follows the reader will always know what parts of the text are founded on fact and what is surmise or guesswork. It is the reality of the lives led by the Magyars of the Conquest period that I seek to unfold, not the fantasies of some dream-world.

Having myself devoted more than fifty years to the topic, I am sometimes depressed by the thought that virtually every educated Hungarian seems to fancy himself an archaeologist of sorts. Symptomatic of this are periodic attempts to 'prove' the antiquity of the Magyar people by appeals to 'evidence' of the most outlandish nature – whether it be supposed links with the lost continents of Mu or Atlantis, or references in the hermetic texts of the Arvisuras, or claims that the Hungarian language is the key to deciphering Egyptian hieroglyphs, or assertions that the ancestral figures of Hunor and Magyar may be discerned in an Assyrian depiction of a prince hunting in his chariot – and such attempts are by no means confined to our emigrant communities but thrive in Hungary too. This, then, was a further reason for writing the book. I am well aware, however, that my own standpoint, which is simply that, in the words of our seventeenth-century soldier-poet Miklós Zrinyi, we Hungarians are 'not a whit inferior to any other nation', will not go far enough for those who believe that we have our Magyar ancestors to thank for civilizing the world – or even that those ancestors, as the denizens of some distant galaxy, were the bringers of 'advanced culture' to our benighted Earth.

In describing the Magyars during the period around their entry into the Carpathian Basin, I take the whole region into my perspective even though the modern frontiers of Hungary have shrunk to just its central core.[3] Today's map is not that of Conquest-era Hungary – or, for that matter, of Hungary when the Magyars first entered the country. I also wish to make use of the findings of environmental geography, for mankind is not just master of the animal and plant kingdoms but has been shaped at least as much by them in turn. In this I learned from Béla Hankó, wise man of zoology, that animal species introduced into the Carpathian Basin alter within just a few generations to acquire subtly new traits due to the changes in climate, vegetation, and mode of rearing. This must apply to man as well: it is just that we have not yet found the measure of the changes that have taken place for our own species. I shall have no more success, but the intention is there.

One further thing by way of preamble. This book is by a researcher who for half a century has been preoccupied with this one period and with the Magyar people. I have never been able to content myself with mere surveys of the latest findings in my field but continually have felt the need to pose fresh questions, to keep casting a sceptical eye on my own and others' earlier work. And I have often found that what was once regarded as established fact sustains other explanations.

I have striven, as best I can, for complete objectivity and dispassionateness. I cannot deny, however, that in the process of writing, sober objectivity may have given way, on occasions, to love for my chosen subject and respect for our ancestors. I hope this fault is pardonable and that, to borrow a phrase from the Árpádian epic of our great poet Mihály Vörösmarty, by aiming to 'make later centuries see in fitting manner' our forebears – the Magyar people of the two Conquests of Hungary – I may yet win favour with the Muses.

Gyula László

THE CARPATIAN BASIN IN THE COQUEST PERIOD

The idea has become deeply rooted in the literature on Hungary's history and archaeology that the face of the Carpathian Basin was little more than an untouched wilderness until it was transformed by regulation of the River Tisza during the early nineteenth century. There is some truth in that, but it is misleading nevertheless to think of the land as having been a 'wilderness' even when the Árpádian Magyars entered it in the late ninth century. The dire state of neglect attested to by the land surveys performed in the 1770s, in the reign of Joseph II, was largely a relic of the Turkish occupation, for it was barely a century before that the Alföld (Lowland) plain had been liberated from the Turks. What the surveys showed, then, were not the primeval conditions but the havoc that had been wrought under the Turks, when the land was abandoned to the rule of scrub and marsh. The Middle Danube basin had been inhabited by various agricultural peoples for three or four thousand years before the Magyars entered it, and they had already radically changed the face of the country, modifying it to human needs over the course of those millenia.[4]

In the Neolithic Age farming tended to be limited to patches of cleared land near to the dwelling places and was associated with rearing of domestic animals. This form of economy did not change greatly later on, in the Copper and Bronze Ages, except that larger territories were brought under cultivation as villages began to emerge and thus fields had to support an ever-growing population. The Iron Age was already an era of largescale construction (Nagytatársánc, Jakabhegy, etc.), with the primeval landscape now being altered by the appearance of villages, fortresses, and great barrows (kurgans). This activity grew apace under the Celts, whilst under Roman rule it proceeded as far as the building of roads, towns, aqueducts, and chains of fortifications, at least in Panno-

---

1. Route followed by the Magyar tribes on their way to the Carpathian Basin.

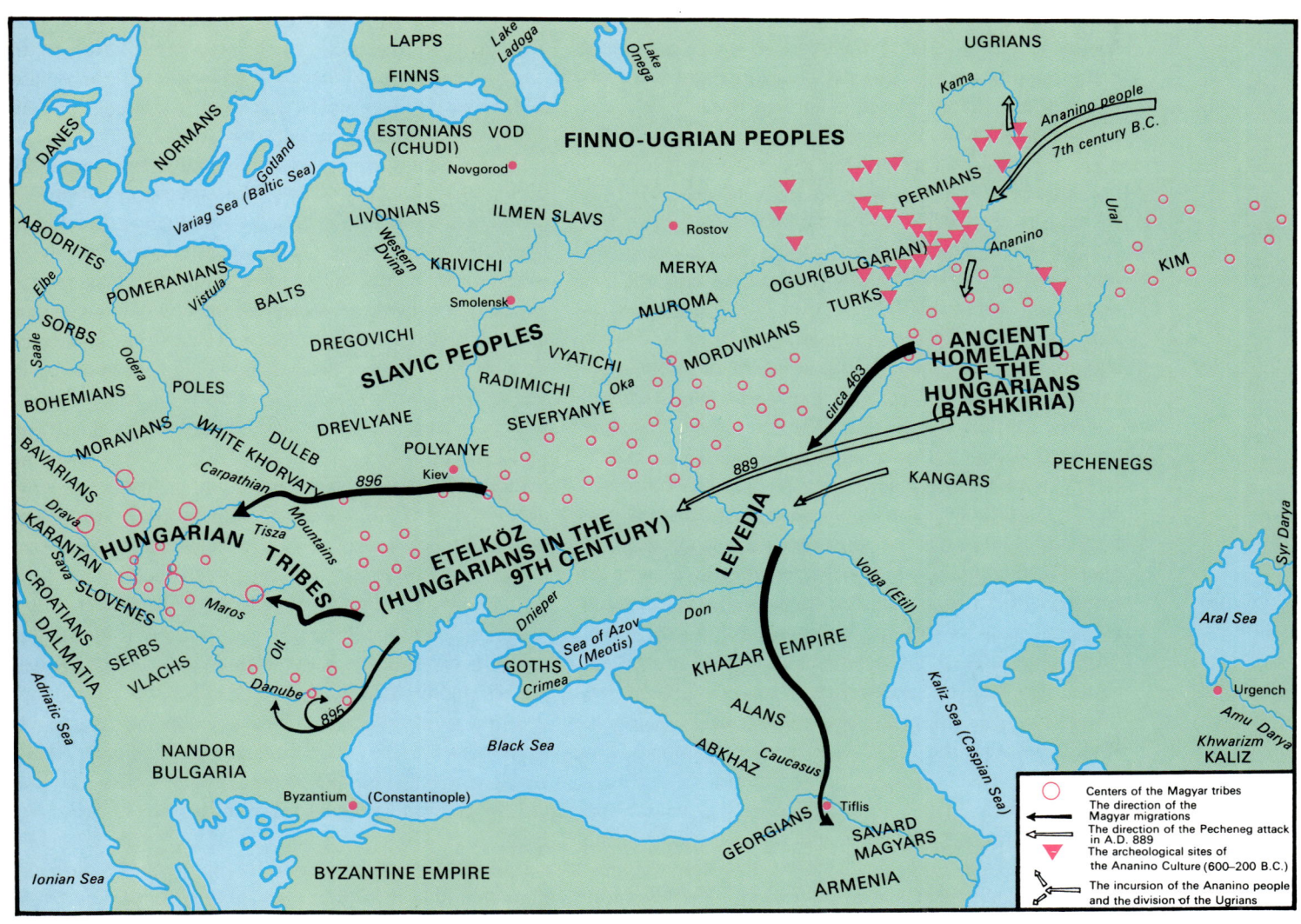

nia (Transdanubia). Other parts of the country remained largely as they had been, though here too massive constructions were undertaken, notably the so-called Csörsz ditch comprising several hundred kilometres of defensive lines. Meanwhile the influx of peoples into the Carpathian Basin from north, east and west continued. In Transylvania, under the castle-building Dacians and the one-and-a-half centuries of Roman domination, something of a counterbalance to Pannonia emerged.

It would be a mistake to believe that the great movement of peoples across Europe during A.D. 309-700 was associated with a reversion of the Hungarian countryside to the wild. To give just one example, it is now accepted that viticulture, established by the Romans, was not abandoned with the arrival of the Lombards and Avars; indeed, it manifestly survived to the time when Árpád's people conquered the land. The 'late Avars', or Onogurs, settled in extensive villages, which called for – or perhaps were made possible by – a high level of agriculture and animal husbandry. Some of these villages had populations of a thousand or more, necessitating amongs other things the development of a road network of sorts. Livestock breeding, by and large, was at a similar level to that in the Hungarian village at the beginning of this century. Obviously, just as the indigenous population did not die out with the arrival of the Magyars, nor did their animals.

This should serve as proof enough that Árpád's people did not occupy an untamed wilderness but took over a terrain that had already been shaped by man. The countryside certainly differed markedly in character – and hence opportunities, from its present form, which reflects not only the regulation of its waterways but also deforestation of the Alföld (both by the Turks as well as earlier ages) and climatic changes, but it sustained arable farming and animal-rearing mode of life which the Magyars themselves adopted and which has continued ever since.

The Middle Danube basin is the most westerly of the wooded steppe-lands of Europe. It was no accident that Scythians, Sarmatians, Huns, Avars, Magyars, Cumanians and Pechenegs did not migrate further westwards whereas Germanic peoples did so, with the Goths proceeding as far as Spain, the Vandals into North Africa, and the Lombards into Italy. The latter were primarily agricultural peoples whilst the steppe-dwellers were primarily nomadic pastoralists. Thus the Magyar occupation of the Carpathian Basin conformed to established pattern, and as their marauding campaigns, both before and after the Conquest, covered the length and breadth of Europe, if they had found a territory that suited them better, clearly they too would have moved on.

In some respects the country that was setttled by the equestrian Magyars under Árpád was reminiscent of, though not identical to, the vast prairie tracts of their erstwhile homeland, the Etelköz, on the Pontic steppes. The Carpathian Basin is ringed by mountains and this imposed limits on their grazing grounds in winter and summer. It was no use their migrating southwards during the winter for there the snow cover and the cold were just as bad as in the north; conversely, it was no use their moving northwards in the summer because the heat was the same and the grassland was just as parched as in the south. To side-step the problem, a doubling between grassy plain and forest came to take the place of the annual north-south treks of their earlier transhumant way of life. Traces of this can still be found in the duplication of many place-names, with the same toponyms, in the same order, recurring at the foot of a wooded hill as on the plain. Attention was first drawn to these regularities by Bálint Hóman, István Györffy and László Makkai.[5] The restriction in pasturage led to important changes in animal-rearing practices as, despite their smaller extent, the new grazing grounds had the great advantage that their grass was ten times lusher than it had been in the old homeland. György Almásy wrote of the Bashkir and Kirghiz steppes that the grass there is shrub-like in habit and not like the continuous expanses of meadow found in Hungary.[6]

Let us now turn to the geography of the territory settled by the Magyars and what we can learn from those who lived there centuries before the waterways were brought under control. We may start with the anonymus notary to King Béla III, who possibly wrote his *Gesta Hungarorum* around the turn of the twelfth century.[7] Several scholars have cast doubt on this work's authenticity as an account of the nation's past, considering it more a medieval romance than a proper history, but the same cannot be said of its geographical descriptions, even if they were written in the light of the limited knowledge of those times. At the fortress of Ung, Anonymus tells us: *The leader [Árpád] and his people beheld the fertility of the land, its abundance in all kinds of game, and how well stocked in fish were the Tisza and Bodrog rivers; and for these reasons they were inexpressibly delighted at the land.*

At much the same time as Anonymus was writing, Otto, bishop of Freising, who passed through *Hungary* with his crusader army in 1147, described the country as 'God's own paradise', whose plains were irrigated by 'noble streams and waters', the game of its forests beyond counting, and 'its beauty as enchanting as its luxuriant land is fertile.'[8] A detailed account can be had from Hungaria, written by Miklós Oláh, archbishop of Esztergom, in 1536.[9] This text depicts the country as a Canaan flowing with milk and honey, from its description of the richness of the black soil to its listing of wines, fruits and fauna. Its reference to great herds of horses and cattle confirms the observations of an earlier visitor to Hungary (in 1433), the knight Bertrandon de la Brocquière, who mentioned the vast herds of horses that ranged the open plains of the Alföld.[10] Other early sources provide similar testimony.

One reason for this luxuriance is undoubtedly the fortunate position of the Carpathian Basin.[11] It lies approximately equidistant from the North Pole and the Equator and thus within the temperate zone, whilst its remoteness from the sea is also a major climatic factor. 'Sparse woodlands, marshes, and willow-beds besides river flats are interspersed with steppe-lands of great extent,' writes one geographer. The annual flooding of the rivers, nowadays awaited with such trepidation by those who live near the dikes that hold the waters back, in older times was a veritable blessing because its deposits of mud, richly charged with organic matter, fertilized the land but did not threaten the settlements, which were built on higher ground. Vast reed-beds and boggy marshlands afforded refuge for the inhabitants of the hamlets, on their hilly prominences, against enemies; by retreating there they managed to ride out the devastations wreaked by Tatar and Turkish armies. The same water-meadows were an ideal habitat for hunter and fisher, but these, and all other aspects of rural life, were changed by the land-drainage and waterway-regulation schemes of the modern age. Such reclamation added new productive land to the Alföld but also impoverished its human and animal populations, rendering them more exposed. Places where trains and automobiles now speed along without hindrance in olden days had to be crossed by canoe, and only those who knew the secrets of the marshes would dare to enter these environs. When pastures could no longer be replenished they became exhausted, thus precipitating a parallel crisis in the herdsman's life too. The oakwoods of these marshy regions fell victim to clearance long before land reclamation took place, as the timber was required to build the fortresses of the border-defence system. As a result of all these changes, the movement and composition of the atmosphere itself has altered over the course of the last millenium, and along with it the history, the very lifebreath, of the present populace.[12]

It was not only trees, vegetation and men that were modified by the gradual changes in environment; certain of the animal species that had lived there also had to adapt or died out. Their bones have survived as relics among the finds at old settlements (in domestic refuse) and burial sites, from which we know that the region once sustained aurochs, bison, buffalo, elk, brown beer, lynx, beaver, musquash, rats, moufflon, sheep, goats, swine, horses, dogs, cats, donkeys, poultry, turkeys, coneys, pheasant, hazel-grouse, mallard and, of course, roe- and red-deer. Nowadays, apart from the deer, only the smaller species live on in the wild. It is noteworthy that domestic animals account for some 95% of the bones found at early settlements, whilst hunted game occurs only sporadically.[13]

These were the flora and fauna that greeted the Árpádian Magyars on their entry into Hungary. But what kind of people was it that battled its way across these lands and settled down as victors among the indigenous inhabitants, most of them presumably Onogur-Hungarians? Since they differed in their way of life from the latter population, the Magyars concentrated on occupying territories that their predecessors had made little use of. Consequently, the 'aboriginals' were left to their own devices, largely undisturbed, or rather, as defeated and subject peoples, were accomodated into the Árpádian state.

What did Árpád's people look like, anthropologically speaking? Or, to put the question in its commonly posed form, which of the present-day ethnic groups corresponds to the 'true' Magyar type? The natural historian, Ottó Herman, devoted a book to the subject under the title, *The Physiognomy and Character of the Magyar People*.[14]

Who, then, are the descendants of the 'original' Magyars in today's Hungarian population? Even to raise the question in this way is inappropriate, because it implies that Árpád's people was itself ethnically pure and of uniform appearance, whilst differing from the inhabitants whom they found here. Fundamentally misguided enquiries of this kind were seen as of burning importance particularly in the pre-World War II era of racial mythification, when some became so detached from reality as to teach that 60% of the Hungarian population was of 'Germanic type' and arrogantly proclaimed that they were the progeny of the 'master race'. Others have argued for a Greek origin, others again hold that the Magyars were the direct legatees of Sumerian civilization and language, whilst some extol the Árpádians as preservers of the culture of the submerged Oceanic continent of 'Mu', or profess themselves able to decipher – and with ease – Egyptian hieroglyphics as codes for the Magyar language. I shall not continue the list of cock-eyed and fanciful notions which have so often attracted impressive trains of adherents.[15] Let me simply recall a line from a Hungarian folksong that folklorists are fond of quoting: 'The true Magyar type is neither brown nor white.'

Measurements of the skeletal remains from graves of the Conquest era – that is, the graves of Árpádian Magyars – and from the so-called commoners' cemeteries that were started half century later, have been compared with anthropomorphometric data for the present-day Hungarian population.[16] According to this evidence about 60% of the Conquest Magyars and today's population are of similar build to Turkish peoples. Anthropologists also observed some time ago that the Mongoloid elements which are discernible in the modern population can be traced back to the original inhabitants of the country, the Onogurs. As it is impossible to believe that the Mongoloid features were in some mysterious manner held back from being expressed up until the time that Árpád's Magyars appeared on the scene, one is bound to conclude that a significant proportion of Hungary's Onogur population must have survived the arrival of the Magyars and, after interbreeding with them, formed the basis of the Hungarian people of the Middle Ages and our modern era.

This is one of the thorniest problems for anthropological research in Hungary – all the more as the cemeteries of the Árpádian Magyars are so small, whereas those of the Onogurs contain many hundreds of graves, and in some instances a thousand or more. This raises the question whether the small population of Árpádian Magyars in fact ever did assimilate into the native Onogur-Hungarian population. That, in essence, is the basis for my own hypothesis of a 'double' Conquest or occupation of Hungary by related Magyar peoples. However, we should not get ahead of ourselves, for up to now we have been dealing just with the manifestations of life – plant, animal and human – in the Carpathian Basin.

We may summarize this short chapter, then, by saying that Árpád's people did not colonize a land in its primeval condition but one that had been inhabited and cultivated for millenia – a land, moreover, where their immediate predecessors, the Onogurs (i.e. late Avars), were already present and, as we shall see, with a sparse Slavonic population dwelling among the mountains of its periphery. Let us turn, then, to the historical aspects of the Árpádian Magyars.

THE CONQUERORS: ÁRPÁD'S MAGYARS

It has already been mentioned that the Árpádian Magyars were not of uniform stock; rather, several racial strains commingled in their ethnic character. This inevitably leads to the question, eternally raised by Hungarians, of what were the origins of their people? When and how did they emerge as a people? The answers supplied by different lines of enquiry are not consistent. Thus written chronicles, linguistics, anthropology, archaeology, and so on each provide a different testimony and it is hard to steer a 'true' course in the tangle when we lack the reassuring hand of a reliable helmsman. Let us look at the various testimonies in order.[17]

Up to the middle of the last century there were essentially no real doubts about the early history of the Magyars, because their Old Testament and Scythian origins were explicitly vouched for by the chronicles. Nobody questioned this and the country's nobility was proud to proclaim its descent from Hunor and Magyar, whilst Attila the Hun was celebrated as the foremost of their glorious ancestors. The Bible taught that after the Flood only Noah and his family survived and that mankind was descended from Noah's three sons, Shem, Ham and Japhet. Now, according to Anonymus, Japhet's son was Magog, and it was from the latter that the Magyar nation took its name, and from his progeny that 'mighty King Attila' was descended. Attila was succeeded by Ügyek, and Ügyek's son was Álmos, whose later descendants became the kings of Hungary. This line of descent passed down through the Scythians, who thereby were direct ancestors of the Magyars. Anonymus relates of the Scythians, with evident narrative relish, that:

The Scythians were wise and gentle, they did not till the soil, and there was almost no crime amongst them. Moreover, they did not have houses built by craftsmen but merely tents made from felt. They consumed meat, fish, milk and honey, and had aromatic wine in plenty. They dressed in pelts of the pine-marten and the skins of other wild animals. Of gold, silver, and pearls they had as much as there are pebbles...

Philologists have shown that this description was taken from a western European manuscript entitled *Exordia Scythica*, and there they have been content to leave the matter, although it would have been and still is – pertinent to ask what reason Anonymus had for borrowing a description of Scythia. The answer, obviously, is that the idea of kinship with the Scythians was already implanted in the Hungarian nobility's mentality.

This idea was further elaborated by Simon Kézai, a priest at the court of King Ladislas IV the 'Cuman', in his own *Gesta Hungarorum*, composed around the year of 1283.[18] Here we find the story of Hunor and Magyar of Japhet's house – a marvellous relic of the ancient folk history of the Hungarians. It was from this that János Arany drew the inspiration for his enchanting canto, *Legend of the Wondrous Stag*, which he wrote to make up for the presumed loss of a Hungarian national epic. Here it must be noted that the Stag legend had already been recorded in the tenth century by the Saxon chronicler Widukind, a friar at the abbey of Corvey, so it was an ancient tradition among the Hungarians and there is no need to look to Gottfried of Viterbo for our chronicler's sources, as some historians have believed. In the Stag legend the history of the two related peoples, the Huns and the Magyars, begins with the brothers Hunor and Magyar, and there is also reference to connections with the Bulgars and Alans. To quote directly from Kézai's version of this, one of the most beautiful Hungarian legends:

After the Flood had destroyed all flesh except for Noah and his three sons, Shem, Ham and Japhet, seventy-two tribes were descended, from these three when the Flood had ceased ... the giant Menrot, the son of Thana of the house of Japhet ... moved to the land of Evilath after the confusion of languages, a country which in those days was called Persia. There his wife Eneth bore him two sons, Hunor and Magyar, from whom the Huns and Magyars were descended.

It can have been no accident that the Khazars, too, were supposed to have descended from Japhet and Magog. Could it have been that a wish on the part of Magyar 'notables' to be considered equal in rank to their erstwhile Khazar suzerains dictated this identity of genealogy to their chroniclers? Or even that many of them were actually Khazars? 'Now one day,' Kézai continues his account:

...they happened to go out hunting, and in a desert place a stag leapt out before them. They gave chase, whereupon it fled before them into the marshes of the Maeotis [i.e. around the Sea of Azov]. There it quickly vanished from their sight and although they searched for a long time they could find no trace of it. At length, having wandered through these marshes, they realized that the land there was very suitable for cattle-grazing, So they returned to their father and, having obtained his permission, migrated to the marshes of the Maeotis with all their possessions and settled there. Now the Maeotis region borders on the province of Persia, though apart from one small passage it is surrounded on all sides by sea. It has no rivers, but is rich in grass, wood, fowl, fish and game. It is difficult to approach and leave. Nevertheless they reached the marshes of the Maeotis and remained there for five years without stirring. In the sixth year they began to roam, and in a deserted spot they came upon the wives and children of the sons of Belar, who were living in tents, their husbands being away from home. They seized them and made off with them as fast as they could, together with all

their possessions, to the marshes of the Maeotis. Now among the children they captured there happened to be two daughters of Dula, king of the Alans. One of them Hunor took as his wife, the other became the wife of Magyar. It is from these women that all the Huns are descended... And after they had spied out the province of Scythia, they moved with their children and livestock into that homeland...

[trans. G. F. Cushing]

Historians have pointed out some interesting aspects of this descent myth. The customs of taking women from outside the man's tribe (exogamy) and the man moving in with his wife's kindred, and the memory of contacts with the Bulgars (Belar) and Alans (Dula) are hinted at in mythological terminology but nevertheless refer to real events. The role of the two brothers is particularly noteworthy because in the descent myths of other pairs of related peoples – Tatars and Mongols, Onogurs and Kutrigurs, Voguls and Ostyaks – the two branches always stem from two brothers. Linguists see the word 'Onogur' as the source for the name Hunor, so that the myth speaks of the Onogurs and Magyars as kindred peoples.

However, we must not lose sight of the fact that Anonymus was not writing a chronicle of the Magyar people as a whole but of its aristocracy. This has usually been brushed to one side by historians, who have identified Anonymus's text as dealing with the Conquest and ancient history of the nation. Kézai follows the same tradition, as do later scribes, including the authors of the two most widely read texts – János Thuróczy, with his *Chronica Hungarorum* of 1488, and Gáspár Heltai, whose Hungarian translation of Antonio Bonfini's *Rerum Hungaricarum Decades* was printed under the title *Chronica az magyaroknac dolgairól* (Chronicle of the Affairs of the Magyars) in 1575. Nevertheless, it is by no means certain – at least in principle – that the Hungarian common people and its ruling class shared the same origin, and it is my belief that the distinction is worth making as it clarifies many issues that have hitherto been unresolved. An extreme example of this is the difficulty of otherwise explaining how nomadic warriors and herdsmen like the Magyars became sedentary farmers, but this is a point to be taken up later on. At any rate, Hungarians themselves, especially those of the nobility, firmly believed that their ancestors were the Scythians and the Huns. And even as the Finno-Ugrian school was winning the argument academically, major poets like János Arany, Endre Ady and Árpád Tóth continued to insist that the Hungarians had their ancient cradleland in Asia and that they were Turkic in character.

When first propounded in the late eighteenth century, the thesis of a Finno-Ugrian origin provoked an outcry amongst educated Hungarians. What it asserted, as will be discussed below in more detail, is that the Magyars had descended from the Finno-Ugrian ethnic group, and that the prevailing belief in a Scythian-Hunnish connection was simply a romantic fantasy. Neither the Scythians, nor the Huns, nor the Avars, it was suggested, were related to

the Magyars, the closest kindred peoples were the Voguls (Mansi) and Ostyaks (Hanti). All other opinions were labelled unscientific and firmly to be rejected. A century and a half of systematic linguistic researches since then have indeed demonstrated undeniably strong ties between Hungarian and the Finno-Ugrian family of languages. This view ultimately shut out the opposed school of thought, argued with great passion by Ármin Vámbéry, that the Magyars were a Turkic people whose language had been Finno-Ugrianized. I do not wish here to resurrect the details of the polemic between the 'Ugrians' and the 'Turks', as the two factions have been nicknamed,[19] but I have my own reservations about the linguists' position on the grounds that other views are still tenable, as even distinguished Finno-Ugrian scholars such as Dezső Pais have conceded.

How, then, is the affinity of Hungarian to the Finno-Ugrian linguistic family accounted for? First of all, it is claimed that the Magyars are a people of Finno-Ugrian origin which attained a separate linguistic and ethnic identity in the course of a stepwise splintering of a once-unified Finno-Ugrian tribal grouping. In this view, there was in the beginning a single 'Uralic' people, comprising the future Finno-Ugrian and Samoyed peoples, in which the seeds for the later linguistic divisions may have existed as dialects. The first group to break away from this Uralic community, around 4000 B.C., was that of the proto-Samoyeds. They migrated eastwards to the Siberian territory where they have lived to the present day, eventually fragmenting into five major linguistic units. The original homeland of the still-unified proto-Finno-Ugrian people was along the Kama river, as is indicated by the fact that the names given to trees in the languages of this group refer in part to the mixed deciduous forest species of Central Europe, in part to conifers indigenous to the

Siberian taiga. These two forest types co-occur only in the Kama region, where the taiga protrudes into the predominant Central European forest habitat. The Uralic people, and later on the proto-Finno-Ugrians, were crammed into this small territory, and not long after the Samoyed emigration, a proto-Finno-Permian block began to move westwards, leaving a proto-Ugrian remnant behind (whether this was to the east or west of the Ural mountains is a detail that is still hotly debated). One group which splintered away from the proto-Finno-Permians as they began this westward trek formed the basis of the modern Zyryan (Komi) and Votyak (Udmurt) peoples, whilst along the River Volga two tribes of Mordvins, the Moksha and Erzya, together with the Cheremis, broke away to leave a proto-Finnic core which made its way to the Baltic Sea where it eventually fragmented into Finns, Estonians, Vepsians, Vodians, Karelians, and others. In this manner a chain of Finno-Ugrian linguistic communities is supposed to have arisen, with the Magyars originally staying within the proto-Ugrian group but later, around 1000 B.C., cutting itself adrift and beginning an independent existence.

This hypothesis, as it has been elaborated by successive generations of linguists, admittedly has a rational appeal, supplying a plausible explanation for the linguistic links between the Finno-Ugrian peoples. Each of these peoples, the linguists contend, has lost most of what was once a common word-stock, replacing it with a welter of words that have arisen by process of separate linguistic evolution to serve their respective communication needs. Notwithstanding that process, a core vocabulary of essential words of common etymology has been retained in all the languages.

What alternative interpretation can archaeology bring to this otherwise almost universally endorsed hypothesis? Before broaching this, let it be noted that the Finno-Ugrian kinship of the Magyars has been assailed in a great variety of ways, especially by certain Hungarian emigrants in the West, but also here in Hungary. I should emphasize, however, that the evidence of systematic affinities in vocabulary, grammar and phonological features cannot be gainsaid. Nevertheless, the linguistic case has been constructed on false premises, which admit – indeed, necessitate – a different manner of approaching the problem. Let us look at the main objections which can be raised against the premises.

1. First of all, the hypothesis postulates a densely interspersed group of ancient Uralic peoples which later set off on a migratory route and eventually dispersed. Anthropological studies of primitive peoples, however, have shown convincingly that when it comes to dependence on a hunting and fishing economy one cannot possibly speak of a large population densely packed into a small area. Approximately one hundred square kilometres of land are required to provide the means of subsistence for a single family of 8-10 members. What is more, this cannot be just any randomly chosen area but can only comprise the narrow bands of land and forest bordering streams and rivers. In reality, even the smaller settlements of the present-day Ob-Ugrians are spaced some 20-30 kilometres apart along the river banks. Thus the belief that vast areas of forest can be designated as an 'ancient homeland' is mistaken.[20] Accordingly, the linguistic hypothesis starts from a premise that is false and should not be used to support the linkage of the languages in question.

2. From this putative (though, as we have seen, unrealizable) *Urheimat* there are supposed to have been emigratory streams to both the east and west, with smaller groups peeling off and later going on to develop as separate peoples. That should be a matter of historical and archaeological record – a matter on which linguistics is unable to offer evidence. Each people's past material culture – or at least what remains of it – would have been preserved in the ground and should thus be accessible to excavation. By collation of the finds one should then be in a position to reconstruct the movements of each people's culture. In this respect the known archaeological finds provide not a shred of support for a west-to-east or an east-to-west migration; there are a few scattered manifestations, but it would be a gross mistake to interpret these as indicating a corresponding movement of peoples. Quite apart from that, archaeologists of the individual Finno-Ugrian peoples generally admit that their people developed in much the same locality as they now inhabit, give or take a little. Indications of migration in the archaeological record may well be a mark of actual movement of a people, though not necessarily so. A phenomenon of this kind does, in fact, occur with sites on the Baltic coast and near the Ural mountains, in the form of so-called 'Sperrings' ware, but this could have evolved in each area independently of the other; in so far as there is any connection between the areas, the data are more consistent with a west-to-east migration. The Sperrings pottery evidence is vital because several leading Soviet researchers (Foss, Chernetsov) have come to the conclusion that the decorations on the bowls and other ware constitute clan symbols; thus it was not the pottery itself so much as the clans which 'migrated'. Alas, even in this respect there is no good evidence for a series of offshoots along an east-to-west migratory axis.[21] Thus the conjecture that the nascent Finno-Ugrian peoples splintered and embarked upon their independent existences in the course of an east-to-west migratory movement remains unproven and, moreover, seems improbable.

3. Let us turn to the proposition that each of these separate peoples came to forget most of the word-stock of their originally common language, and that the vocabulary not shared with the other Finno-Ugrian peoples happened to develop after they had fragmented. This is, of course, pure speculation, even though it has acquired the status of dogma by dint of repetition. If one carefully studies the postulated 'forgetting' process, it is found to be just as poorly attested; what evidence there is tends to contradict the hypothesis. It is well known that the vocabulary of so-called 'primitive' peoples is much more detailed than that of peoples used to abstract modes of thinking. Accordingly, the vocabulary of the putative Uralic people must have been huge to cater to all aspects of their life. One must ask, therefore, whether it is reasonable to suppose that this enormous vocabulary was oblit-

3–4. Árpád Feszty, Ignác Ujváry, Pál Vágó: *The Magyar Conquest* (details from the *Feszti Panorama*) – *Árpád and his Chieftains, Attacking Magyar Horsemen.*

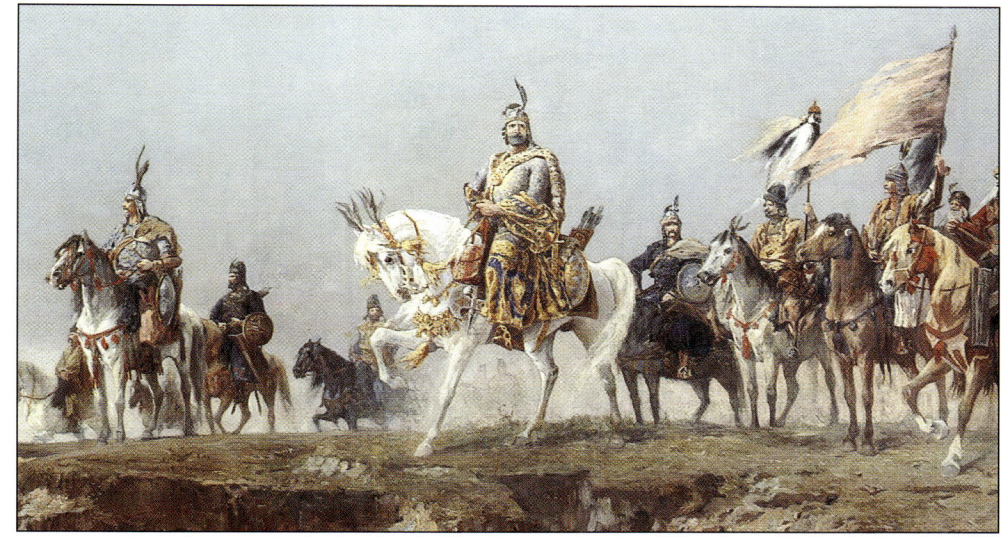

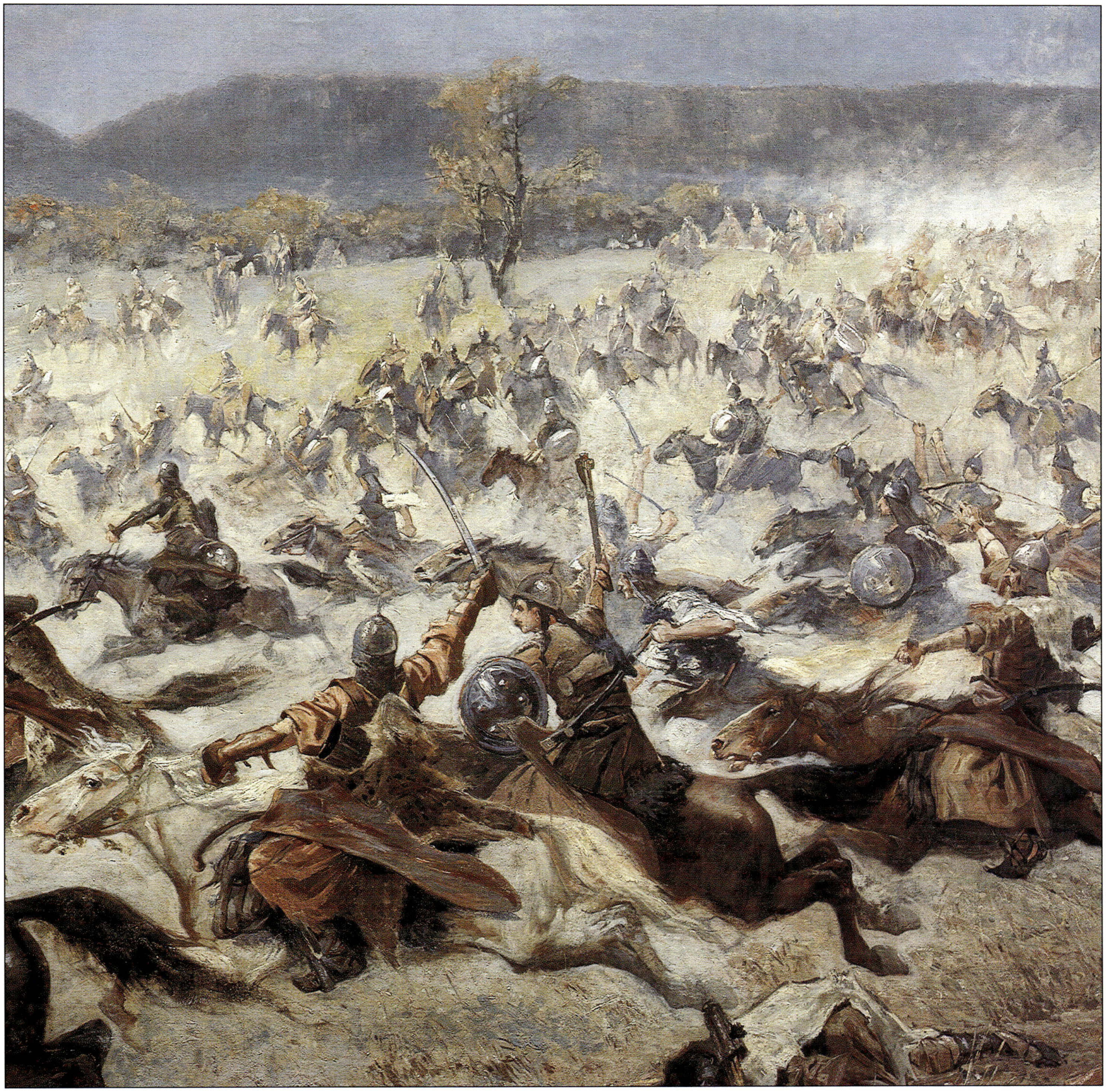

erated from the memory of each of the descendant peoples once they began their 'independient existences' so that each of them had to coin completely new words for the same large range of items. Would it not be simpler to suppose that it is the non-congruent word-stocks and grammatical features which were primitive, whilst the Finno-Ugrian features were innovations or borrowings? This does not detract a whit from the great and successful endeavours of Finno-Ugrian linguistics; it can accomodate everything that the linguistic historians have been able to determine, but is intensely sceptical about the historical inferences that they have made. A distinguished linguist, critical of my earlier book on Magyar prehistory, has reproached me for dabbling in linguistics. All I can plead is that, to the contrary, it is the linguists who have been dabbling with history.

To summarize, then, there is no evidence that the various Finno-Ugrian peoples had to re-invent much of their basic vocabularies during their respective 'independent existences'; rather, it is more natural to suppose that essential words would be the least likely to be forgotten. Following on from that, we should not overlook one of the lessons of physical anthropology, namely, that the Magyars had nothing in common with the people who are linguistically their closest kinsfolk, the Ob-Ugrians. Some investigators, such as János Jankó, noticed this almost a century ago, and certainly, had the linguists not diverted attention that way, prehistorians would have had no reason to seek the ancestry of the Magyars among the Ob-Ugrians.

Something should be said about the systematic phonological shifts that occur between related languages. It is indeed true that the phonetic form of a given word in the different Finno-Ugrian languages alters in a regular manner. Yet whenever any word is adopted by another language it is assimilated to the particular articulation and phonetic structure of that tongue. It is therefore at least equally plausible that this is why certain words sound one way in one Finno-Ugrian language and slightly but systematically different in another. This in turn leads straight to a second proposition: namely, words of the common Finno-Ugrian vocabulary did not 'evolve' serially from an ancient Uralic stock but they were originally loan-words, receiving a different articulation in each language according to the phonetic laws of that idiom. That is to say, the words did not evolve phonetically but assumed a different phonetic shape, according to specific rules, in each different linguistic environment. The same process operates, as anyone can observe, with loan-words in all living languages.[22]

The question now arises as to what was the source of the essential words that are common to the Finno-Ugrian tongues? Are we still justified in calling them related languages on account of these homologies? To put it another way, what was the language which loaned its stock of words for items of vital importance to the various vernaculars that existed along the northern perimeter of the forest belt and thereby brought them into relationship with one another?

Here I am obliged to fall back on a conjecture first put forward in an earlier work. My starting point is the evidence that characterizes what is called Swiderian culture, named for the late Palaeolithic site by the River Swider in Poland where it was first defined, penetrated, to greater or lesser degree, all the archaeological cultures of the northern perimeter of the forest zone. Swiderian culture extended from central Poland up to the Ural mountains and is divided into a number of subgroups on the basis of certain variations which are irrelevant for our purposes (the stratum of Swiderian culture was overlaid by Kunda-Sigirian culture, which in turn was succeeded by Neolithic pottery cultures). To reiterate, a Swiderian legacy, which shifted out of southern Russia as a branch of Eastern Gravettian industry, is present throughout the late Palaeolithic cultures of northern Russia in the third millenium B.C. What I envisage – and archaeological cross-evidence supports this – is that peoples dwelling in the territory to the north of Swiderian culture proper developed contacts with that culture and thereby acquired a stock of essential words. In this way various 'pidgin' languages could have developed in such a way that they were mutually inter-related, and perhaps even mutually comprehensible, in terms of the Swiderian 'lingua franca'.

This hypothesis serves to explain a great many things. For instance, Swiderian culture would supply a 'bridge' to account for the known link between proto-Indo-Germanic and proto-Finno-Ugrian peoples. It would also free us to treat those words which have been interpreted as having evolved during the 'independent existences' of the various Finno-Ugrian peoples, and which otherwise have nothing in common with one another, as belonging to the original word-stock of each people.

None of this runs counter to the hitherto established Finno-Ugrian ties, which are linguistic and not anthropological. But what it boils down to is that there was never a proto-Finno-Ugrian people as such, only a number of disparate peoples which became 'kinsfolk' by virtue of the fact that they all borrowed certain linguistic features from Swiderian culture. In effect, the position that the linguists have posited as being occupied by a Uralic people can be reconciled with the idea that the archaeologically demonstrated Swiderians provided, through their own idiom, the basis for the development of a chain of linguistic affinities. This naturally leads us on to ask what was this ancient Uralic or ancient Swiderian language like? We cannot give an answer to this but, considering that the Hungarian people, despite the decimations of a thousand years of adversities, is still twice as numerous as all the other Finno-Ugrian peoples together, it is surely not fanciful to speculate that it was the Swiderians who formed the nucleus from which the historical Magyar people gradually emerged. I would emphasize again that this new, and perhaps startling, line of conjecture not only does not conflict with the available linguistic evidence but, as a matter of fact, through its very acceptance of that evidence, has been able to generate further hypotheses.

5. Bertalan Székely: *Blood Contract*, 1896–97.

THE PROTO-MAGYAR CRADLELAND
BY THE KAMA

It was mentioned at the start of this chapter that linguists have identified the original homeland of the Finno-Ugrian peoples as being located in the Kama region[23] of the Urals on the grounds that this is where the tree species characteristic of both the Siberian taiga – the Siberian spruce [*Picea obovata*], Arolla pine [*Pinus cembra*] and larch [*Larix*] – and the Central European mixed decidu- ous forest – elm [*Ulmus*], oak [*Quercus*], alder [*Alnus*], lime [*Tilia*], etc., – coincide, and the names for these species in the languages of the various Finno-Ugrian peo- ples have common roots (though not consistently so, as will be noted later). This seemed to be an impeccable conclusion until attention was paid to the actual testi- mony of tree-pollen analyses, and these showed that the linguists had failed to take into account changes in the vegetational zones over the millennia. Plant pollens, due to their tough, waxy outer skin, persist almost indestruc- tibly in the soil so their analysis can reveal precisely what kind of vegetation, and in particular what kind of forest, covered a given area at different times. By collation of pollen analyses performed by the Moscow Institute for Plant Physiology, it has now become clear that the only time when the Siberian taiga and the Central European mixed deciduous forest were in contact was during the second millenium B.C. – and this is too late to have a bearing on Finno-Ugrian prehistory. So the territory sought by the linguists as the location of the putative

'ancient homeland' never existed. Around 5000-6000 B.C. – the period to which the 'Uralic' era had been dated – the taiga was still thousands of kilometres away from the Ural mountains and the mixed deciduous forest had only just begun its northward advance. More recent- ly, the linguist Péter Hajdú has re-examined the tree- name evidence, coming to the conclusion that the *Urheimat* was further to the north, in the tundra zone.[24] There is still a problem even with this suggestion, howev- er, in that no human life at all existed on the tundra dur- ing the period in question. The environmental geographi- cal approach has therefore proved to be just as unservice- able in support of the Finno-Ugrian hypothesis as the assumptions of a densely populated territory or migratory movements.

We need to separate out, once and for all, the well- founded evidence of linguistic affinities from the ama- teurish historical deductions that have been drawn from them by armchair scholars. The apparent contradiction, or *cul-de-sac*, that the linguists have driven themselves into is resolved if one turns to the Swiderian theory and at the same time notes that it is the appellations of the eastern tree species which occur among the more easterly Finno-Ugrian tribes, those of the deciduous trees which occur among the westerly peoples – in other words, each people named only the species in its immediate habitat.

In my opinion, then, the antecedents to the formation of the Magyars as an ethnic group should be sought somewhere in the region between central Poland and the Urals. It stands to reason that differences in dialect could have existed, indeed probably did exist, in a population that was spread out across the vast territory occupied by Swiderian culture. Whatever may have been the case in reality, this idea would extend our perspective on proto-Magyar prehistory back to the late Palaeolithic era.

It is more difficult to conceive what happened after that. Swiderian culture petered out some 5,000 years before the Christian era and persisted only vestigially in the lands to the north of the territory where it had flourished. In other words, the Swiderian-cum-Uralic people dispersed among the various subgroups of a Kunda-Sigirian population inhabiting the territory above the Russian foest belt (this has been shown in the archaeological record). We next find a slow advance towards the world of pottery vessels, the Neolithic Age, by which time fairly well-defined Combed and Pitted ware groups were established. If these patterns actually did represent clan symbols, then this may be the period of emergence of the individual Finno-Ugrian ethnic groups. Thereafter nothing that could be described as a general migration of peoples took place in these territories, so there is no support for any idea of a westward movement of Finno-Ugrian groups. Research into events of the millenia that intervened between this early prehistory and the Magyar conquest of Hungary has prompted a range of illuminating theories, but to survey these would lead far away from my present goal and into a continual stream of further questions.

There is a great deal that is uncertain about the speculations presented above, but then how can it be otherwise? None of us is blessed with total insight into the mists of the distant past. At all events, by the end of the eighth century A.D., when the Magyars burst on the European scene and we obtain the first written intelligence of the people who were to take over control of the Carpathian Basin, the Magyars had made their entry into history as a fully-formed, militarily strong ethnic group. It is to them – a people described by reliable Byzantine and Arabic sources as being one of the races of 'Turks' – that I confine my remarks in what follows.

WRITTEN SOURCES ON THE CONQUEST

The history of the Magyar conquest of Hungary and of Árpád's people has usually been written on the basis of Anonymus's description, for all the strictures that must be placed on his 'romance'.[25] This and all other Hungarian chronicles, however, were written down 300-400 years or more after Árpád's people had occupied the country, and they relied chiefly on the clan traditions of nobiliary families. A search for source material that was contemporary with the Conquest accordingly began more than two centuries ago. These endeavours were crowned in 1898, as a mark of the millenary celebrations of the Conquest, by the publication of the invaluable *A magyar honfoglalás kútfői*, 'Authorities on the Magyar Conquest' – which collected the texts of all the relevant sources in Hungarian translation. This important book was for a long time out of print and could only be consulted in libraries, but in recent years its main contents have been resurrected in a new popular edition prepared by György Györffy, the distinguished scholar of early Hungarian history, thus making new, critical translations of the sources relating to the Árpáds available to a wider public.[26]

Let us look at the Byzantine sources first of all. It lay in Byzantium's interest to obtain accurate intelligence about the peoples who threatened the northern borders of the empire so that it could prepare to deal with them in full knowledge of their idiosyncrasies. In his treatise *Taktiká*, Emperor Leo VI the Wise (886-912) provides copious details on the arts of war employed by the 'Turks', his name for the Magyars. 'They have a liking more for fighting at a distance, setting ambushes, encirclement of their enemy, simulated retreat and about-turning, and for the scattering of fighting formations,' he writes, among other things, these being the same as the tactics employed by the historical Turkic peoples. Leo's son, Constantine VII Porphyrogenitus (913-959) describes the Magyars with the freshness of recent experience, for he tells us that he gained his information directly from Árpád's great-grandson, Tormás, and the army commander, Bulcsu, who had happened 'just lately to be with us.' He lists the names of seven Magyar tribes: after the horde of Kavars, a group of dissident Khazar tribes that had placed themselves at the head of the Magyars, was the tribe of Neke [Nyek], second that of Megere, third Kourtugermatos [Kürtgyarmat], fourth Tarianos [Tarján], fifth Genach [Jenő], sixth Kare [Kér], and last that of Kase [Keszi]. These tribal names, in the form of the parenthesized equivalents of the Greek transliterations, survive in Hungary to the present day.

Alongside the Byzantine reports, the other significant sources are Arabic. These too needed to be authentic for it was on their strength that trading caravans and Islamic missionaries journeyed to the East and armies set off in search of conquests. The Arabic geographers in turn gathered new information from the leaders of these ventures. The most important of these sources for our purposes are Ibn Rusta (c. 930) and Gardìzi (c. 1050). The former records:

Between the country of the Bajanakiyya [Pechenegs] and the country of the Askal, who belong to the Balkariyya [Volga Bulgars], is the first [i.e. outermost] of the Magyar boundaries. The Magyars are a race of Turks and their king rides out with with horsemen to the number of 10,000 and this king is called Kanda [Künde or Kende]... They possess leather tents [covered yurts or wagons] and they travel in search of herbage and abundant pastures... The country of the Magyars contains many trees and much water and their ground is moist and they have many fields... The Magyars worship the sun and the moon.

[trans. M. Smith]

Gardìzi's remarks on their marriage customs have the directness of an ethnographer's report:

It is a custom when marrying that when a woman is sought in marriage a dowry is appointed in accordance with the wealth in cattle, less or more, belonging to that man. When they sit down to appoint that dowry, the father of the maiden brings the father of the son-in-law to his own house and whatever he has in the way of sable and ermine and grey squirrel and stoat and the belly of the fox... and brocade, he collects all of these skins together to the quantity of ten fur garments and folds them inside a carpet and fastens them on the horse of his son-in-law's father and speeds him to his house. Then whatever is necessary for the maiden's dowry which they have agreed upon such as animals and money and goods is all sent to him [i.e. the maiden's father], and at that time they bring the woman to the house.

[trans. M. Smith]

This splendid description might well have served Arabic traders as a guide to the kind of goods that they should take with them to the land of the Magyars, and what they could obtain in exchange.

The *Primary Russian Chronicle*, attributed by some to Nestor, recalls that the Magyars undertook two Conquests of Hungary, first under the name of 'White Ugrians', during the time when the Avars occupied the country, and a then second during the reign of Grand Prince Oleg.[27] We shall return to this piece of information further on.

The Legend of St. Methodius, from the early 880s, contains some fine lines about a 'king of the Ugrians' (i.e. Magyars):

But when the king of the Ugrians arrived in the region of the Danube, he wished to see him [i.e. Methodius]. And although some said that he would not live through this with-

6–7. The sabretache from Galgóc with detail.

out the ordeals of torture, he went to him. But the king received him respectfully as befits a high priest, with due ceremony and rejoicing. And speaking with him in a manner as was proper for men of such rank to speak, embracing and kissing him and bestowing valuable gifts upon him, he dismissed him with these words: 'Reverend father, do not fail to remember me in your holy prayers'.

This Magyar 'king' was evidently familiar not only with diplomatic proprieties but must also have had a good knowledge of Christianity.[28]

Lastly, we should not overlook the available western sources. Most of these saw the Magyars as hostile and so tended to write down even hearsay as authentic fact; nevertheless, they do provide us with precious documentation. This is particularly true of the vivid and sympathetic account of the deeds of a band of 'marauding' Magyars in Switzerland as written down by Ekkehardt Junior, the eccentric friar of the monastery at St Gallen, around 1060.[29] The 'hero' of the tale is a simple-minded monk, Heribald, who, instead of taking flight with his brother friars on the approach of the Magyar army, calmly awaited its arrival. He had a fine time amongst the formidable warriors and they in turn evidently took a liking to him:

Now there were in the monks' common cellar were two barrels of wine, which were filled to the brim… One of them [i.e. the Magyars], brandishing his axe, would have cut the hoops, but Heribald, who by now moved about amongst them with great familiarity, spoke out: 'Desist, my good fellow; for what shall we drink once you have departed?' Hearing these words from the interpreter, the Magyar laughed and asked his companions: 'Touch not my fool's casks. ' In this manner they were preserved … Their captains feasted copiously in the cloister-garth; and Heribald, too, ate and drank: his fill along with them, as he was wont to tell in later years, as he had

never eaten and drunken before… The Magyars tore and devoured with their bare teeth the half-raw shoulder-blades and other joints of the cattle which they had slain, after which each would cast the gnawed bones in sport at one another. The wine was placed in the midst, in brimming goblets, and each drank as much as he desired… Giving release to their high spirits, they danced and wrestled with one another before their captains; some contended in arms to demonstrate their skill in the art of war.

[after G. G. Coulton]

Heribald said to those who interrogated him later about his experiences:

I do not recall that I ever saw happier people within our monastery than at that time. For they provided food and drink in the greatest abundance. Whereas before then I had scarcely been able to prevail on our dour cellarer even once to give me drink when I was thirsty, they gave me plentifully at my bidding.

The unparalleled immediacy of this memoir is amply complemented by other western sources which deal more with military campaigns than with daily life. Among these, the chronicle of Widukind (925-1024), which concerns the history of the Saxons, is of great interest as it refers to the Magyars in a rather unusual set of circumstances. Widukind relates that they had settled down in Hungary before the campaigns of Charlemagne; their people was one and the same as the Huns and Avars, who were now called Magyars. Regino, abbot of Prüm in Carolingian Lotharingia (Lorraine), is generally regarded as the most important of the western sources, for under the entry for the year 889 in his *Chronicon*, he reports on the emergence of the Magyars, who had earlier lived in the Scythian realms. He speaks of a Pecheneg attack on them and of their horn-tipped arrows against which 'it is scarcely possible to find protection.' Regino also gives credence to certain malicious rumours when he opines

8. The sabretache from Rakamaz.
9. The sabretache from Szolnok-Strázsahalom.

that the Magyars are not men but live in the manner of wild beasts.[30] Other contemporary sources deal mainly with the battles of the Magyar 'marauders', and we can therefore omit reference to them here.

EVALUATION OF THE SOURCES

It is obvious that the majority of our sources speak about the same ruling class as that described by Anonymus. The *Taktiká* is concerned purely with information on their modes of fighting, Constantine confers with Magyar aristocrats, and even the Arab traders wrote primarily about the wealthy people with whom they could do business. The sources are thus one-sided, lacking precisely in a sense of the life of the ordinary people. At the end of the last century, the historian Gyula Pauler, drawing mainly on the testimony of lesser western sources, established the date of the Conquest to have been A.D. 895. He took no account of the fact that Kézai had put it to 700, and the *Chronicon Pictum* to as far back as 677, nor did he pay any attention to the *Russian Primary Chronicle,* which set the time of the Conquest by the White Ugrians to the reign of Heraclius and the entry of Árpád's Magyars to the era of Oleg. The date 895 or 896 has, in fact, taken root in Hungarian historiography as the 'fully authenticated' one. It is typical of this prejudice that when, in a lecture given not so long ago, a professor in Slavonic linguistics presented a dozen or so references to the ethnic name *Hungarus* deriving from the eighth and ninth centuries, one highly respected Hungarian linguist retorted to me that these could not have been Magyars because the Magyars did not reach the Carpathian Basin till 896. Even the documentation of '*Strata ungarorum*' and a '*Marcha uengeriorum*' in the ninth century was unable to shake his set belief in this dating of the Conquest.

We need to ask what it was that prompted the Magyars to leave the homeland, the Etelköz or Levedia, that they had between the Don and Dnieper rivers, and occupy Hungary. Besides population pressure, the Hungarian chronicles supply a mythological cause: proliferating numbers of eagles had begun to decimate their livestock. However, both Byzantine and western sources provide a more plausible reason, which is that the Pechenegs, taking advantage of the absence of the Magyar armies on campaigns in the west, fell upon the defenceless camps they had left behind in the Etelköz, slaughtering the women, children and elderly, and thus forcing the remnants of the race to flee:

Everything was lost
That once united: judge, soothsayer, priest, altar,
A band of widowed old men and a host of
Orphaned youngsters; had the Magyars come to this?
[Gyula Illyés, 'Árpád']

This information is vouched for by two reliable sources, Constantine Porphyrogenitus and Regino.

For a long time I suspected that all this was mere boastfulness on the part of the Pechenegs who were Constantine's informants, because after all, approximately equal numbers of male and female burials have been found in cemeteries of the Conquest period in Hungary, and the women have Oriental accoutrements. More recently, however, I have been puzzled that whilst almost exactly similar male burial dress has come to light east of the Carpathians, and close equivalents of the Magyar partial horse burials (i.e. where just the skull and lower legs are placed in the grave) are likewise known from the Volga region further eastwards, this is not the case for the jewellery in the female burials. Indeed, what we find is that the male burials show not the slightest traces of animal-pattern decorations, whereas the female graves yield beautiful zoomorphic pendants of a type that was prevalent up to the late Avar period. With this background, let us then examine more closely this question of the Pecheneg-inflicted defeat.

Czech-Slovak scholars have long held the view that the whole of Hungarian territory, up until the arrival of Árpád's Magyars, was under settlement by Slav tribes. Thus if, after their loss at the hands of the Pechenegs, these Magyars did indeed carry out their conquest of the country in the manner of Cossak bands, then plainly they would have had to marry women of the indigenous – hence presumably Slav – population. That, however, would surely have led inexorably to the complete Slavization of the Magyars within two or three generations, as the children's mother-tongue would literally have been the mother's tongue. I recall a visit to Hungary that Professor P. N. Tretyakov, the eminent archaeological expert on the Slavs of the Volga basin, made in the early 1950s. After hearing a goodly number of Hungarian scholars trying to impress on him the view that the entire population of Hungary at the time of the Conquest was Slav, Tretyakov, intensely sceptical, asked simply, 'Then how come we here don't all speak Slavonic?' That is a fair comment.

The only way round the dilemma is to suppose that the women encountered by Árpád's Magyars were already Hungarian speakers. Extensive support for this is found among the serf names which feature in eleventh – and twelfth-century documents: these are predominantly Hungarian.[31] This implies that the subjugated native population must itself have been Magyar. A parallel may be drawn with what happened to the Bulgar Turks. Despite conquering a Slavonic population on the Lower Danube, the Bulgars ended up being rapidly Slavized. In Hungary, Árpád's armies, also Turkic in culture and almost certainly speaking a Turkic vernacular, were Magyarized. This is a question to which we shall return later, but we should register the fact that whilst the names of the Magyar chieftains were almost exclusively Turkic, those of the serf and slave classes were overwhelmingly Hungarian, and no amount of quibbling can alter this fact.

Another point relevant to the issue is the consideration that whereas only one or two dozen graves are uncovered in Árpádian Magyar cemeteries, burial grounds with several hundred, even a thousand, graves are found at the sites of late Avar-Onogur settlement, that is, in cemeteries of the first Conquest. The simple thought suggests itself that a large crowd readily swallows up a few individuals.

Our historical sources raise a further 'awkward' question over the existence or nonexistence of Magyar tribes. The difficulty is that whereas Constantine Porphyrogenitus lists these tribes by name, the Hungarian chronicles are completely silent on the matter. This seemingly insurmountable discrepancy was explained away by older schools of historiography with the claim that by the time the chronicles were written down the very memory of the tribes had been lost from the Hungarian collective consciousness. It is hard to take this seriously, however, when villages bearing those very tribal names survive to the present day and, what is more, are scattered about fairly evenly throughout the Middle Danube basin. The number seven obviously had mystic significance (the seven tribes). Place-name researchers have noticed that there are other toponyms including presumably tribal appellations – for example, *Székely*, *Varsány* and *Tárkány* – which are distributed just as widely as the names in Constantine's list. In this connection, Dezső Csalány has mapped out the types of archaeological finds that have come to light in the vicinity of villages bearing tribal names.[32] In a total of sixty cases he found that these were late Avar-Onogur cemeteries but in no case was he able to establish the presence of either an Árpádian Magyar cemetery or a later commoners' burial ground. This implies that whatever tribes there may have been in Hungary, they were not Árpádian Magyar, but Onogur tribes. I should, perhaps, also note that linguists have been able to find only one or two tribal names of demonstrably Finno-Ugrian origin, the remainder presumably being Turkic. This, however, would tend to redirect attention towards Árpád's people.

To date, research work has failed to locate the areas in which Magyar tribal organizations set up their camps after their entry into Hungary, which has prompted the thought that by the time of the Conquest, the tribes were no longer closed formations and, indeed, may even have had no significance at all. The whole phenomenon remains one of the great puzzles of Hungary's history. Archaeological data complicate the picture still further for neither in the relics of the Árpádian Magyars nor in the material of the commoners' graves has any sign of tribal distinctions been discovered, although differences in dress would be the very thing to attest to a tribal life. From anthropometric data Kinga Éry was able to demonstrate the existence of three major, more or less distinct, populations in the ninth century, but only three and not seven, let alone ten.

Some completely new perspectives on the settlement problem have been opened by György Györffy in his linking of certain tenth-century duchies (*ducatus*) to earlier tribal territories, or 'countries', that could be considered as falling under the rule of individual chieftains.
Men-Marót's Khazar-inhabited duchy of Bihar was the same as the country of Zolta, heir to the supreme leader; Gyalu's duchy of Transylvania the same as the country of the tribal chieftain Gyula; Galád's duchy of Maros the same as the country of the tribal chieftain Ajtony; Salan's duchy in the cis-Tisza region the same as the country of Ond; and finally the country of Zobor, in Nyitra County, became another duchy through its occupation by the sons of Hülek: or, more accurately, of Árpád's son, Üllő.

The term 'tribal chieftain' used here, implying as it does the continued existence of tribes in the Conquest period, might be better expressed as 'leader' Nevertheless, it is plausible to suppose that in the Conquest period there were as many 'countries' as there were leaders (seven?) who entered Hungary, together with their peoples, under the supreme commander, Árpád. It was over these semi-autonomous provinces, or 'countries', that the central command had to try to exert its authority. The leaders of each of the regional power-centres, or 'peoples', were clearly the ones who made the blood pacts referred to in the chronicles, and it was with their influence that the later kings, Géza and Stephen I, had to contend.

More information about the blood pact might help us to resolve this 'fruitful uncertainty'. We do not know for sure if its terms were as recorded by Anonymus, but the four centuries of rule that resulted for the Árpádian dynasty are testimony to the reality of the pact, as is the fact that even subsequent rulers attempted to bolster their claims to the throne by proving collateral descent from Árpád.

The earliest traces of the custom of making blood pacts amongst steppe-dwellers are found with the Scythians, but the most characteristic examples are those known from *The Secret History of the Mongols.*[33] Such bonds between men of different kindreds were stronger than consanguine links. We may conjecture that an act of this kind set the seal on an alliance between seven Magyar tribes or 'peoples' – or rather ten, if the three Kavar tribes are included – and at the same time marked the ending of their tribal separation whilst also signalling how Hungarian territories were to be carved up for military occupation by each people. What does seem certain is that the blood pact welded the tribes into an ethnic entity, the Magyar people. So much for the 'birth certificate' of the Magyars, of which Constantine wrote:

And the Magyars consisted of seven tribes but at that time they had no ruler, either of their own kind or foreign, but there were certain voivodes above them.

It would be reasonable to think that these tribal associations might have lent some local colour to the regional dialects of the Hungarian language. However, nothing has come of efforts to demonstrate this sort of influence. In the course of a thousand years there has been much internal movement of Hungary's inhabitants, most notably after the ending of Turkish occupation in the late seventeenth and early eighteenth centuries, when the Alföld was re-populated from all corners of the country. Following Géza Bárczi,[34] all we can say for sure about the main dialectal phenomena is that they are of relatively modern origin. These include use of an 'ő'-sound in the Drava region, in southern Dunántúl (Transdanubia), around Szeged and eastwards into the Danube-Tisza interfluve; the 'í'-sound used in the Nyírség (north-eastern Hungary), Szatmár County and western Dunántúl; the splitting of 'é' into diphthongal 'ie', also in western Dunántúl; and the adoption of an 'ä'-sound in the Palóts dialect. Bárczi specifically warned that 'it would be a serious methodological error to extrapolate the present state of the dialects back into medieval times,' – and here we would want to go back to the Conquest period! It must have been the case, though, that any dialects that might have been spoken were closely similar, at least to the degree that speakers would have had no difficulty in understanding one another. When all is said and done, therefore, no trace of a former tribal organization has been preserved, even in the Hungarian dialects.

Our information about the centuries directly preceding the Árpádian conquest comes primarily from Constantine Porphyrogenitus. He it is who tells us that the Magyars lived for a while in an alliance with the Khazars and that, as allies of Byzantium, they attacked the Bulgars. Another source (Georgios Monacos) informs us that the Byzantines held negotiations with Árpád and a certain Kuszán (Kurszán or Kusal), from which it has been speculated that the latter may have been the supreme ruler whilst Árpád was the army commander and thus that the Magyars had a system of dual kingship. Western sources speak about a Magyar campaign in northern Italy, but it is the Hungarian chronicles that deal with the Conquest itself. Since the present work aims to fill in precisely those aspects that are missing from the sources – that is, to describe the life of the people – I shall be giving relatively little weight to the historical events themselves, which anyway have been fairly well covered by other authors. Anonymus describes how the Conquest steadily proceeded according to Árpád's command; how he broke the resistance offered by the indigenous population, whether militarily or by dynastic pacts (his own son, Zoltán, married the daughter of Mén-Marót); and then how he began to play various sides against one another in the struggles between the western powers (his 'raids'). The question that are of greater interest here, however, are: Who exactly did the Árpádian Magyars find living in Hungary when they took it over? And what were their relationships with these autochonous populations?

In the ninth century the territory of Hungary fell within the spheres of influence of three powers. In the north, up to the line of the Garam river, the kingdom of Great Moravia held sway, whilst the south, between the Drava and Sava rivers and into the Bácska region, was controlled by southern Moravians. The Carolingian Empire had driven a wedge between these into Pannonia (i.e. the Dunántúl), with the Danube acting as the border with Bulgarian Khanate, which had suzerainty over the lands to the east (the Alföld plain and Transylvania). These spheres of influence were not, however, reflected in the distribution of the respective peoples. The Bavarian colonizers introduced by the Carolingian occupation vanished without trace after the Magyar Conquest and the true mass of the native population was represented by the Onogur-Hungarians who had arrived around A.D. 670, in the late Avar period. The Onogurs spread essentially throughout the Middle and Upper Danube basins and formed a series of alliances with the Carolingians and Byzantium in succession, around the years 811, 832 and 860. Formerly historians used to believe that Onogur armies attacking from bases in southern Russia were involved but they were actually Onogurs dwelling in Hungary. It is from these Onogur-Hungarians that we get most of the early Hungarian place-names in the Carpathian Basin, i.e., those featuring in the earliest extant documents from the Árpádian era.

Anonymus reveals that he too must have had some knowledge of these antecedents, because he writes that Árpád's people were called *Hungari* after the fortress of Ung. In other words, he knew that this was the name that had attached to the 'Turks' once they were on Hungarian soil. Furthermore, he reports that Álmos took with him a number of peoples when he set off from the old Magyar homeland in the Etelköz to occupy Hungary. This might explain the hitherto unsolved problem of why Árpád's people were known under a variety of names in the sources: Magyars, Onogurs, Bashkirs, Turks, and Savartoi or Savards. At one time all these names were taken as referring to a single ethnic entity, the Magyars, but it is highly likely that the Magyars emerged from a meld of peoples which formerly had had separate identities.

An excellent survey of the history of the Conquest, following the version given by Anonymus, can be gained from a map prepared by Dezső Pais. This shows the routes taken by Árpád's armies and the way they fanned out across Hungary. Directly after the Conquest a number of different 'countries' were established within the occupied territory, and this is what lies behind the tradition of the sealing of a blood pact between tribes. The chiefs of these 'countries' tried to preserve their autonomy over against the central authority, the eventual upshot of which was a series of campaigns conducted against them by Duke Géza and especially by King Stephen I (e.g., those against Koppány, Ajtony, Gyula, and later on, Aba and Vata). Árpád's successors organized Hungary's border-defences, deploying certain auxiliary peoples (Székely, Pechenegs, Kavars) as frontier guards and constructing a fortified line which is now beginning to be uncovered in the form of 'burned' earthworks (these extend the length of entire county districts in Transylvania and also elsewhere).[35] It used to be the view that the policing of these marchlands was limited to roads and passes, but today we can see that the whole settlement territory, the new Magyar 'homeland', was girdled by a series of fortified places.

Studies of the social and administrative structure of Árpádian Hungary have provided some rewarding insights. Here, too, it is simplest to show this diagramatically, using a figure prepared jointly by György Györffy and István Dienes.[36] An important detail, and one which is observed only in the early Árpádian era, is the existence of what are called 'service' peoples, that is, settlements differentiated by their obligations to specialize in certain crafts or services. These were worked out in detail by Gusztáv Heckenast.[37] Mention should first be made, however, of the use of a 'decimal' system as the administrative unit not only of King Stephen (e.g., his decree that one church was to be built by every ten villages, the establishment of ten bishoprics, etc.), but equally of the late Avar-Onogur state. Analysis of maps of late Avar-Onogur cemeteries has shown that, in general, each arrow find symbolized ten freemen. This kind of decimal organization is not found amongst the Árpádian Magyars, suggesting that King Stephen simply adapted to his own purposes a system that predated the Magyar conquest. As Hans Göckenjan has pointed out,[38] it was also a common principle of military organization amongst eastern peoples. Much has still to be investigated in this area, but we can be certain that this decimal principle did not emerge as the result of a single royal proclamation.

The Árpádian state and the rule of the Árpád dynasty thus slowly took shape. Its administration rested on the army, on decimal organization, and eventually, under Géza and Stephen, on Christianization. In dealing with the adoption and propagation of Christianity in Hungary it is necessary first of all to dispel the notion that the Christian states of the west, and above all the monastic orders, can take all the credit for spreading a more civilized culture to the country. Undoubtedly there is much truth in this, but it is simply misleading to suggest that all was pagan and barbarian before Stephen's reign, whilst after it everything became Christianized and civilized in the western mould. We shall go into this in more detail in the final chapter on religious beliefs; suffice it to say for now that the pre-Christian Hungarian vocabulary was already adequate to translate the entire Bible text, and the process of conversion drew mainly on this extant 'pagan' word-stock for its exegesis of the new faith. This alone must be taken as indicating that the Hungarian language was already rich in expressions for religious concepts prior to the conversion and that these concepts in turn did not fundamentally differ from those of the new creed.

In reality, the Magyars had been living in a veritable sea of monotheistic peoples for several centuries prior to the Conquest – amongst them Christians of the Caucasus and Maeotis, Judaicised Khazars, as well as many converts to Islam. These same peoples also accompanied the Árpádian Magyars in the occupation of Hungary. We know this because Ibrahim ibn-Yakub, a Jewish merchant, recorded that when he visited the fair at Prague on his journey back to Spain from Kiev, he had met Turkish, Jewish and Mohammedan traders who had travelled there from the land of the 'Turks'.[39]

It is appropriate also to touch briefly on a similar misconception that the Árpádian Magyars were a race of nomadic pastoralists and that some crisis led them to abandon this way of life for sedentary farming once they had entered the Middle Danube basin. This theory, which held sway as a virtually obligatory teaching in the early 1950s, cannot be substantiated and, moreover, is falsely grounded. The occupations of farmer and animal breeder both call for their own separate skills, expertise and experience that take centuries to develop, and neither is given up or acquired so lightly, from one day to the next, least of all on orders. The Árpádian Magyars had their own farmers from the beginning and others already inhabited Hungary when they arrived; the animal-breeding, horse-riding segments of their society was needed to provide warriors for the army, not as serfs. Again, this will be dealt with in greater detail in the later chapters on agriculture and animal husbandry, but we may mention here one of the more recent hypotheses which attempts to reconcile the opposing views. György Györffy has proposed that high-ranking Magyar leaders used to move between winter and summer camps along the river valleys, in much the same way as the Mongol khan and nobles of the Golden Horde in a later century. Györffy cites as evidence the use of the same clan and personal names for sites on the upper and lower reaches of rivers.[40] The difficulty with this suggestion is that it is hard to imagine how such pastoralism could have been carried out in the flood plains of some rivers, whilst in other areas the density of settlements was such that little grazing ground can have been left for horse and cattle herds that were merely in transit.

MAGYAR VILLAGES OF THE CONQUEST ERA

When we come to describe their cemeteries later, it will be seen that the leaders of the conquering Magyars buried their dead in clan groups. This was also the organizing principle of their settlements. The simplest, and most regular, pattern was for those who carried out the most responsible work to settle to the right, and junior members to the left, of the clan head (the converse held in the afterlife). There is only one Conquest-period clan whose male lineage is known to us, that being Árpád's family, which was recorded for posterity by Constantine. Nevertheless, the clan principle becomes clear when the locations of the settlements of the leader and his sons are mapped. Árpád occupied the centre of the country, with Levente(?), Jutas and Tarhos in the Dunántúl (Transdanubia) to his right, and the two youngest sons, Üllő and Solt, on the Alföld plain to his left. The same organi-

zation can be shown as continuing in the second and third generations.[41]

We can now turn to the archaeological data. The chapter title is slightly misleading inasmuch as there is just one Conquest-period Magyar village, Felgyő, for which we have detailed information, and even this is incomplete because it has been possible to excavate only small areas of the site.

The conventional school of thought used to assume that no Árpádian village could have existed. It was supposed that the Magyars, being nomadic pastoralists, could not have had permanent settlements or villages because they would have been constantly on the move in

---

10. Protective ditch around a yuhrt after excavation.

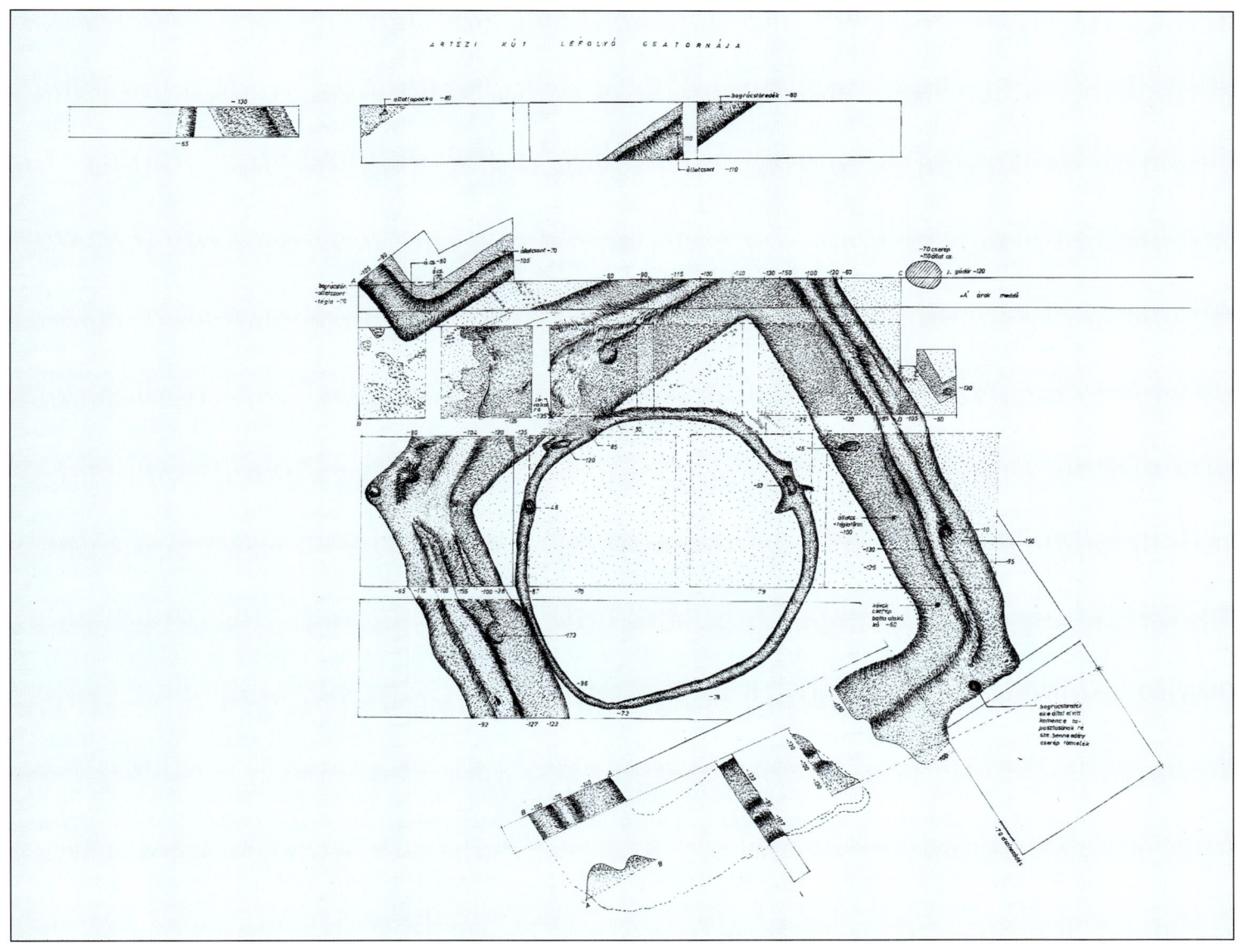

search of fresh grazing grounds. Once the myth that the Magyars were no more than nomadic horsemen had been challenged, however, it became necessary to locate the settlement sites of the Árpádian Magyars – a task that was originally entrusted to me by the Archaeological Committee of the Hungarian Academy of Sciences, perhaps on the tacit understanding that something that had not come to light in 150 years of excavations in the country would be a fitting object for my attention. The support that ensued for excavations was meagre, to say the least (over twenty years it amounted perhaps to as much as excavations at Roman-era sites received annually). We could only look enviously at the seemingly limitless funds available to our Slovak colleagues, on the opposite bank of the Danube, for their work on early Slav settlements and the high-culture kingdom of Great Moravia. Rouma

---

11–12. Cross-section of the ditch at the excavations at Felgyő; the ground-plan of the church of Geda-Halom.

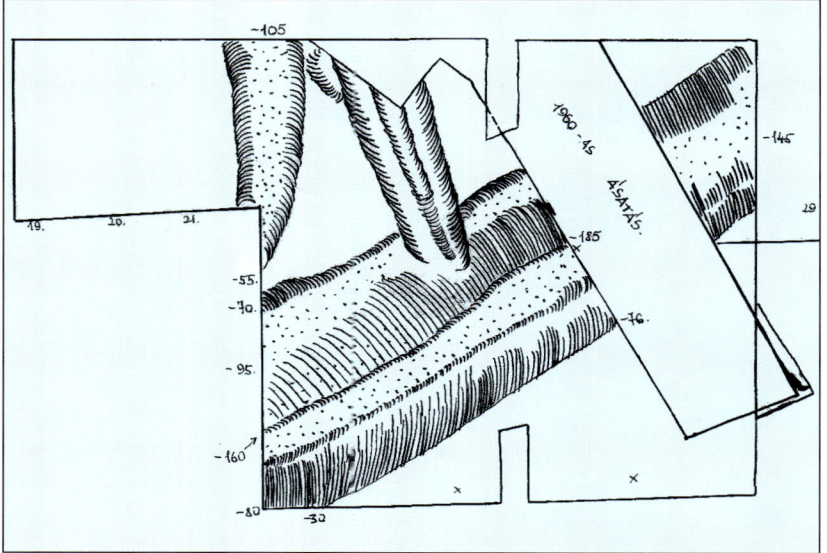

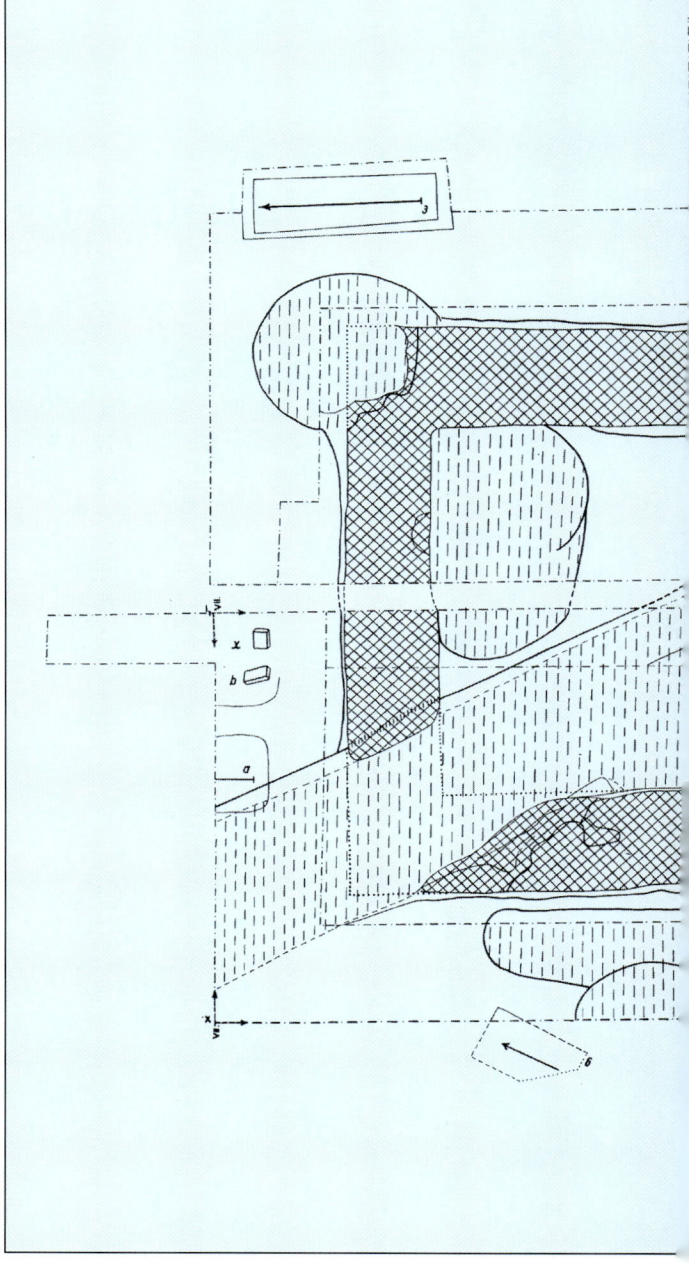

nian archaeology likewise was attracting large sums for diggings at the castles and settlements of the Dacians. Meanwhile we had to patch and mend as best we could and failed even to gain a protection order for our thousand-year-old site because a new socialist village was under construction there. For all the restrictions these circumstances imposed, they had compensatory spin-offs – for example, in the kilometres of ditches for watermains that were dug up, like so many 'exploratory trenches', which greatly helped us to fix the boundaries of the old settlement. I ought also to acknowledge the grants awarded by the Museum Service of Csongrád County and, later on, the Agricultural Museum, Budapest, which helped to swell the Academy's pittance.

The old ideas about the nomadic Magyars suffering some kind of crisis in their pastoral life-style continued to exert a baleful influence on the picture of the early Magyar village that began to emerge. For some time it had been fashionable to say that by the time of the Conquest, Magyar dwellings had advanced no more than 'from *yurt* to shack'. This assertion is laughable enough nowadays

but it was sustained for a while by the over-hasty conclusions of some linguists who had tried to trace the history of Hungarian housebuilding terms back into the Finno-Ugrian past and ended up envisaging some amazingly primitive shelter. Clearly, the concept may have had some validity for conditions that prevailed five or six thousand years before the Conquest, but to project this into the Conquest period itself was methodologically unsound.[42] Ethnologists were closer to the truth with their opinion, briefly put, that Conquest-period Magyar settlements must have been more nearly like nineteenth-century Hungarian villages than the clusters of rudimentary tents in which the Magyars' kinsfolk, the Voguls and Ostyaks, dwelt until recently. Sadly, the timescales of linguistics are extraordinarily precarious: correct as many of the etymologies undoubtedly are, they are not anchored to a firm chronology and thus have led to historical deductions which are as faulty as those in the sphere of prehistory.

As the material from our excavations at Felgyő has not yet been published in full,[43] I shall report here some of the main findings.

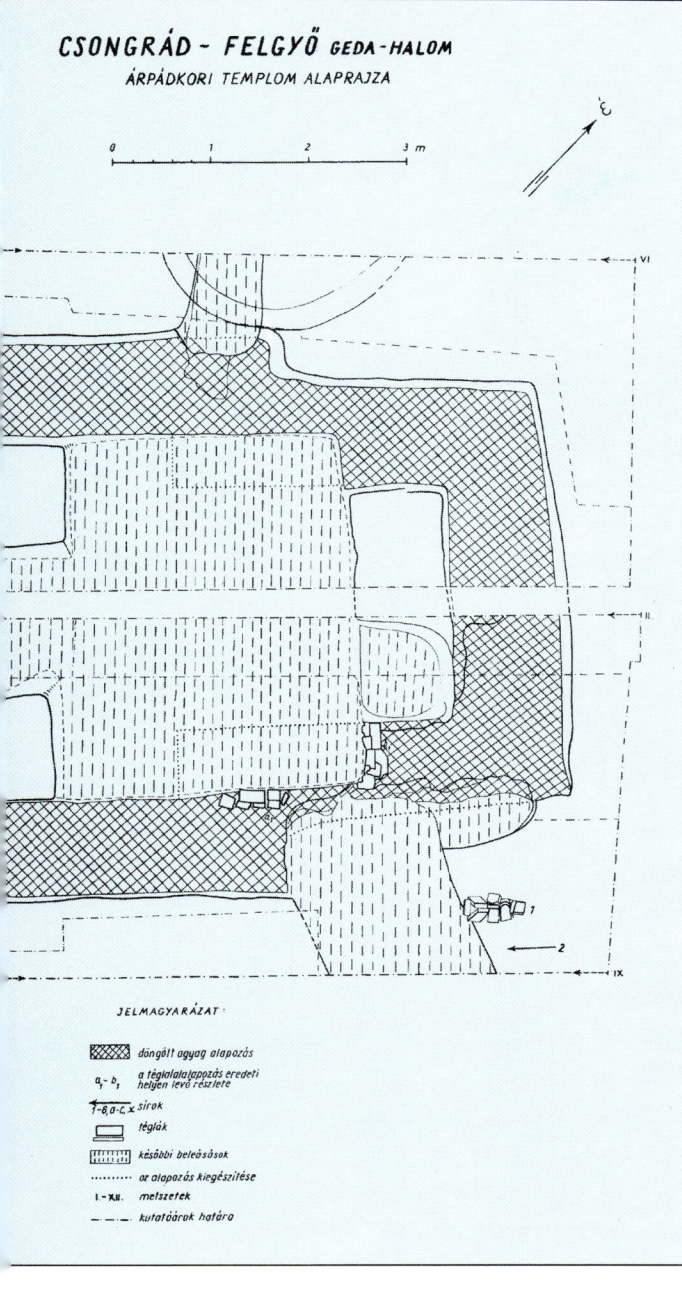

CSONGRÁD - FELGYŐ GEDA-HALOM
ÁRPÁDKORI TEMPLOM ALAPRAJZA

JELMAGYARÁZAT :

döngölt agyag alapozás

a téglalatalappzás eredeti
helyén lévő részlete

1-8,a-c,x sírok

téglák

későbbi beleásások

az alapozás kiegészítése

I-XII. metszetek

kutatóárok határa

of the village itself, containing brick-lined graves, pits with wooden coffins, bodies wrapped in felt cloths (these may have been meant to evoke the *yurts*) and finally – though this is still only a tentative interpretation – graves with mud-packed walls. This suggests that an individual's abode in life was supposed to be perpetuated in death.

None of the dwellings had foundations; they were constructed on levelled ground,. The small church, on the other hand, had immaculate clay foundations. The hill on which it stood which we believe may have been a prehistoric barrow, had been banked up twice over to raise the house of God higher above the cluster of moated dwellings,. Unmistakeable signs of earth-moving activity were found around the hill in the form of B810 gullies, now partially eroded where the topsoil had been removed down to the yellow hardpan layer,. Similar traces of 'collective work' were found in the ditches around *yurts*.

Burial grounds dating from four different periods – late Bronze Age (Vatya culture) Sarmatian, early-late Avar, and Conquest era – were found within the village area. The last of these yielded a double-bladed sword, which makes it more likely to date from the latter half of the tenth century; a spur with terminal cone points to the same period. For all practical purposes, then, Felgyő seems to have been continuously inhabited since village settlement started in Hungary. It had two attributes to thank for this. First was ready access to water, for the village was situated alongside a stream called the Vidre and was also within the flood-plain of the Tisza river, whilst a series of hillocks provided high ground for settlement. Second, Felgyő stands at the point where the main East-West route through Hungary, from prehistoric times onward, crossed the Tisza. To this day, the towns of Csongrád and Szentes, on either side of the river, are connected by the ferry at Bód. The sword and spur indicate that its owner was a military man, possibly a sentry at the ferry.

As to the village itself, each dwelling was surrounded by a fairly large ditch system enclosing 700-1,000 square metres (approximately one-eighth to one-guarter of an acre). These had been carefully dug as double-lipped ditches but they followed the lie of the land rather than having a run-off. In older times, at least when the water-table was high, the ditches would obviously have been filled with water so that the dwellings had individual moats. We may guess that dense thickets of reeds, sedges and bulrushes fringed the ditches and even that a wattle fence or hedgerow was set on top of the inner mound. Each enclosed compound was a self-sufficient unit, with a dwelling in one corner and the remaining space given over as a sort of 'garden' to cultivation of crops and vegetables. It may be supposed, though we have come across no traces of such a structure, that there would have been a bridge to pass over the ditch, at least at one point. As no dung heaps were found, we assume that most animals were not not kept inside the enclosures, in which case they must have been held outside the village, on the surrounding lands. At most one or two saddlehorses may have been kept next to the dwelling (a curry-comb was found buried in the mud at the bottom of one of the ditches).

The inhabitants of Felgyő cultivated wheat, rye, millet and grapes and kept poultry, swine, horses, cattle, sheep, goats, and guard- or shepherd-dogs. In this respect, they do indeed seem to have been the thousand-year-old counterparts of early twentieth-century Hungarian peasants – an impression that is strengthened by what we have learned of their abodes. They had *yurts,* but these were surrounded by wide defensive ditches and so could not have been intended for use as mobile quarters; more likely they were comfortable permanent dwellings. The village also had habitations made from logs, wattle-and-daub, and bricks. Alas, we were unable to uncover the full ground plan of the village, so we can only suspect that these differences in house-type point to social stratification of the population. We believe that the *yurts,* which would have belonged to the high-ranking, formed a single row with the various other types of dwellings arranged alongside or around them. The majority of the abodes did not have an internal hearth; the fire-place was located in front of the dwelling. It was highly instructive to find that the Christian-era cemetery was virtually a mirror-image

These findings lead us to imagine that the old village consisted of a central core of enclosed compounds with some system cf outlying camps for open-range herding of horses and cattle. We can read in the Legend of St Gerard, and also from Bertrandon de la Brocquière's account, about the huge herds of horses that belonged to Ajtony. At Felgyő István Méri has discovered a stable that was set into the ground, but this dates from several centuries after the Conquest.

The ovens which we found dug into the ground, apparently ouside the dwellings, pose another problem. There are two ways that we can imagine them being used. Either they really were exterior to the habitation, in which case there must have been at least a makeshift structure over them to provide protection against rain and snow (otherwise their shutes would simply have become waterlogged), or else they were built as part of the dwelling but the structures above them have disappeared without trace. Even nowadays, the summer kitchen, with its oven, is a familiar feature besides the homes in many Hungarian villages; indeed in Transylvania, for example, the oven for baking bread is normally out in the courtyard, completely detached from the house. We shall need to excavate much larger, continuous areas at Felgyő, however, if we are to gain a better picture of this aspect. Ovens, some with a lining of stones, found in the corner of earth huts had such a narrow aperture that earthenware pots could not have been inserted in them. There are also several places where four or five ovens are set around a common pit, from which it might be deduced that they were shared by a cluster of families, perhaps to reduce the fire hazard.

A surprisingly large number of millstone fragments were uncovered during the excavations at Felgyő – so many that one suspects that every family may have had its own mill. They were carved from solid rock and had plainly been transported to this Alföld village along some trading route (possibly by boat or raft). There is no way that the millstones could have shattered of their own accord; they must have been broken up by human hand. One cannot help recalling those reports of landowners in western Europe who smashed the grindstones of their serfs in order to force them to have their grain ground at the landowner's mill, thereby making it easier to extract tithes.

These findings already tell us something about the early Árpádian village, and more recent excavations are now adding to this knowledge. At present, however, we know very little about the system of settlement in its entirety. We have already seen that it was not on a tribal basis, but we can gain only a vague idea of the principle that did operate from the existence of the decimal organization. We do not even know if the Árpádian Magyars settled amidst existing Onogur-Hungarian villages, in the same manner that Cumans were to settle in Hungary during the thirteenth century, or whether a quite different course was taken. There is reason to discern some regularity in their seeming preference for the sandy bluffs overlooking rivers, in contrast to the more loamy meadows and ploughlands preferred by the Onogur Hungarians. The chronicles relate an episode when Árpád's emis-saries bought lands from 'Svatopluk', king of Great Moravia, in exchange for white horses with gilded bridles and saddles (in the steppe world, donation of 'gifts' was tantamount to formal purchase); what the emissaries asked for was grass, sand and waters of the Danube. Here it is the sand that I would emphasize, because Árpád's people did indeed settle on sandy soil.

The wider outlines of the settlement process in Árpádian Hungary are only just beginning to be filled in now that a concerted effort is under way to survey the individual counties archaeologically, partly to authenticate known sites, partly to identify new sites. One of the first areas to be studied in this way was the Szentes district. The fruit of this is a topographical map prepared by Julia Kovalovszky on the basis of her exemplary coverage of both banks of the Tisza,[44] to which István Méri greatly contributed his meticulous work. It can be seen from this map that the settlements or villages are distributed in close proximity to one another along the former line of the river banks. In order to interpret the results of these surveys it must be appreciated that the presence of settlements is disclosed primarily through the collection of finds that come to the surface. As graves are dug deep in the ground, it is rare for grave goods to be encountered in such work; houses, on the other hand, are superficial structures, whilst the discovery of domestic refuse tips or large amounts of pottery fragments is a sure sign of settlement.

It has already been mentioned that the late Avars, or Onogurs, preferred heavier, loamier soils, the Árpádian Magyars, the sandy alluvium of river banks. In some cases, this would have resulted in a separation of their respective settlements by areas the size of a county. However, this view has recently been challenged as outdated on the grounds that the topographers themselves have shown that there are many late Avar sites where Árpádian Magyars also settled down. In my judgement this is a misinterpretation of the data. To begin with, the region extending westwards from Kapuvár (western Hungary) into the Upper Danube basin takes in many large late-Avar cemeteries, but not one Árpádian Magyar burial ground. It is the same in the Dunántúl counties of Somogy and Baranya in south-west Hungary, where Onogur cemeteries are associated with Hungarian village names, as well as in Szabolcs County in the north-east and in the Csallóköz (now Velky Zitny Ostrov) on the Slovakian side of the Danube. Even in places where Onogur and Árpádian Magyar cemeteries are in close proximity, as in the district of Hódmezővásárhely (Csongrád County) – that is, places which, on the evidence of the map, seem to speak against my hypothesis – we still find the Magyar conquerors on the water-crossed dune areas, the late Avars on the wide loess plains.[45] I believe, therefore, that my original observation has stood the test of time.

That is where we stand at present with regard to the occupation and settlement of Hungary during the Conquest era. However, one aspect that we have yet to touch on is where Árpád's armies and the Magyar people crossed the Carpathians to enter the country. Hungarian chroniclers record three routes: one via the Vereckei Pass, a second through Transylvania, and a third via the lower reaches of the Danube. It is more than likely that the various peoples flooded into the Carpathian Basin by all three routes, 'country' by 'country', in the same groups as they and their ancestors had occupied the Etelköz beside the Black Sea. There is even some documentary evidence for this inasmuch as Kézai records that the headquarter sites occupied by the Magyar 'captains' were well separated from one another (this may be how we should interpret the seven earthwork fortresses constructed in Transylvania). Settlers may then have fanned out from these centres, with the final share-out of territories only occurring after the whole country had been colonized. We have no way of tracing how these expanding ripples of settlement took place – for instance, whether newcomers prodded those who had reached Hungary before them into moving on, or whether they leapfrogged them to claim the next zone of land for themselves.

In view of the need for wood and timber to make everyday implements, it seems quite possible that the paired settlement names referred to earlier do not represent winter and summer quarters but recall a time when each population had one settlement on the plain, by a river, and a second settlement in a wooded area. The small, 'classical' Conquest-era burial sites of Árpádian Magyars could be memorials to a re-settlement process. But then where have the human remains of the clans that participated in this process disappeared? The population of Hungary must have been in a state of upheaval for a good half century after the Conquest; all we can be sure of is that the generations which succeeded the small groups buried in the 'classical' cemeteries moved on to other areas. Only future anthropological study will be able to tell us if cemeteries discovered at a distance from the 'classical' sites conceal the remains of another, earlier Magyar group. An alternative approach might be to try and date cemeteries and their graves by decennials and thus determine whether given sites were burial grounds for two, or even three, similar peoples that successively settled an area further and further away from the 'ancestors'.

These are not just academic matters as they have a bearing, for instance, on the religious beliefs of the Magyars, including their concept of an afterlife. The indications are that clan members would have wished to join up with their earlier generations for life in the next world – or, to use a Székely expression for eternity, 'whilst the world and two suns exist'.

Let us look at what we can learn about the early villages from contemporary law-books. According to Article 34 of St Stephen's Second Decree, which was promulgated in the 1030:[46]

Every ten villages shall build a church and shall bestow on it for its benefice two household servants, and moreover one stallion and mare, six oxen and two cattle, with thirty-four younger animals.

Article 19 of King (St) Ladislas IV's Decretum at the Synod of Szabolcs, from 1092, states:
If the people of a village, abandoning its church, should move to another place, the bishop is empowered, and it is the king's command, to force them to return to the place they have left.

And lastly, King Kálmán (Coloman the 'Bookman'), in Article 13 of his second synodal Decretum, from around 1116, ordered:
Whatever village has a church should not move far away from that church; if it should move away, it must pay a penalty of ten coins and return to its place.

What we should understand here by the word 'village' (villa or villani in the original Latin text) is a collectivity of all properties and pastures. By another article (No. 25) of his Decretum of 1092, St Ladislas tried to restrain the perpetual shifting of his peoples by laying down that the dead could only be interred around a church. Each village must initially have represented the settlement of a single extended family or clan, since early villages had no more than 25-40 inhabitants. The head villager (Hu. *folnagy*) would probably have been the clan chief. The early Hungarian laws treated villages as single units, carrying collective responsibility. For instance, Article 63 of Kálman's First Lawbook (c. 1100) orders that 'if a traveller's horse should be stolen in a village, the villagers together must compensate him for the loss'. And elsewhere there is the instruction that 'In place of ten members of a family, one may submit himself to the trial by red-hot iron'; in other words, one person (presumably the clan chief) was taken to represent the collective unit.

This leads us on to the problem of identifying the Árpádian Magyar cemeteries. We do not know what it was that prompted the people who started these cemeteries to move on. However, one is reminded, for instance, that Ob-Ugrian clans would usually migrate to a new place after two or three generations; if they chose to stay, they had to restore the fertility of the land. Unfortunately, we are in no better position to know what dictated the movements of the Onogur-Hungarian populations that preceded the Árpádian Magyars. We can deduce that they, too, moved on after two or three generations (this is generally what any given cemetery corresponds to in size), but even here we have no means of sorting the population out from first to last. Nor have we yet started to investigate the connections which may exist between the cemeteries of communities which bear the same tribal name. Hungarian archaeology is therefore still very much at the beginning of exploring the early history of its people.

BURIAL CUSTOMS

For too long Hungarian archaeology was preoccupied with the chronological and ethnic classification of remains found in cemeteries rather than looking at the sites as a whole. A decisive break with this tradition was signalled by the publication of my 1944 monograph on the life of the Conquest-period Magyars and a subsequent volume on Avar society. In these I expressed the view that cemeteries should be treated as, in effect, the villages or abodes of the dead, where the same laws and customs prevailed as in communities of the living.

To stay with this view of burial grounds as integrated units, it has been shown for a growing number of cemeteries that the characteristic 'griffin-and-tendril' ornamentation of the Onogur-Hungarians survived the invasion of the Árpádian Magyars, even into the second half of the tenth century, when the 'S-terminal' temporal rings began to appear. There are sites, like that at Visznek (Heves County), where both late Avars and Conquest-era Magyars are buried. One aspect of settlement that we must come to terms with, therefore, is the demography of the Árpádian Magyars. The figure of around 400,000 that historians have estimated as their population pays no regard to the small size of the Magyar cemeteries. The Onogur-Hungarian population in the late-Avar period could be counted in hundreds of thousands; their burial grounds of hundreds and sometimes a thousand or more graves are proof enough of their vastly superior numbers relative to their Árpádian conquerors. The historian's estimates rest entirely on a single Arabic source (Gardìzi) who speaks of 20,000 Magyar horsemen, though it is always advisable to treat such round numbers with caution, for in many instances they mean no more than 'a lot'. The so-called commoner's cemeteries can hardly come into the equation as these were only opened from around the mid-tenth century. We must therefore face the evidence that Árpád's people occupied the sandy areas along the river banks and essentially left the Onogur-Hungarians as they were, living on the plains.

Before discussing the cemeteries of the Árpádian Magyars in any detail, a few words should be said about burial in general. In all ages this has been a paramount concern of surviving family members. In older times this concern was inspired by fear that the dead would return to haunt the living; in our own age, by love and respect for the deceased. When we look at the way the cemeteries of the Árpádian Magyars are arranged, we are bound to conclude that they conceived of death as a continuation of life in this world, not only for the individual but also for the community (or clan). It is a secondary matter whether they thought of the afterlife as an unbroken continuum with this world or as its mirror-image.

Burial began with the digging of a grave, which in itself fixed the orientation of the body. The Árpádian Magyars laid their dead to rest in an aligment, whereas Onogur-Hungarians usually chose a north-east/south-west direction, sometimes north-south. The reason for these choices (direction of the rising or noon-day sun, ancestral homeland, etc.) is not known, but the Magyars certainly adhered to them strictly. Now this seemingly insignificant item of certainty permits us to draw some sweeping inferences in respect of the population of tenth-century Hungary for in some of the commoner's cemeteries the graves are not oriented east-west but north-east/south-west. This implies that the people who practised northeast/south-west burial survived into the era when the serving class was marked by the wearing of temporal rings.

Béla Szőke, who made an enduring contribution to the archaeology of tenth-century Hungary, divided the finds of that century into three groups, each of which corresponded to a different social stratum.[47] The first group comprises the solitary burials of high-ranking personages and the small clusters of clan burials, which to my mind represent the predecessors of the later ruling class or nobility. The second group represents some form of middle class, whilst the third comprises the serf burials.

Let us take, first of all, the clan burials. Typically, these are of wealthy warriors, who merited partial horse burials, and womenfolk decked out in relatively rich jewellery Warriors' graves contain a bow, quiver, sabre and usually also a weapon belt, embellished with mounts. At one time, following Nándor Fettich,[48] it was believed that everything of artistic value in these graves – the ornamental plates that covered the flap of the pouch, or sabretache, that was suspended from the belt, the mounts on the belts themselves and on sabres, helmet crests, etc., must have been fashioned by Khazar craftsmen working in the Magyars' earlier homeland in the Etelköz and manifestly under the influence of Norse art. This view is now known to be mistaken, because the bulk of these decorated objects were manufactured in Hungary itself. Another suggestion which has been advanced, in this case by György Györffy, is that objects bearing decorative palmette motifs were the work of Kavar goldsmiths, but the geographical distribution of such finds does not match up with the known areas of Kavar settlement. This is not in itself a decisive argument, because the products of Kavar craftsmen could have reached all the territories settled by the Magyars through the trading channels of the day. Nevertheless, I suspect that these gold objects were produced to individual order and so, with the possible exception of the studded belts, they were not ordinary commercial goods. Furthermore, as will be shown later, we

13. The sabretache from Bezdéd.

can distinguish at least three 'schools' of ornamentation on these objects, which implies that they were the products of different workshops. From this we may speculate that there were a number of goldsmiths' workshops in operation, scattered throughout Hungary.

To return to our description of the grave goods, the burials of high-ranking men often contain equine remains – regularly just the skull and lower legs. As has been established from careful observations (e.g. at Zápolya Road, Kolozsvár [Cluj], in Transylvania), these parts were not simply cut off the animal's body, but the horse was flayed so as to leave the skull and lower-leg (cannon and pastern) bones attached to the skin; the whole bundle was then interred with the dead man.

There were several different ways in which this subsidiary horse burial was carried out; these evidently represent the once-separate traditions of the peoples which melded to form the Magyar people.[49] In one method of partial burial the horse-bones and tackle are found together in a bundle at the foot of the human skeleton. This indicates that the horse-skin was buried with harness in place at the dead man's feet. There is also reason to think that this burial took place after the human interment, with the foot of the grave being re-opened and the

horse-skin lowered into this pit. Ethnographers came across this same type of funerary custom among the Turkic-Tatar peoples of Central Asia, where the rites preceding the horse-burial allowed cemeteries to be picked out from afar as the horse-skin and harness were initially hoisted high on a pole erected by the grave. After forty days, or some such pre-determined time, the grave was re-opened and the skin laid at the foot of the deceased (this manner of insertion can be clearly deduced from the position of the horse-bones).

A second method of interring the horse skin left no visible mark on the grave mound itself. In this instance, a much wider pit was dug. The flayed horse-skin was first stuffed with hay or foliage before equipping it with the horse tackle and then laying it on the left side of the body (horses are always mounted from the left side). When such a burial is uncovered, the horse's skull is found near to the human skull, its fore-legs somewhat lower down, and the hind legs at the foot of the grave; stirrups and remnants of the saddle are seen around the middle.

The third method was what used to be called a 'stirrup burial', in which just the wooden saddle, with stirrups attached, was placed in the grave. In one variant of this the saddle was put under the dead man's head, as if he were a herdsman sleeping out on the plain.

One further comment should be added before we look in detail at the Magyar burial customs, and this relates to quivers and arrowheads. Both will be

14. The gold coin of Constantine "the Red", obverse and reverse sides.
15. The gold coin of Leo "the Wise", obverse and reverse sides.
16. Western coins from Conquest-period graves.

described more fully in a later section on bowmaking. Here I wish to explore a different aspect. The quivers of the Árpádian Magyars are known to us from the pieces of iron framework that have been preserved in the graves. The dimensions indicate that the quivers had capacity for 25-40 arrows, but the most that has been recovered from a Conquest-era grave is eight, and some graves have yielded only one arrow. Obviously, there was some reason for not filling the quivers, and this has turned out to be one of our most valuable clues in deducing the clan basis of overall cemetery organization.

The graves of the Árpádian Magyars were not dug particularly deep compared with those of the late Avars or Onogurs – on average, about a metre and a half in depth, or even less in the commoners' cemeteries. The graves were arranged in a slightly arched north-south row, with the heads at the west so that the skull faced east. It is fairly common to find that the bones in these graves have moved from their natural position, even though the graves are otherwise intact. The only way we can explain this is by supposing that some sort of plank was placed over the corpse when the grave was filled in so as to prevent the soil from falling directly on the body. After the passage of two to three years, when the tendons would have rotted away, the skull might roll to one side under its own weight, or a gopher or mole burrowing through the grave might nudge some bones out of its way. Movements like this cannot occur if the soil is pressing directly on the skeleton.

Evidence of deliberate opening of graves to obtain the human skull, rather than for simple plunder, is seldom found with the Árpádian Magyars; it is much more common among the Onogurs. This directs our attention to the realm of superstition (perhaps belief in vampires) as does the finding of the remains of a dead woman whose left foot had been amputated, together with the lower part of her ornamented boot, and placed a good half-metre away from the rest of the body in the wide grave-pit (Hencida, grave 5).[50] The latter is an isolated case, so we should not read too much into it in respect of the religious beliefs of the Conquerors; it may have been the custom of just a few superstitious families, their way of protecting themselves against the return of the dead.

The classical examples of clan burials are those from Szabolcs County (north-eastern Hungary). The cemetery that I shall present here is the one excavated at Bezdéd by András Jósa (1834-1918), a physician and man of great learning as well as the founder of the County Museum at Nyiregyháza. His exacavation report, 'modern' for its day, includes accurate maps of the grave locations and descriptions of the goods in each individual burial, together with their positions in relation to the skeleton. This offers us a splendid opportunity to interpret the findings. In fact, the Bezdéd cemetery material was the first to which I applied the 'interpretative mapping' approach which has since been almost universally adopted both here in Hungary and elsewhere. What is the basic principle of this method? When we have an authoritative record of a dig at, say, a cemetery, the graves will have been numbered in sequence of discovery, from first to last. This process may yield accurate, professional descriptions

us a great deal not, of course, about the chronology of the graves but certainly about the type of site that a person was allotted in the cemetery, or 'village of the dead', as I would put it.

This idea about how to approach the analysis of cemeteries was originally sparked by two personal recollections. One was that in my father's Transylvanian home-village of Abásfalva, in what was the former Hungarian county of Udvarhely, the cemetery really had been a copy of the living village: clans that lived alongside one another in the village were buried in their own groups in the cemetery. The second stimulus was that when I was at the Transylvanian Scientific Institute in Kolozsvár, I had a room next to the ethnographer László Kovács, who was working on the burial sites in the outskirts of the town. This gave me a daily opportunity to observe the customs and usages that the burial ceremony demanded. The idea of getting cemetery maps to speak for themselves which emerged immediately clarified for me the burial customs of the Árpádian Magyars and, later on, those of the Onogurs. After that, use of the method percolated into all areas of Hungarian archaeology and, with the observations on clan burials in Transylvania and the Little Alföld that were published by Károly Kós and László Timaffy, into ethnography, too.

The cemetery at Bezdéd was excavated by Jósa in 1896, the year of the millenary celebrations of the Conquest, and published that same year.[51] A total of 18 graves were uncovered; no further burial places came to light despite a thorough search of the cemetery area. Most of the graves lay at a depth of about one and a half metres. The richest grave was in the centre, and for its description, together with comments on the goods, I shall quote directly from the notes that I made 40 years ago:[52]

[Grave no.] I/8, the 8th to be uncovered during the excavation. Male. Around the skull were found two stirrups, a girth buckle and a bit with cheek-pieces, Paperthin silver foils lay on the skull but disintegrated on exposure of the grave [these may have been pinned over apertures in a winding-cloth over the eyes]. A guiver was placed by the

and yet still give an unintentionally distorted view of the site as a whole. To take a relatively simple example like the Bezdéd cemetery, where there were only a few graves, the grave that was by chance the first to be disclosed is designated No. l. As the excavation proceeded (in older times by digging exploratory trenches), the next grave to come to light was called No. 2, and so on, depending on the order in which the patches indicating burial sites were identified. Thus the numbering merely reflects the sequence in which the graves were found, not the order in which the burials were carried out, and this is a major difference. It is necessary to get away from this method of numbering the cemetery map, and the only way of doing so is to sketch on the map, either on or next to each grave site, all the artefacts associated with it (belt, sabretache plate, weapons, armlets, etc.). This allows us, first of all, to distinguish the male and female graves (though nowadays this would be done directly by an anthropologist working on the dig), then to see the relationship between 'rich' and 'poor' graves and, in larger cemeteries (e.g. those of the Onogurs), the tribal distribution, social hierarchy, etc. Once put in this more graphic form, such a cemetery map can tell *dead man's left shoulder, and Jósa found 8 arrowheads in it. A sabre was likewise placed on the left side, its hilt reaching the armpit. Below the left hand was found a leather pouch covered by a finely worked plaque of gilded copper. In the same area a steel kindling tool, iron awl and a knife blade were also found. There was a silver ring on the right hand and a whetstone nearby. At the foot of the grave, about 30 cm above the left leg, was a horse's skull and slightly below that its leg bones.*

Note: Burial was therefore carried out by placing the saddle and harness under the dead man's head (hence their discovery beside the skull), whilst his weapons were stowed on his left side. Thus he was not buried wearing a weapon belt. The equine bones were interred at the foot of the grave.

That was as far as I went at the time, but looking through my notes on the remaining horse-burials in the cemetery, I see that in these instances the animal's bones were found 50 cm or 30-35 cm away from the left leg, 55 cm or 25 cm away, higher up, 30 cm above the skeleton's left leg: in other words, the above description exemplified all the other graves. Based on the grave goods, all the burials to the left of the central grave were males, those to the right were all females.[53] It was conspicuous that on both sides a grave-sized plot had been left unused, plainly indicating that each body was interred at a predetermined site in the cemetery.

The next observation related to the numbers of arrowheads found in the quivers. There were eight in the central grave, then, progressing leftwards, (child's grave?), 7, 6, ?, ?, and 4; thus the numbers decrease as one passes further to the left. As I had seen the same at several other burial grounds, this finding threw a particularly strong light on the arrangement of the cemetery, for the arrows clearly functioned as a sign of rank among the Árpádian Magyars (among the Onogurs its significance was military, a relic of their decimal organisation). It was also interesting to note that one of the males on the left-hand side had not received a horse-burial but this was included in the corresponding female grave on the right side. This suggests the Árpádian Magyars may have operated some principle like that enshrined in later Hungarian law, which permitted a woman to inherit where there was no male lineal descendant, though we cannot be sure about this.

Starting from the central grave with its sabretache plate, its seems that to the left we have a series of male graves in order of decreasing wealth, whilst to the right is a similar series of female graves. As there are only eighteen graves, this raises the question of what happened to the later generations. Evidently, they moved on to new quarters and opened a new burial site there.

The cemetery at Bezdéd is just one of several 'classical' burial grounds, of which several variants are known. In one such variant the male and female graves lie alongside one another (presumably married couples), but here too the poorer the individuals, the nearer they are to the periphery. There are also cemeteries (e.g. at Szeged-Bojárhalom and Hencida) where a female grave is found at the centre of a small group. Finally, we have a number of sites where only a single male or female was interred. The solitary male graves obviously contain leaders such as tribal chiefs, whilst the females may have been their spouses.

The male grave excavated at the earthwork fortress of Zemplén (now Zemplin, Czechoslovakia) was of the latter type, and is of interest because of the great tragedy that was woven into it at the time of its discovery through a complete misinterpretation of the find.[54] It was claimed that this was where Álmos had been laid to rest after his 'reactionary' son, Árpád, had arranged his assassination. The grave was undoubtedly that of a high-ranking leader, and an Árpádian Magyar at that, but he may have been no more than the lord of Zemplén fortress. I used the word 'undoubedly', but I should give some idea of how we acually ascertain whether a grave or cemetery dates to the Conquest era, or any other period.

There is truly no doubt about our ability to recognize the graves of Ápádian Magyars. This is primarily from the practice of partial burial of the horse-skin with skull and legs, from the design of the horse tackle (stirrups, bit) and from the belt mounts. Furthermore, the coins that are frequently found in graves of this type, among them Arabic silver *dirhems*, gold *solidi* from Byzantium, and some from the West – were invariably minted early in the tenth century, that is, the period to which the Árpádian Magyar invasion is dated. Apart from these items, a host of lesser characteristics are valuable aids to identification. These include the ornaments of female dress and, amongst the men's weapons, the sabres with their recurvate hilts and blades bearing cutting edges both on the front and the upper part of the back, the narrow bows with bone reinforcements, the broad, lanceolate arrowheads, etc. The earlier Onogur burials are differently oriented, the men's belt mounts, bows, sabres and stirrups are different, as is the women's dress and, in fact, just about everything else, including the way that the sacrificed horse was interred whole. The word 'undoubtedly', therefore, is no exaggeration.

The rich burials of Árpádian Magyars stop suddenly around A.D. 1000, to be succeeded by commoners' graves and evidence of continuous cemetery use over many generations, as attested by coinage of the Árpádian-dynasty kings. Several commoners' cemeteries have been completely excavated, among them those at Fiad-Kérpuszta[55] and Halimba,[56] and it is clear that their populations originated from a different region than the people of the partial horse burials. Károly Mesterházi, the researcher most recently concerned with this matter, concluded that the ancestors of this 'rank-and-file' folk did not come from the Volga-Kama region, the presumed homeland of the high-ranking grave occupants, but from the Donets Basin; moreover, they and their wattle-and-daub huts could be found not only in Hungarian-speaking areas but across Central Europe.[57] We should cautiously heed the valuable suggestion, first made by Béla Szőke, that these sites might represent cemeteries of the Hungarian common people, but this needs to be further corroborated before it can be accepted. Previously, József Hampel and many Yugoslavian scholars had held them to be Slav cemeteries of the Urnfield (Bjelo-Brdo) culture.

The population associated with the commoners' cemeteries seems to have differed from the Magyars of the horse burials. Their burial grounds, like those of the Onogur-Hungarians, are large, containing several hundred graves, and here too we find members of a clan buried in rows. At Halimba finds of Árpádian-dynasty coinage could be used to show that the cemetery had been expanded outwards from a central 'core'. More vessels have been recovered from commoners' cemeteries than at 'classical' Magyar sites, suggesting that the custom of providing the dead with drink or broth was practiced at a number of places. Reference has already been made to the orientation of burials, but Sarolta Tettamanti has recently published an interesting study which demonstrates – for example, from the different ways that the hands of the dead were positioned (extended, clasped in prayer, etc.) – that a diversity of burial customs was prevalent, obviously pointing to variations in religious beliefs.[58] However, the final word on these cemeteries will only come from anthropological analysis of the skeletons, because of the absence of artifacts from so many of the graves.

We have few data on the relationship between burial grounds and settlements, but there is a general impression that they were separated by water (a stream or marshy area). One explanation for this might be that in Hungary, as in ancient Greece and many other places, it was believed that the dead had to cross a stretch of water in order to gain access to the next world. But to return specifically to the small, 'classical' burial grounds of the Árpádian Magyars, we have seen that these are a direct reflection of the size and structure of their settlements, which can be equated with their clan organization. We go on in the next chapter to look more closely at what anthropologists can tell us about these clans.

17. László Hegedűs: *Blood Contract*, 1908 (detail).

FEATURES OF CLAN ORGANIZATION[60]

Social collectivities numbering some 15 to 20 individuals – precisely the size of most of the 'classical' Árpádian Magyar cemeteries, with the sole exception of a site excavated by Béla Kürti at Szeged-Algyő, which contained upwards of forty graves[59] – are known to anthropologists and sociologists as 'greater families' or clans. The size is determined by the economic organization of clan life; it is the maximum that the joint resources of the greater family will support. Once the population reaches the critical size, the clan is obliged to divide into smaller units, each of which takes its due share of the common property and sets up as the nucleus of a new clan. The characteristics of clan organization in Árpádian Hungary are best examined under a series of headings.[60]

1. Patrilineal descent That this principle operated is confirmed by the early written laws of Hungary and the customs of its people, which have known parallels amongst the Turkic-Tatar and Finno-Ugrian peoples.

2. Collective ownership of property The clan was not just a unit of two or three generations of blood relatives but also held property in common. Property was not inherited as such, it simply existed and was utilized as an indivisible entity by successive members and generations of a clan. Value was not placed on the land itself but on the people who lived off it, which is why the early Hungarian kings, in their deeds of foundation and gift, did not grant lands but vassals who were listed by name. There are also data to show that if a group of vassals subject to the Church died out, then the Church lost its property rights in that village.

Károly Tagányi established that in villages belonging to a land-collectivity the land was the property of the collective, though everyone had rights to a certain piece of the land (it could be taken away if received in gift).[61] Unclaimed areas around a village would be partitioned by drawing lots by arrows, each person taking as much as his number of arrows entitled him to. The clan marked its property with its own badge or, to use the Mongol-Turkic expression, *tamga;* new clans that sprang from an existing clan did not take a completely new *tamga* but slightly adapted the old one. Gyula Sebestyén did some splendid work in tracing links of this kind among the Székely in the Csík region of Transylvania.

3. Power of the clan patriarch The head of a Magyar clan was absolute master within his clan in the same way as a king within his country; he was free to dispose of other clan members as he pleased. Thus he could not be called to account even if, for instance, he put his wife to death for adultery, as women were the clan's property just like any other chattels (Article 13 of St Ladislas's Decretum of Szabolcs). This power survived in practically undiluted form amongst the people of the Göcsej region, in south-west Hungary, up to the end of the last century, as we learn from a remarkable monograph by Ferenc Gönczi:[62] *The master demanded strict order: he was a veritable tribal chieftain and despot. All members of the family owed him unquestioning obedience... He would address all of the household using the intimate form te ['thou'], but everyone else, including his brothers and wife, had to address him formally either by maga ['you'] or 'your worship.'*

4. Inheritance When the head of the house died, we read about the Göcsej, either a son or son-in-law, or possibly a nephew, would be chosen by the surviving members of the household as their leader and master. In other regions of Hungary, some test of aptitude for the position was also part of this process. Amongst the early Árpádians either the eldest male in the family or the first-born son or a des-ignated heir-apparent succeeded to the 'throne'. Árpád himself, for instance, had as his successor his youngest son, who acceded to the throne when barely thirteen years old.

Among peoples related to the Magyars, clan chiefs were allowed to keep their position only as long as they remained 'fit for the job'. On closer investigation, this turns out to signify not fitness for physical work, but the retention of sexual potency – a custom which becomes especially noteworthy in connection with reigning princes. Among the Khazars, for example, the senior king was sacrificed if some misfortune befell his people, although other information suggests that the incumbent was permitted to rule for up to forty years, when he was sacrificed. It would seem that Álmos met an end of this kind in Transylvania, since, in the words of the *Chronicon Pictum,* 'he could not enter Pannonia', and a similar phenomenon may be discerned in the attempt that was made to assassinate King Stephen in his old age. The rationale for these events was that the welfare, happiness and success of the people were symbolized in the person of their ruler, who therefore had to surrender his office when his powers began to fail. In just the same way, the clan chieftains personified the prosperity of their clans, though we have no data to suggest that they were killed when they began to age.

Special rights must have appertained to the youngest son in a clan. It can be deduced from certain statements in the chronicles and from early Hungarian laws that boys became fully fledged members of the clan between their tenth and fifteenth year (in cemeteries, too, belt mounts have been found in the graves of adolescent boys). Moreover, according to the Hungarian legal code, in the Middle Ages it was the youngest son who inherited the father's house – a custom which cannot help but remind one of the great part that youngest sons always play in Hungarian folk tales.

18. Mór Than: *Attila's Feast*, 1865.

5. Division of work The extent of a clan patriarch's power has already been touched on, but it can be further judged from the records of trials by fire ordered at Nagyvárad (now Oradea, Romania), which reveal that even as late as the thirteenth century it was possible for the patriarch to sell his own children or use them as security against a pledge. We can be sure, from consideration of Hungarian folk customs, that the head of the clan was at one time also its priest. Be that as it may, the everyday duties of the clan proceeded according to his wishes, with division of labour amongst both men and womenfolk. Ferenc Gönczi observed in the Göcsej region that:

It was the business of two of the men to deal with the plough-horses, a third looked after the oxen, a fourth was the cow-hand, a fifth was responsible for the calves and sometimes helped with the pigs… Among the womenfolk… the one next in rank to the senior woman of the house had to bake and to wash up the pots, a second fed the fattening pig, a third tended the pigs that were turned out in the open, a fourth milked the cows, a fifth took care of the fire, gathered wood, swept the floors, etc.

Of course, there must have been a great many changes in the details of such duties over the thousand years that had elapsed since the entry of Árpád's Magyars into Hungary, but this way of ordering and delegating labour was in principle a heritage of that distant time.

6. The position of women We shall see later on that the rites of marriage had a place for acting out a simulated abduction of the bride (with the parents' consent) and for pay-ment of a bride-price. For the moment, though, let us keep to the woman's role within the clan. The clan matri-arch stood in roughly the same position of power over the clan womenfolk as her spouse did over the men. She, too, was at once the clan's 'priestess' with custody of the spells for keeping evil spirits at bay, securing harvests, and other domestic charms, as Zsigmond Szendrey verified from his examination of the material in Hungarian ethno-graphical collections.[63]

The division of labour has already been dealt with, but we should also note that at meals the womenfolk did not sit at the table but had to eat standing up, with their backs to the men, as is also the custom among nomadic peoples in Asia. A woman coming to a clan was treated as that clan's chattel. To ensure that she remained so, the institution of the levirate, by which a dead man's brother was required to take his wife, was customary because a woman's dowry was reckoned to become an integral part of the clan's property only after the passage of 'seven win-ters and seven summers'.

7. Cohesion of the clan In a settlement, new units of the extended family, denoted by the Hungarian terms *had, szer, szeg* and *zug*, would be crowded into a given area of land, in much the same way as the dead in the common-ers' cemeteries. When a clan had to split up, usually because of population pressures, its head would break a loaf of bread into as many pieces as there were new clans in order to signal the start of negotiations over how the communal property was to be shared out. Usually, one may be sure, this would not have proceeded harmoni-ously but would have been accompanied by quarreling and protest. It is this that left its mark in the Hungarian expression '*kenyértöresre került a sor*' 'the time has come to break the bread'.

8. Rank and left-right distinctions The same division into groups of the right and left that we have observed in the cemeteries played a part in clan life as well, especially at meal-times, when it was manifested in the seating order at the table. The clan patriarch sat at the centre with his eldest son on his right, the youngest son on his left. It is evident, however, that placing was a function of the responsibility attached to a man's work, for a servant or hired hand might be seated next to the eldest son if his duties were important enough.

This right-left distribution has its precise equivalent in certain Árpádian Magyar cemeteries where the two flanks of the burial group are not segregated by gender but both are ranked from the centre outwards in order of increasing poverty, with the left side always the higher ranking. From this it may be inferred that the Magyars envisaged the next world as the inverse of this life. The same can be seen within individual graves, where weaponry was placed on the opposite side to that used in life – a right-left and left-right transformation that also occurs in the beliefs about the afterlife held by some Eastern kinsfolk of the Magyars. This inversion has left its traces in some aspects of Hungarian folk beliefs.

Magyar clan organization was reflected not only in the seating arrangement at meals but also, for instance, in the way food was apportioned. The head of an animal was always served to the clan chief, meat from the animal's right flank to those sitting on his right, that from the left flank to those on the left. One task for archaeologists in the future will be to look out for what animal parts were placed in different graves. Hitherto the only such attempt to be made has been in the Onogur cemetery at Felgyő (byJános Matolcsi and archaeological assessments by Emese Lovász).In my 1944 book on the Conquest-era Magyars, I endeavoured to explain the subsequent evolution of the Hungarian state as a projection of clan organization. Today I see that this was an oversimplistic view of matters, as I had not recognized that the Árpádian Magyars already had a highly stratified society, manifested in the dichotomy between yurt-dwellers and hut-dwellers, between rich and poor.

19. Caftan ornaments from Szeged-Bojárhalom.

AGRICULTURE, ANIMAL HUSBANDRY

Opinions on whether the Árpádian Magyars were *yurt* or hut-dwellers have tended to polarize according to whether the Magyars are seen as having been either pastoral nomads or a settled peasant folk. In fact, neither of these two extremes is right, because both assume that the Magyars could be regarded as ethnically uniform, whereas in all likelihood they were a motley of farmers and warriors. If this were accepted, there would be no need for the contortions that have been employed to make farmers out of nomads, a nation of peasant cultivators of crops out of warrior tribesmen. A parallel can be drawn with the Cuman leaders who, in the thirteenth century, fled into Hungary from beyond the Carpathians, bringing with them many tillers of soil and animal breeders. One such was Vajk, founder of the Hunyadi dynasty which supplied Hungary's fifteenth-century kings (his name was the same as St Stephen's pagan name up to his coronation), who settled in Transylvania along with the Vlach people. But this apart, the Onogur-Hungarians, who were already living in Hungary when the Magyars arrived, can be assumed, from their extensive villages, to have been mainly agriculturalists; as a defeated people they would presumably have continued to farm for their new masters.

Since the 1950s, a similar – and peculiarly important – role has been ascribed to the indigenous Slav population who are also supposed to have pressed into the service of their Magyar conquerors. According to one of the standard history text-books:

In the course of the inevitable changeover to agriculture the Slavs taught the Hungarians a more advanced method of tilling the land, with the use of an iron cutting share... The adoption of the Slavonic word-stock relating to arable farming is another sign of how the slow conversion of Hungarian herders to agrarianism proceeded.

Considering that the Magyars had known and practised tillage farming in their earlier homeland for a good millenium and a half before they entered Hungary, I can only regard the above statements as deliberate distortions, not as serious scholarly comment. In fact, the relevant vocabulary – words like *tarló* 'arable land [later 'stubble']', *búza* 'wheat', *árpa* 'barley', *eke* 'plough ', *sarló* 'sickle', *boglya* 'haycock', *szérű* 'threshing floor', *szór* 'winnow', *őröl* 'mill, grind', *dara* 'coarse meal' – were already present in the Hungarian language long before the Conquest. Iván Balassa's investigations into the history of the Hungarian terms associated with ploughing[64] are pertinent here, for the early occurrence of words like *szánt* 'till', *köldök* 'foot, prop', *szarv* 'stilts', *eke* 'plough', *talp* 'sole, chip', *ekefő* 'beam', *szántóvas* 'point, share', *csoroszlya* 'coulter', *vezér* 'mouldboard' is evidence that the ploughs in use were relatively sophisticated for their age. Admittedly, some of the

new terms could have been – and probably were – borrowed from the Slav farmers among the villagers.

Several centuries after the Conquest, the Hungarian chroniclers sought a reason for the adoption of farming by Hungarian villagers. Simon Kézai produced the following reasoning, though we can read his own doubts between the lines:

Whosoever flouted the order [to mobilize for war] without sufficient reason was either cleaved in two by the sword, in accordance with the law of the Scythians, or publicly declared an outlaw, or thrown into bondage. Only crimes and transgressions of this kind could raise barriers between one Magyar and another. Otherwise, since all Magyars were descended from one father and one mother, how is it that we should call one a noble yet the other a non-noble unless it were that he had fallen into servitude as sentence for such misdeeds?

A clear contrast is drawn here between Magyars and serfs. Naturally, one can believe that some nobles were punished by reducing them to serfdom, but it is absurd to pretend that the entire peasant population could have arisen in this manner, for even in later centuries the nobility comprised but a small percentage of the total Hungarian population. However, one cannot help but notice that this same 'small percentage' also characterizes

20. Silver horse trapping decorations from the grave at Ártánd.

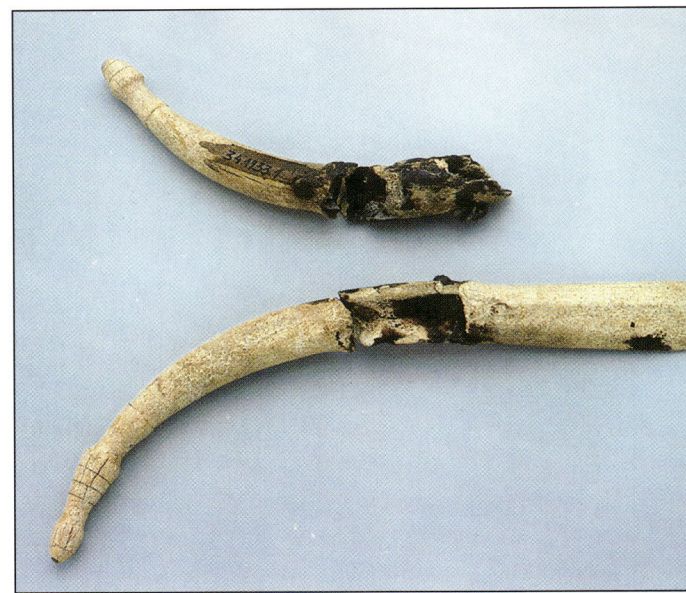

21. Horse trapping from Pilin-Leshegy.
22. Bone mouthpiece from Tiszaderzs.
23. Carved bone mouthpiece from Kiszombor.
24. Iron bridles from Muszka.

the relation of the small burial grounds of the high-ranking clans to the huge cemeteries of the Onogur-Hungarians and the later common people. Hungary's peasantry was not drawn from the ranks of Magyar mounted warriors and herdsmen but partly from the indigenous Onogurs and Slavs whom the Magyars found on their entry into the country, partly from the farmers and allied peoples who migrated along with Árpád's armies. Each population retained its own occupations, one providing the country's soldiers and nobles, the other staying on the land.

To accept this dichotomy in tenth-century Hungarian society is to reconcile the contradiction that we find in one of our principal Arabic sources, Ibn Rusta, who writes, on the one hand, that 'they possess leather tents and they travel together in search of herbage and abundant pasturage' and, on the other hand, 'they have many cultivated fields'. It is a mistake to interpret this as meaning that the nomads and the farmers were one and the same; they were two quite distinct social strata. The foundation charter of Pannonhalma Abbey, thought to date from A.D. 1001, refers to farmsteads, vineyards, vegetable plots, wine and fishermen in a way that suggests they were already long established – or at least that they had not suddenly appeared in the tenth century. From the foregoing it is apparent that the old schma of 'from nomad to farmer, from yurt to house', must be regarded as invalid.

Judging by the plant seeds that have been excavated at early settlements,[65] agriculture in Hungary seems to have included the following crops: wheat, rye, millet, peaches, flax, buckwheat, hazelnuts, grapes, walnuts, oats, wild and sour cherries, lentils, vetch (chickling pea), pea and hemp, along with field bindweed and the corn cockle. These were cultivated in the enclosed compounds that were discovered during excavations at Felgyő. We know from documents of the Árpádian era that a wealthy man would have yoked six to eight oxen to his plough, whilst the poorer folk would been lucky to have two. This would naturally affect the depth of ploughing anf hence the yields obtained from the land.

At sites of Árpádian-period settlement, 90-95% of the bones that have been recovered are from domestic animals, only 5% are from game. As the majority of the sites were inhabited by the needier segments of the populace, these figures could be construed as indicating that non-nobles were forbidden to hunt, as they certainly were later on during the Middle Ages. The horse and cattle herders, shepherds and swineherds of Hungary were always male; only poultry-keeping was women's work.

Of the large animals the horse is the one that is usually highlighted because it has become almost a dictum that the Hungarians are an equestrian nation. Horses, white ones in particular, were sacrificial animals, the flayed skin being given to accompany a dead man to the next world, whilst in Transylvania the horse even figured as an ancestor in the Székely descent myth. Horse-keeping depends, in part at least, on having access to suitable grazing grounds, so that György Almásy's observations on the differences between the prairies of Asia and the Middle Danube basin assume considerable importance:

There is no comparison between the pastures of Central Asia and those of Europe because their productiveness is often one-twentieth that of the same-sized European pasture, so that in order to keep the same number of cattle there, ten or twenty times as much grazing land is required as in Europe... where it is impossible to employ a regimen of alternating pasturing and stabling. They cannot gather a sufficient quantity of winter fodder... Nomad-ic peoples are largely reliant on settled peoples for grain production.

In return, Almásy adds, 'they receive meat from the nomads'.

It is now deeply ingrained in the Hungarian consciousness that the open-range style of stock herding displayed at Hortobágy and Bugac on the Alföld plain has been passed down from the Conquest era. The very epithets rideg 'inclement, rough' and szilaj 'uncurbed, wild' which are often used in this connection give some

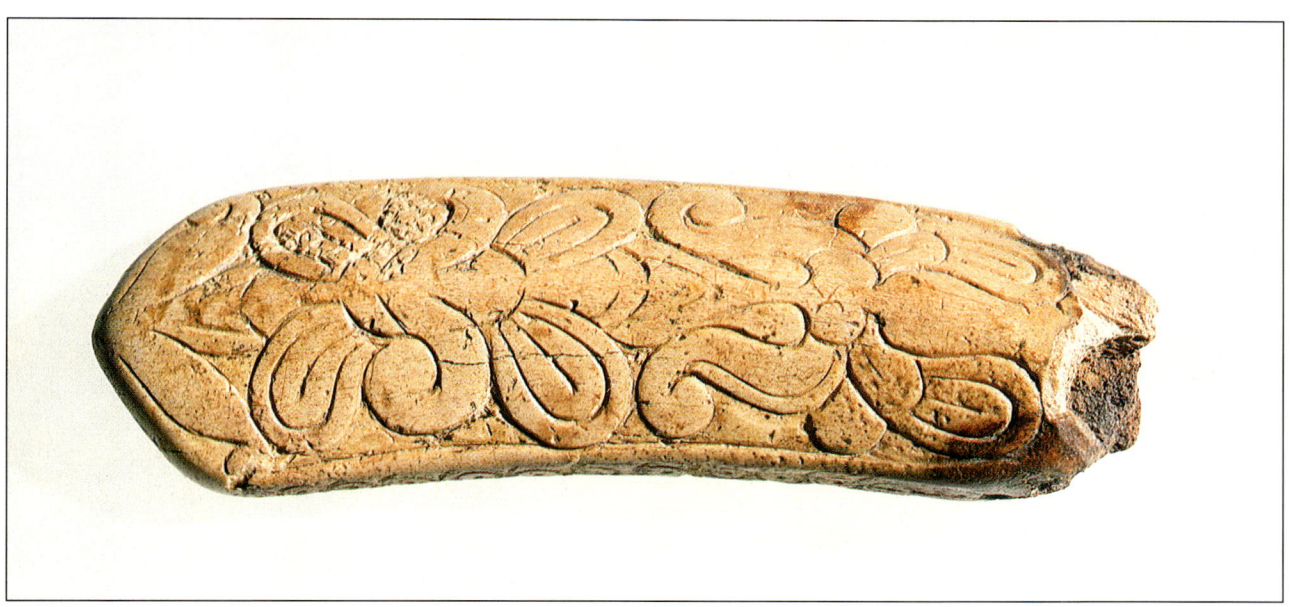

idea of its peculiarity, which was well captured by István Györffy in his book on the history of the Nagykunság region of the plain:

The herds of wild horses, cattle and swine grazed the whole year round in the open and even in the winter were not brought together... It was impossible to drive a wild herd. Camp would be struck wherever night overtook them, so that the herdsmen could not build permanent huts for themselves. At best they might improvise a little shelter, but even this only in the winter; otherwise they would sleep out under the open sky... There were some 'wild' herdsmen who had not been into a town for thirty years.

It is hardly surprising that the herdsman came to embody personal freedom in popular imagination.

Many Hungarians, scholars included, visualize the everyday life of Conquest-era Magyars as having been something like that, though it is a misconception. The herding life of the Alföld evolved only centuries later, on grasslands that had been left to run wild during the Turkish occupation of Hungary. Let me remind you again of what Ibn Rusta had to say about the nomadic herders of the Conquest era: 'They possess leather tents and they travel in search of herbage and abundant pasturage.' The records of the Magyar raids into foreign lands clearly show that Hungarian horses were hardy animals, well able to withstand heat, cold and relatively long periods without water, and seldom allowed the luxury of a stable. Their bone remains are well known to us from Magyar graves of the Concquest period. Béla Hankó pictured them as being 'on average only 140 cm [14 hands] tall at

the withers, with a small, lean head, blazing eyes, wiry hocks, and muscles of steel.' To this may be added some remarks by János Matolcsi, who has been giving expert advice on the bone finds at my own excavations:

The very excellence of Hungarian horses in the Middle Ages attests to the great expertise and high breeding standards of our forebears. This is worth emphasizing becuse in respect of the origin of the Hungarian horse the view has become prevalent among the general public that a breed's good reputation is due to some sort of noble progenitor... The sole archetype of the Hungarian horse, as of all other breeds, was the Eurasian wild horse [i.e. Equus caballus przewalskii] which is why Csaba Anghi stated that the blood of their Mongolian Taki stock showed up in horses of the Conquest-era Magyars.

The late Vera G. Molnár published the evidence that the long felt cloak, or *szűr*, worn by Hungarian herdsmen was already part of the dress of steppe peoples in ancient times.

The type of shepherd-dog used in the Conquest era is still a matter of debate but we may be closer to knowing the truth when the half-dozen canine skeletons excavated at Felgyő have been fully examined. At all events, it would appear that the komondor, kuvasz, puli, and harehound are among the older Hungarian breeds.

Early sources also make reference to the keeping of camels in Hungary. Anonymus, for example, writes that when Álmos began his migration he received some camels, amongst other rich gifts, from the prince of Kalich. King Béla III, on the other hand, donated 'four packed camels' to Emperor Frederick I Barbarossa when the latter set off on the Third Crusade.[66] There is nothing surprising about this, as we have documentary evidence that a number of the royal and princely houses of western Europe attempted to naturalize the camel in their lands, but the wet climate did not suit the animals and they died out. We know, however, that no camel bones have come to light among the animal remains at Conquest-era settlements in Hungary, so we may suppose that, at most, the species may have had a place in some sort of 'zoo' at the ruler's court, more as a curiosity than as a regular pack-animal.

Hunting, Fishing

What little we know about hunting in the Árpádian age is but a faint reflection of the presumed reality. The contest with game is not a matter of weaponry, or even nerve, alone; it also involves experience and skill. The hunter needs to know the habits of his guarry, its quirks, its tracks by day or night, its watering places, and innumerable other aspects of the animal's life if the hunt is to be successful. Besides his bow, arrow and spear, the Árpádian hunter very probably set up cunning traps and snares along the paths used by animals, ingenious contraptions that would be triggered by a touch on a tautened line, and maybe hunted with nets.

The most spectacular and popular form of hunting was falconry. A well-trained bird would be the pride of its owner and its fame might spread afar. So highly esteemed was the hawk that, according to Hungarian chroniclers, it formed one of the devices in the insignia of Attila and the Magyar princes. Indeed, under the name *Turul,* it was revered as the Árpádian dynasty's

clan ancestor which, after rebirth, had begat Hunor and Magyar with their mother Emese.

On the beauty of falconry and the conduct of the chase I again turn to the account given by György Almásy of his travels in Central Asia at the turn of this century.[67]

25. Hunting brothers from the drinking horn from Chernigov.
26. Belt strap in the shape of a bird from Karos.

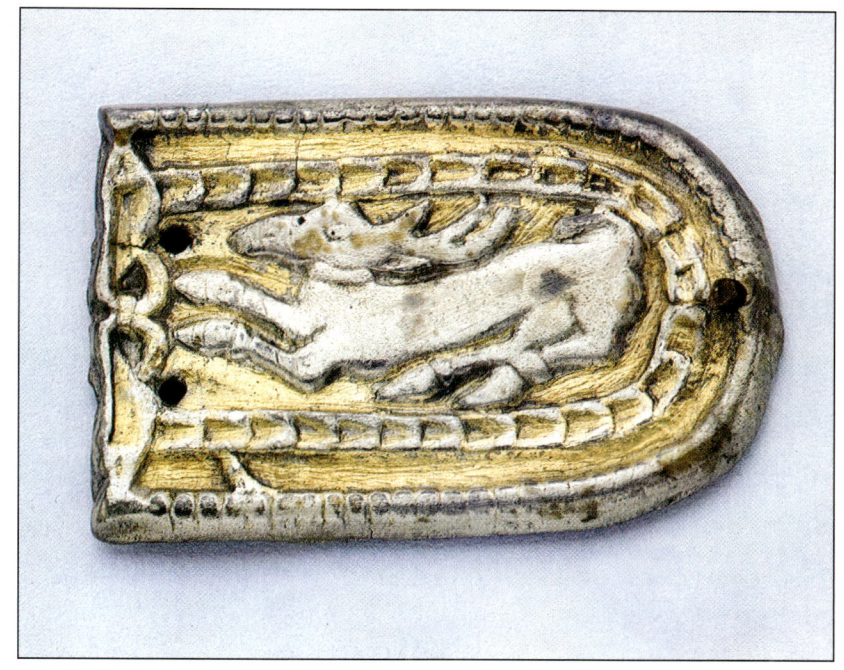

Once the horseman had released his bird, he galloped along in its track, giving it encouragement and also striving to be near at hand when the quarry was killed; all the time he would whoop and scream 'Ahi, ahi!' at the top of his voice… Completely absorbed in the thrill of the moment, riding exuberantly at breakneck speed, the horseman was the animated, bubblingly vital focus of this passionate scene… The proceedings were always the same. The hawk would swoop down over its rabbit prey which, in mortal fear, would race off straight as an arrow in flight. The bird would then fly a little higher, drop at lightning speed and with one movement fasten on the rabbit's backbone, just above the shoulder-blades, and with a second grip its head. At this instant the rabbit would usually turn a somersault, as if hit by a shot, and then fall prostrate and still. The needle-sharp claws kill the animal like a dagger, usually on the first strike, whilst the hawk drops on its victim so violently that the latter's bones crack and shatter as if they were being crushed in a press. The victorious bird perches stiffly, without moving, as though giddy, on its felled prey; its yellow eyes enraged, it glowers angrily, dazedly around, its wings lowered to cover its prize.

The falconer lures the bird back onto his thickly gloved fist with a piece of raw meat and then the whole process starts again from the beginning.

Hungary was famous for its falconry, and a manual by a Hungarian master falconer was read in the West as one of the standard treatises on the subject into medieval times. The falcon and its victim was also a common and skilfully rendered subject of steppe art in olden times. Scythian-era goldsmiths particularly excelled at it, but the falconer's figure also appears later on silver platters, just possibly modelled after the handiwork of a Magyar craftsman.

If a hunter had to be familiar with the nature of his game, this applied even more to the fisherman.[68] Each species of fish has its own haunts and habits, one preferring the surface, another deeper waters, a third the mud of the river or lake bottom, and so on, and the fishing tackle has to be adapted to these differing needs.

Among the techniques known to Conquest-period fishermen in Hungary were artificial weirs, set across river channels to divert the fish swimming upstream into a trap. They also had wicker fishbaskets, or weels, and similar gear, which were smaller-scale implementations of the traps used with weirs. These devices caught fish passively, but the use of large seine or drag nets and other active netting methods required the coordinated work of a gang of fisherman. At one time it was thought that the ten fishermen mentioned in the foundation charter of Tihany Abbey, on Lake Balaton, denoted an early fishing team, but Károly Gaál has pointed out that similar groups can be traced to the properties of the Benedictine Order at a number of other places, suggesting that we may be dealing with a monastically-based fishery organization.[69] Fish were also caught from canoes or rafts by bow-and-arrow or harpoon and, in smaller streams, with bare hands or small baskets; fishing with hooks seems to have been of lesser importance.

Ethnographers and linguists who have explored the history of Hungarian fishing have traced the origins of the tackle and procedures back to Ob-Ugrian times. However, it must be borne in mind that fish have not changed their habits over this sort of time period so it is not inconceivable that similar fishing methods could have evolved quite independently in the trans-Ural region and in Hungary without there being a historical link between the two.

The primary demand for fish came from monks and priests, with their need to observe fast-days. It is extremely rare to come across fish-bones at the Conquest-era settlements known to me. Nevertheless, fish were dried or salted for storage, to eke out the diet in leaner periods, and they also had uses other than as a food item. Fish-glue was a valued material of the bow-maker, whilst the fat which can be rendered from fish was also a much esteemed product.

*

We have almost no information about *bee-keeping* in the period of interest. Virtually the only evidence that it was cultivated lies in Hungarian toponyms that incorporate the root *födém* 'roof, cover' (certain wild bees construct a cover above the nest to protect it from rain). Bees would have been kept, or their nests in the wild rained, not just for the honey but more especially for the beeswax, which was an important exchange and export commodity.

CRAFTS

BOW-MAKING The purpose of the curved bone or horn plates that were unearthed from both Árpádian Magyar and Avar-period graves was a matter of dispute for quite some time. Early guesses included trimmings for cloaks and decorations for sword or sabre hilts until Károly Sebestyén puzzled out, from careful consideration of the excavation data, that they were none other than reinforcing strips from the handle and tips of the recurved, or reflex, compound bow.[70] This was the decisive weapon in the armamentarium of the Conquest-era Magyars, the close-combat spear or sabre serving only to finish off what would already have been largely accomplished by bow and arrow.

Already by those times the bow could look back on a very ancient past, having figured in the cave art of Spanish hunters of the Mesolithic period, but subsequently it became chiefly a weapon of nomadic hunters. The reflex bow in particular was a temperamental weapon due to the manner of its construction, being made from several layers of different materials that had to be tightly glued and bound together, so that if it was soaked the bow became unusable. For this reason the Magyars carefully protected their bows by carrying them in leather quivers, and warriors would avoid having to go into combat in rainy weather.

Bow-making called for highly-skilled artistry, not so much because of the lively gilded ornaments applied to

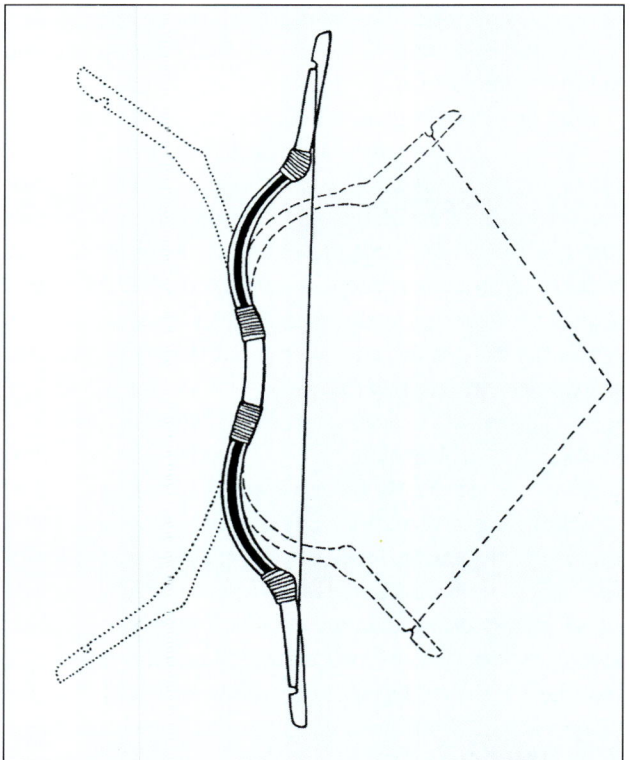

the leather sheath that covered later examples of the weapon, but because of the need to get its balance and distribution of forces absolutely right. Following Sebestyén's elucidation of the function of the bone plates, Jakucs and Professor Fábián made reconstructions of the Magyar bow, drawing on observations of living Turkish craftsmen who had continued to make this type of recurved weapon. The procedure is as follows. A springy, three-inch-thick branch, which can be bent back evenly from a C-shape into the reverse, is selected. The bow is carved from the branch so that its two limbs are of equal weight and elasticity about the belly. The grip and the ends of the limbs are tapered down and then two or three layers of ox sinew, obtained by soaking and separating bundles of tendons stripped from the leg bones, are glued to this springy wooden core. Over this are fixed long strips of cow-horn. Fish glue is used as the adhesive as this retains its elasticity. Finally, to stiffen the tips of the two limbs and the grip, these parts are covered with bone-plaques, carved from antler horn, which are closely grooved to allow them to be tightly bound as well as glued. When completed – a process that might take up to several years – the bow is braced in the reverse direction to its natural bend and then strung. The pull of such a weapon – around 25 kg was normal – was two or three times greater than that of a simple bow, so considerable strength was required to draw it. Generally, the bone-plaques on the two tips would be exact copies of one another, matching in their curvature, but some asymmetric bows were also made, with the plaque on the lower limb longer and less curved than on the upper. This design was particularly suited for shooting to the rear on horseback because it allowed the bow to be rested conveniently on the horse's crupper.[71]

A bow, expensive as it was, was interred along with its owner. It was put into the grave alongside the body in one of three states – slack, strung, or broken into pieces – each of which presumably signified different attitudes to the other-world, though we have no way of knowing what these were.

To turn to the arrows, these were of several types. Iron-tipped arrows (ones with wooden tips may be conjectured to have existed but would have perished in the ground) had flat, lanceolate more precisely, rhomboid – heads, usually with a slightly raised central 'rib'. The centre of gravity of the arrowheads varies, being to the front in some, at the centre in others, towards the back in yet others. Arrowheads of swallowtail and needle shapes are

28. Arrow from the Conquest period.

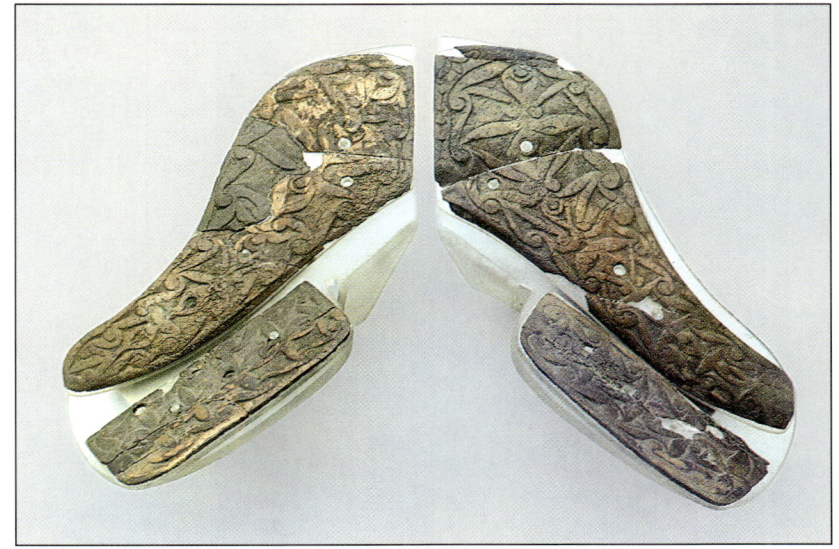

also known. The variously shaped and weighted arrowheads were designed for different purposes, some insight into these being given by Katalin Kőhalmi from her recent studies among the people of Mongolia.[72] The swallowtail type, for instance, is still used today by Ob-Ugrian hunters to shoot water-fowl paddling on the water surface, the bow being drawn horizontally and the arrow released to skim across the water like a flat stone towards its target.

Exactly the same principles of symmetry govern the fashioning of the arrowheads as with the bows: each half matches the other in shape and weight around the axis of the shaft. On one occasion, at a university seminar, I asked a master blacksmith to make such an arrowhead, but the result of about three-quarters of an hour's labour was truly wretched: the crude forging that he produced was a piece of botchery alongside the slender, light arrowheads of the Conquest period. This gave me cause to wonder if the latter might have been beaten out in a mould; at all events, it underlined the high degree of craftsmanship that is implicit even in such a seemingly insignificant artifact as this. The shafts of most arrows were fashioned from wood, although Professor Fábián carried out some successful trials employing reeds for the purpose. The fletching of the tailfeathers, so important for the direction and accuracy of flight of arrows, would have required considerable skill.

Arrows are delicate implements, so a quiver is needed to keep them in pristine condition right up to the moment that they are fired. In Magyar versions of the quiver, as in those of the Avars, the arrows, carefully packed together in small bundles, were laid with the heads uppermost. The quiver, which was broader at both top and bottom to accomodate the shape of the arrow bundles, was provided with flaps on the side which allowed the arrows to be placed inside without damaging them. Since the arrows also had to be protected from damp, the quiver, which in use was suspended from the warrior's belt, had a lid on top which could be opened to withdraw a bundle of four or five arrows at a time, thereby enabling a rapid rate of fire to be maintained.

Archery therefore demanded the joint efforts of several craftsmen: someone able to work with wood and bone, perhaps also to prepare glue from appropriate fishes; a smith to forge the arrowheads (the warriors themselves would do any necessary honing); and a quiver-maker, working with birch-bark or leather, with again some help from the smith to produce the iron frame. Quite obviously, the bows, arrows and quivers would not have been made by individual warriors but would have been 'mass-produced' for the market by groups of craftsmen. The same must have been true for saddles, the item we turn to next.

SADDLE-MAKING The design of the box-like saddles used by the Arpádian Magyars was first pieced together from fragments – pieces of saddle-tree and the bone strips that decorated the cross-woods – that were recovered from the graves at Koroncó,[73] though intact examples of such inlaid saddles have come to light since then. The traditional saddle-making skills somehow managed to last out in Hungary at Tiszafüred, where they continued to turn out exact replicas of the Conquest-period models until the beginning of this century. It was from the last of the Tiszafüred master-craftsmen, Mihály Kuli, that I learned (in 1938) the details of how the saddles were made and the tools that were employed (the tools are now in the collection of the Ethnographical Museum, Budapest).

The components of a saddle are the two halves of the tree, the cross-woods of the pommel and cantle, the leather side-flaps, the stirrup leathers and, for fastening the saddle, the girth, breast and crupper bands. Assembly of a saddle is thus as complex as the bow-making process. To start with, the wood that went into the saddle-tree and cross-pieces would have to be seasoned for years on end to ensure that the finished saddle would not buckle. The saddle-tree was arched in such a way that it rested on the horse's back on an area no bigger than the palm of the hand. The pommel and cantle were lashed to this with wettened thongs that, on the underside of the saddle, ran in recessed grooves so as not to chafe the horse. Once the thongs dried out they bound so strongly that, according to Master Kuli, the saddle might break anywhere else but never at the binding. The pommel was generally fixed vertically whilst the cantle was tilted back at an angle to provide the seat. If the weight of a rider had pressed down on this seat alone, the saddle would have tended to tip back, so, to counterbalance this, the stirrups were slung from nearer the front of the saddle-tree, thus allowing part of the weight to be transferred forward. With this type of saddle, then, the rider was delicately poised on the horse's back.

As to the embellishment of Magyar riding tackle, the equipment recovered from female graves is noticeably more elegant and richly adorned than that from male graves. The same is true amongst present-day nomadic Turkic peoples, where the first thing that the swarms of guests at a wedding feast will admire, or cast a critical eye over, to weigh up how good a 'show' the bride's family are making, is the tackle that has been produced for the bride's horse. Not just the saddle and its attachments, but even the bridle and bit are sometimes exquisite works of

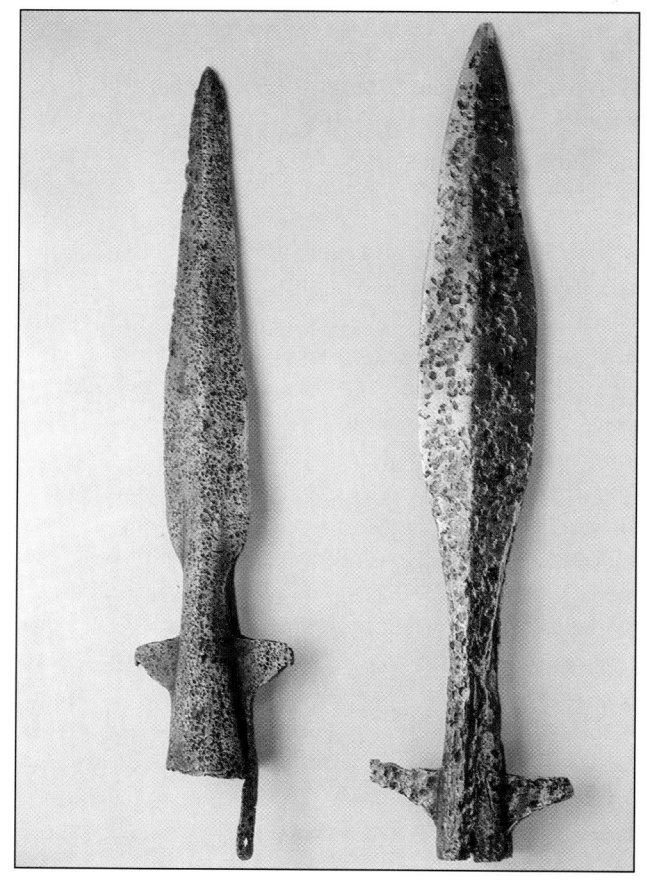

art. From this we may guess that for the Árpádian Magyars, too, the horse trappings were among the most important and splendid wedding gifts. The cheek-pieces of the bit were in some cases gorgeously carved from antler horn, whereas in other cases they were modelled with animal-head terminals, following a Scythian tradition, or they might be masterpieces of Norse craft, no doubt acquired at a correspondingly fancy price. The inlaid palmette designs, in gilded silver, that are seen on some stirrups are truly marvellous. But perhaps these items are also of interest because, seemingly, it was the custom amongst the Árpádian Magyars to bury their womenfolk along with their former dowries (a practice still followed until not so long ago in the Kalotaszeg [Calata] region of Transylvania).

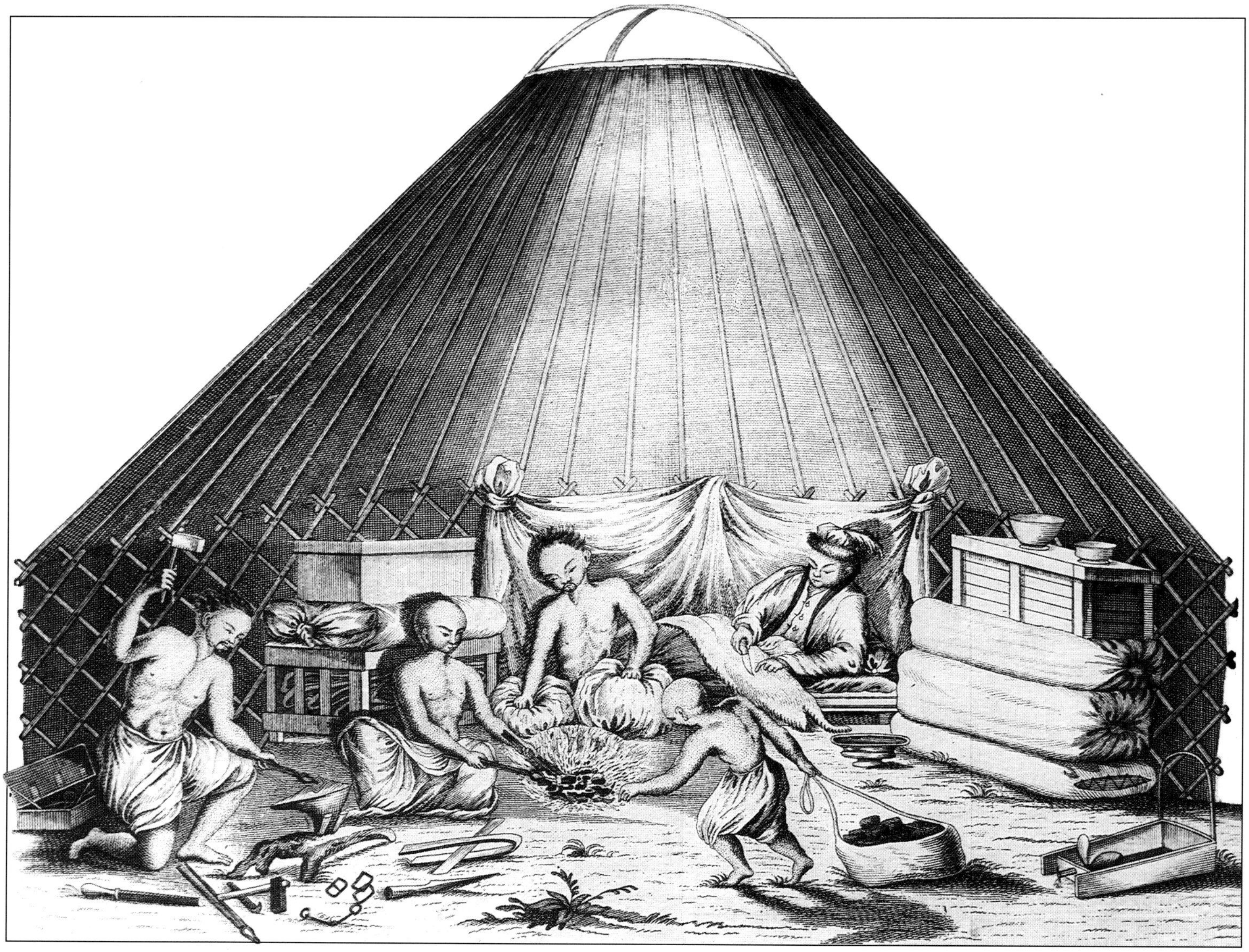

So, with the saddlers, too, we can see the same need for the combined skills of blacksmiths and goldsmiths as well as harness makers, and again it seems reasonable to presume that their wares were taken as merchandise to fairs.

IRONSMITHING The raw materials for the saddler or bow-maker were more or less ready to hand whereas the smith had to get his out of the ground. In the Middle Ages two sources of crude iron were available, ore mined from the earth and limonite, or 'bog iron,'[74] and obviously the same applied in the Conquest period. Iron was needed

in large quantities for the manufacture of arrowheads, stirrups, horse-bits, sabres, spears, quiver frames, curry-combs, buckles, knives and a variety of other objects. We saw already, in the earlier section on arrow-making, the high degree of skill that had to be acquired to produce even a small, apparently simple object like an arrowhead, and this was even more true for the forging of grubbing-hoes, plough-shares and other digging implements. Blacksmithing, like the making of bows, saddles and the rest, was a genuine craft, requiring a well-trained expertise, and that could not be picked up casually any more than could animal breeding or agriculture.

In ancient times blacksmiths, working with fire and iron, used to be highly respected individuals, quasi-priests of their communities. Apart from strict blacksmithing, they often had some understanding of the healing arts and would successfully treat both humans and beasts, though by the time of the Conquest the occupation had lost its religious overtones. We can see this, for example,

in the fact that already during the preceding era the Onogurs had buried their smiths without any particular distinction. It is plausible to assume, however, that their workshops, being fire hazards, would have been located on the fringes of villages.

Whatever the period we talk about, iron, like human nature, does not change, so it is not surprising that black-smithing should have altered so little down to the present day. At most, electrical heating nowadays replaces the bel-lows-blown furnace, but that is not a fundamental change. Legends came into being about the magical knowledge possessed by smiths, yet these legends had a foundation in fact. Wilhelm Radloff, one of the great ethnographers, linguists and archaeologists of the nine-teenth century, was eye-witness to the feat of a smith in the Siberian Altai who, with just a blow pipe and other simple tools, managed to braze together a broken steel needle so that no trace of the joint was visible.[75] Skill of that order is obviously exceptional, but it does demon-strate that it could, on occasion, approach artistic levels. A finely wrought stirrup or steel sword gives us an inkling that the blacksmiths who worked for the Árpádian Ma-gyars must have stood near the summit of their craft.

Iron smelting called for charcoal, and charcoal-burn-ing is a skill in its own right. Blacksmiths obviously would not have carried it out themselves but entrusted it to others who made it their occupation.[76] Thus the more we delve into the life of the Árpádian Magyars, the more we can begin to appreciate that they lived in what must have been a highly stratified society. The views that were circu-lating in 1950s' Hungary, to the effect that the Árpádian Magyars had barely outgrown the primitive tribal system of the steppe-country, now strike one as ludicrous.

GOLD- AND SILVERSMITHING Compared with the blacksmith, the worker in gold and silver had what amounted to almost a 'mobile' workshop. Even nowa-days, Azerbaijani and Balkan master-craftsmen produce jewellery of great beauty with a very limited set of tools, though naturally the more complicated techniques, such as enamelling, granulation and brazing, require more equipment. It seems reasonable to suggest that in Árpádi-an Hungary silversmithing would have been carried out both at fixed centres, especially around the headquarters of princes and other leaders, and by itinerant craftsmen. The latter would have set up a stall at bazaars and, to the wonder of a watching public, fashioned their earpen-dants, armlets and the cruder types of castings. The more intricate techniques like chill-casting could only have been performed with the facilities of a permanent work-shop. However, all that was needed to make a splendid plaque for mounting on the flap of a sabretache, or pouch, or to create a disc-shaped pectoral jewel were, in addition to the balance – an indispensable item of equip-ment for the worker in precious metals – a jar of silver-smith's pitch and a few gravers and punches. These tools would have been prepared by the craftsman himself, as they are to the present day, with each one jealously guard-ing his own set of punches from rivals. It was partly on the basis of the different punch-marks that I was able to

30. Altaic "smithy" (drawing based on the Pallas publication).
31. "Winged" Carolingian spears from Szombathely and Kőszegszerdahely.
32. Double-edged swords from Szentbékkálla and two graves from Sob-Kiserdő.

determine that the pieces of the Nagyszentmiklós Treasure belonged to two distinct sets, produced in different workshops. Itinerant silversmiths from Venice and Byzantium – not necessarily the best ones at that – would show up in Hungary from time to time; certain jewellery with granulation decorations (e.g. finds at Hencida, in Hajdú-Bihar County, and the Tokay Treasure) displays superb craftsmanship.

A precise description of the workshops in a centre can be gained from the treatise *Scedula diversarum artium*, written by Theophilus Presbyter in the late tenth century. There are also extant 'manuals' used by Hungarian craftsmen, though these date from a much later period, the best known of them being the work of a Péter Ötvös (Hungarian, ötvös means 'silversmith') from the town of Kecskemét. It is evident from such writings that all the various processes, as they were handed down by tradition, were associated with spells and other magical practices, for example, to secure the success of an amalgam with quicksilver.

Among the products of the Árpádian Magyar silversmiths were sabretache plates, pectoral discs, helmet mounts and a range of iron objects. They were masters of fire gilding and frequently used this technique to fill in the background on a piece and so bring out the pattern. Engraving and embossing were the two main techniques, besides gilding, for highlighting a design. In engraving, the background is stamped with tiny, circular hollow punches, leaving a smooth pattern of tendrils or some other motif. In embossing, the contours of a design are chased from the back of a metal sheet, using domed punches, which achieves an interplay of light and shade on the front surface. The setting of semiprecious stones within a design or the use of a number of separate mounts to cover the surface (e.g. the flap of a sabretache[77]) were yet other decorative techniques in use. With some sabretaches a mount was only fitted around the central loophole to cover the strap by which the pouch was attached to the belt. (The actual compositional principles utilized in the designs will be dealt with in the later section on horse trappings.)

The most splendid artifacts of the goldsmiths' craft from the late Avar-Árpádian Magyar era are the pieces that make up the Nagyszentmiklós Treasure. As my own monograph on this appeared relatively recently,[78] I shall restrict myself here to just a few remarks of a technical nature bearing mainly on the procedures that were used to create the pieces.

Strictly speaking, the Nagyszentmiklós Treasure is a hoard in so far as it is not the product of a single workshop, or even a single age, but a collection of objects from different sources. It does represent, however, a deliberate bringing together of two originally separate table services. The technique of the repoussé work on the jugs does not differ in essentials from that employed to make sabretache plates except that the decorated surface is spherical rather than planar. The bodies of the jugs may have been raised from a single sheet of gold or else were produced by brazing together two halves, though if the latter, there is not the slightest sign of a joint inside the jugs. In most cases (though not all) the base and neck, as well as the handle of course, were formed separately and then brazed on to the body. The repoussé work was carried out by first filling the jug with jeweller's pitch. The design was then traced on the outside surface and the background between the contours was hammered into the pitch; this forced the waxy pitch behind the contours, pushing the pattern outwards and thereby producing a design in relief that appears to have been worked from the back. The background was then further worked on with engraving stamps, just as with the sabretache plates. On some pieces of the Treasure there are open-work tendril patterns, which originally may have been filled with enamelling (*émail cloissoné*), whilst others have inlays of gem-stones or pastes. Also found on most of the pieces are stamped or engraved inscriptions in a runic script that hitherto has been only partially deciphered.

Models for the Nagyszentmiklós Treasure, and the techniques employed in its production, have been sought virtually throughout Eurasia as far back in time as China and Mesopotamia and as far away as the Caucasus or Byzantium, but the most widely accepted attribution is to the late Avar (Onogur) world. However, even so, like the diplomacy carried out by rulers of the great nomadic empires, it would have taken in a wide range of cultures, and this confluence may have been far from accidental. The court of a leader like the Avar kagan, Bayan, or Árpád himself, had to maintain a truly continental perspective on events. In order to cultivate their far-flung contacts, the presentation or sending of gifts played an important part in the rituals of greeting. For me, this is the root of the 'cosmopolitan' cross-section of styles displayed by the Nagyszentmiklós Treasure.

POTTERY As a rule, the craftsmen of an invaded territory were put to work in the service of their conquerors. Árpád's people unquestionably were conquerors, and this explains the difficulty that we still experience today in distinguishing late Avar-Onogur pottery from the work of Árpádian Magyar craftsmen. It may be taken for granted that, by and large, the same workshops remained in use.

Three techniques were employed by potters of the Árpádian period.[79] In the first, the vessel was hand-formed from a lump of clay; this was the method utilized for most burial pottery, which was often also baked only perfunctorily, presumably in the embers of the funeral pyre itself. The second technique was to throw the vessel on a hand-operated potter's wheel. The clay would have been carefully prepared and the plug to be shaped was sanded underneath to stop it sticking to the wheel (most of these vessels still have sand grains on their base). The decoration on these vessels is neat and pleasing, most often a wavy linear pattern, and there is usually a potter's mark stamped on the bottom. Most of the marks are simple geometrical shapes and convex, formed by a small mould carved either on the wheel itself or on a board fixed to the wheel. Vessels turned on a hand-wheel are easily recognizable because in profile they are never as accurately symmetrical about their axis as wares produced with a rapidly rotating, treadle-operated wheel, which comprise

33. Hair ornaments from Nyíracsád.
34. Hair ornaments from Hencida.
35. Hair ornaments from Bashalom.
36. The sabretache from Eperjes.
37. Silver sabretache from Dunavecse-Fehéregyház.

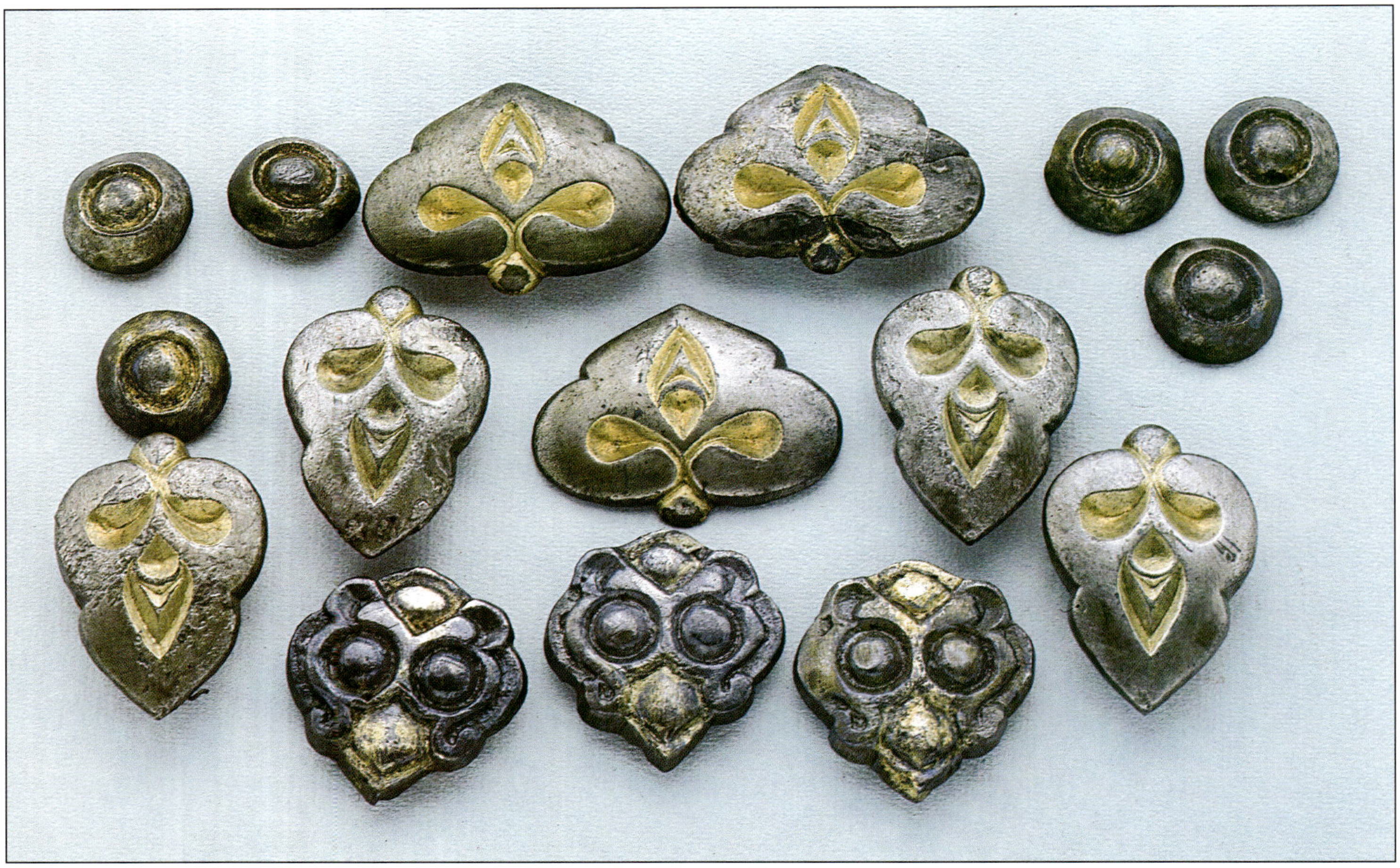

38. Belt ornaments from the Tarcal-Beregszász find.
39–40–41. Shirt ornaments, earrings and half-moon charm from the Tokaji Treasure.
42. Bracelets from Zsenye.

the third group. Both hand- and foot-operated wheels were in use in Árpádian Hungary, so it may be that the pottery fashioned by the older handwheel was better suited to some purposes than the even-walled vessels thrown with the treadle-wheel. There is just a single extant example of a glazed vessel dating from the Árpádian era – an amphora that was presumably of Byzantine origin.

Potters among the modern Hungarian peasantry have clearly retained many traditional aspects of the craft, which makes it highly instructive to read the writings of someone like Lajos Kiss. His book on folk pottery in the town of Hódmezővásárhely describes all stages of the process from extraction of the raw materials and the laborious task of preparing them into a clay paste through to the final baking in the kiln.

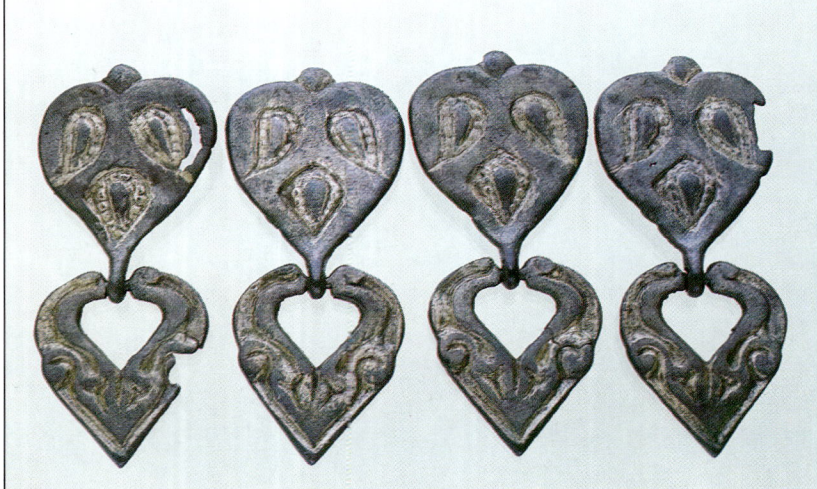

Well-fired earthenware vessels were used in cooking, for storage, and also placed in some graves to hold the food the deceased would need on the journey to the afterworld. In this connection it should be noted that very few Árpádian Magyar graves contain earthenware vessels, unlike those of the late Avars, some of whose cemeteries contain large amounts of pottery, though others have little. In some countries, analysis of the food fragments that remain adhering to the inner walls of such vessels is performed in order to determine their original contents, but this has not yet been done for Hungarian finds. Thus at present we have no way of telling whether the burial vessels contained wine, *kumiz* (fermented mare's milk), or possibly some kind of broth, and our knowledge of early Hungarian cuisine in general is similarly scanty.

One type of vessel which has seemed to date almost certainly to the Conquest era is the earthenware stewpot. Roumanian archaeologists have attributed these to the Pechenegs on the grounds that a few dozen Pecheneg place-names occur in Transylvania, notwithstanding the fact that the same areas equally boast many hundreds of Hungarian names and that thousands of these pots have been recovered on modern Hungarian territory at sites where there can be no question of their origin. Nevertheless, shards of vessels of the same type have very recently come to light in settlements and cemeteries that indisputably belonged to the late Avars or Onogurs. This sug-

gests that the pots, which hitherto were believed to have been linked to the appearance of the Árpádian Magyars, must have been known earlier in the Carpathian Basin. The pots were probably used in milking, but some of them show traces of soot on the underside, indicating that they were also employed as cooking vessels. Since the holes that are bored on the rim of the vessels usually show no signs of wear, we can deduce that the pots were not suspended over the fire but rested on a tripod or on stones.

These reflections on pottery close my account of a few of the male craft occupations in Árpádian Hungary, but I am conscious that there are many others that have not been dealt with. Among these are bone carving and leather-work (there is just one sabretache from which the leather has survived, namely, a find from grave No. 8 at Bezdéd). Veronika Gervers-Molnár[80] was able to demonstrate that the long, felt *szűr*, or cloak, traditionally worn by Hungarian herdsmen was a garment with origins in the antiquity of Eurasian nomadic pastoralism. Nor is there space to do more than mention a range of other tasks, including leather-making and ropemaking, which belonged to the normal domestic duties of the menfolk. Let us instead turn to the female occupations.

FEMALE CRAFTS We know much less about these than we do about the men's crafts, simply because the women mostly worked with materials that were readily perishable – not just in cooking and baking, but also in the preparation and use of textiles such as flax, hemp and felt.

FELT-MAKING No tangible relics have survived, so it is only from a few written documents that we have any record of the felt-covered tents, or yurts, of the Árpádian

Magyars. The most trustworthy of the relics, in fact, is the Hungarian word for felt, *nemez*, which, we are told, derives from an Iranian word that originally meant 'beaten.'[81] This alone gives us an insight into the process of felt-making.

The fleeces of goats (or camels) were first washed and then broken down to fibres by pounding with sticks and also by use of a bow-like implement with a string that, on being vibrated, helped to separate the fibres. The wool was then laid out on the ground for the felting or 'beating' process proper by which the mass of criss-crossing hairs was forced together into a mat of interlinking fibres. The matted cloth was next rolled up and dragged around on rough ground by pulling it behind horses, the constant buffeting on the ground serving to pack the fibres even closer together. After further beating of the unrolled cloth, the felt would be ready. The bulk of this work was performed by girls, all the unmarried females of the family and neighbourhood coming together for the laborious task (a girl would have taken it as a slight if she were not invited to join the group).

Felt had a wide range of everyday uses, not only as an awning for the yurts and covering for their internal walls but also made into horse blankets and saddle cloths. It was also the material of the winding sheets in which the dead were buried. So-called 'white' felts were of higher quality, the 'grey' varieties being used by poorer folk.

SPINNING AND WEAVING Archaeologists at Conquest-era sites occasionally recover scraps of canvas impregnated with green copper-rust. Made from flax or hemp, these fragments conjure up the various stages of their manufacture, which from start to finish was exclusively women's work. After harvesting, the stalks of hemp or flax were steeped, or retted, for a long period in stream water, with stone weights placed on top to prevent them being carried away. Then after drying and 'scutching', or 'swingling', which separated the fibre from the woody parts of the stems, the fibres would be combed and ready for spinning into yarn.

43–44. From the Golden Treasure of Nagyszentmiklós: "ascension" scene from one of the jugs; drinking cup with runic script, drinking cup with ram's head, and omphalos cup.

Practically all these steps would have given further occasion for gatherings of the young women of a community.

Once the yarn had been spun, weaving could begin. The resulting lengths of linen or canvas, roughly two or three spans (50-70 cm) in width, were again thoroughly washed and then spread out to dry on stretching-frames on the ground. Ethnographical data suggest that the long shirts worn in Árpádian Hungary were usually stitched together from rectangles cut from these lengths of cloth.

From the positioning of 'buttons' (metal balls with eyelets) found in graves, it can be deduced that two styles of garment were employed: one that opened down the front, the other fastening to the side at the neck. The first of these was an early precursor of the modern shift, whilst the latter may have resembled the high-necked, sidebuttoned 'Cossack' shirt.

COOKING What little we know about the eating habits of the Árpádian Magyars has been deduced from finds of animal bones at their settlements. Nevertheless, there is reason to believe that the compounds within the enclosures at Felgyő were at least partly vegetable gardens. Presumably, the woman had the task of tending to these plots, as also to the poultry and swine around the dwelling. Likewise, nothing is known about the wild plants that were gathered; however, the very wealth of the vocabulary for plant life suggests that the early Hungarians enjoyed a fairly varied diet with flavours and aromas that differed little from the peasant fare of later centuries. Thus mushrooms, berries, hazel-nuts, walnuts, cornels, strawberries and the fruits of other native species would presumably have formed part of the diet. Salt for seasoning seems to have been transported from mines in Transylvania, as evidenced by the discovery of a double-edged sword near Dés [now Dej], which indicates the nearby presence of a royal or princely army. Ethnographers have also laid particular emphasis on *tarhó*, a dish somewhat like yoghurt or soured cream.

Most cooking was carried out in ovens fired to red heat. To help retain the heat, the bottom of the oven was filled with shards from broken earthenware vessels. These shards were carefully sorted and any pieces that were not suitable for the purpose, like the lugs of the stewpots or the thick bases of some of the cruder jars, would be discarded. This is why it is primarily the latter pieces that are recovered during the excavation of Árpádian settlements.

The *Suidas Lexicon*, compiled around A.D. 1000, cites excessive drunkenness as the reason for the eclipse of the Avars in Hungary. Since an Avar population (the Onogurs) continued to exist in the country after the Magyar conquest, we may presume that their viticulture also managed to survive. Testimony to this is provided by, among other things, the foundation charter of Pannonhalma Abbey, which makes mention of vine-dressers. There can be little doubt, then, that our ancestors were partial to wine, and it seems likely that they also drank fermented mare's milk, or *kumiz*, which was still used by Hungarian herdsmen as a remedy in the last century. The beakers and other small vessels in the Nagyszentmiklós Treasure provide evidence that a variety of spiced beverages were also known. The preparation of alcoholic drinks was only partly women's work, as the milking of mares, for instance, was usually carried out by men (though the Bashkirs are an example of a nomad people where the women do this). To what extent preserved meat was used in the domestic kitchen we do not know, but warriors certainly took it with them on their long campaigns.

DRESS

MALE COSTUME. For our picture of male dress in the Árpádian age, we are entirely reliant on the clues provided by grave goods and an assorted handful of portrayals – the carved stone figure on an impost now in Regensburg Museum, the hunting scene depicted by a silver mount on a drinking horn from Chernigov, the engraving of a falconer on a seventh- or eighth-century silver plate from Perm, but above all the Uigur figures represented in Turkestani wall-paintings.

One source recounts that bishops in the West had a liking for the Hungarian style of fur cap,[82] but no remnants of such headgear have survived. Among the grave goods at Beregszász (now Beregovo, Soviet Union) was the palmette-ornamented crest of a helmet. From this we may speculate that the Magyar helmet was akin to that of the later Mongols or Cumans, covering the head with a dome that would deflect sword-blows from their target. Possibly metal and fur were combined in a cap rather like the *sapka monomacha*, or crown-helmet, worn by Muscovite princes. Whether the hair was tied together under the helmet, as shown by the stone funerary statues called *kamennaya baba* that Turkic tribes set up on the southern Russian steppes up until the early thirteenth century or by the

miniatures in Bulgar manuscripts, is not known. However, it is clear from the chronicles that deal with Vata's rebellion against King Stephen in 1046, and from the representations mentioned above, that the menfolk shaved their heads completely except for a strip at the back where the hair was allowed to grow to be braided in a plait.

It was not uncommon for men to wear ear-rings. In some cases the more ornate piece of a pair was worn by the woman, the other, simpler piece by her husband. Sometimes a thin bracelet of gold or silver is found on the forearm of a male skeleton, its purpose being to tuck in

45. Helmet tip from the Beregszász find.
46. Pair of disks from Rakamaz.
47. Belt-ends from the Vereb find.

the sleeves of the shirt at the cuff; similar bands have also been found around the ankle. These items are reminiscent of the Iranian style of dress in this period. The Árpádian Magyar male did not wear any ornaments on the upper body; these were all on or below the belt for the simple reason that jewellery on the shoulders or chest would have hindered execution of their most important stratagem – firing arrows to the rear whilst retreating on horseback. The belt served to carry everything that the warrior might need in battle, including his pouch, dagger, sabre, bow and quiver.

FEMALE COSTUME. When it comes to building up a picture of the female dress, it is truly unfortunate that as yet we have only a few scattered data which allow us to relate the jewellery retrieved from female graves to the age of their wearer. For as in other ages, and indeed down to the present day, especially in village life, there is little doubt that the details of dress in Árpádian Hungary would have been sensitive markers of a woman's age and social status. The picture that follows is accordingly sketchy, lacking precisely in the important gradations of rank. Here too we shall begin with the head-gear.

Disc-shaped mounts with leaf-like pendants, though more commonly found around the neck of female skeletons, are sometimes seen in a row around the skull, and in these cases were clearly used as head jewellery. Larger discs, gilded like the others, were also hung from the head-dress. We can only guess at who wore them as hair ornaments and who as pendants on a cap, but presumably they were for older girls and married women, respectively. Two types of ornament were attached to head-dresses: one type was worn laterally, over the ears, the other hung down to cover the breasts. The first consisted of a row of bronze discs with open-work décor which presumably were sewn on to a veil; these most commonly have zoomorphic motifs, sometimes palmettes, and they seemingly preserve an Avar-period tradition. The second type was a pair of pectoral discs, suspended by straps from the head-dress. The best-known of these is a disc from the cemetery at Rakamaz (Sabolcs County), which

portrays a falcon grasping a brace of water-fowl in its claws, but other patterns include the use of palmette motifs to form a tree-of-life design. Sometimes a row of beads would be suspended from the pectoral discs.

Ear-rings were worn beneath the veil or shawl that covered the head. Typically these consisted of strings of bead ornaments, but there are also larger decorated discs and crescent-shaped gold pendants with open-work and granulation embellishments, plainly the work of Byzantine craftsmen.

Rows of beads were worn less commonly around the neck. More often the earlier-mentioned disc mounts or rhomboid appendages (the latter possibly symbolizing the mount of venus) were suspended from a rigid torc around the neck; these same pendants might also have been attached to the hems of the chemise. The use of a silver or gold band to tie the wide sleeves of a chemise at the wrist is also seen amongst women. Rings with gemstone settings or simpler designs were worn on the fingers. (Men, especially kings and other leaders, also had finger-rings, not uncommonly in the form of 'magical' amulets to ward off gout.)

The belt was an item of the women's as well as men's attire, the female belts usually bearing a row of square mounts set on their corners, with large, leaf-shaped pendants hanging from them. For women, however, the belt did not have the same utilitarian importance as it did for men; at most a small knife would have been suspended from it. The decoration on armlets was all the more elaborate. Some armlets were formed from finely twisted wire – usually silver, but gold in the case of the one belonging to the Zsennye Treasure (Vas County, western Hungary) – terminating in a pair of opposed animal heads snapping at one another. Flat armbands were adorned with gemstones.

We know that Magyar saddles for both men and women had the same construction, from which it can be deduced that the women did not wear skirts but went about in a baggy trouser-like garment and rode on horseback in the male manner. Footwear consisted either of slippers or, for riding, topboots with decorative mounts. With the

48. Hair ornament with animal figures from Jánosszállás.
49. Earrings of the Saltovo type from Szeged-Bojárhalom.
50. The full saddle of a prince of Transylvania, later
the ceremonial saddle of Francis Joseph.
51. Drawing of the bone plates of the saddle
of Soltszentimre.
52. Reconstruction of the saddle of Soltszentimre
(drawing).

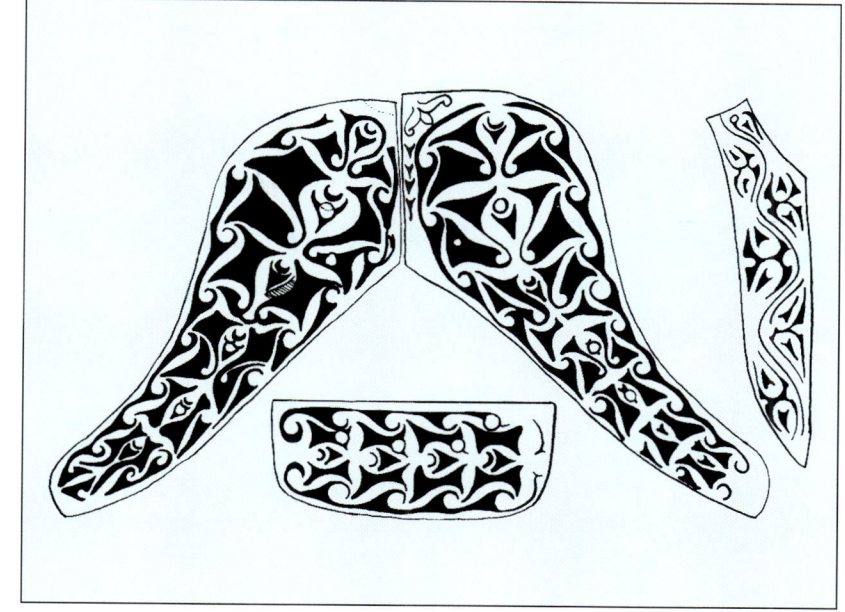

former, the wide trouser-ends would be brought together at the ankle with a metal clip, whilst with the latter, they were probably tucked into the uppers of the boots. The sole was soft, just as with male footwear, because of the need to grip the arched foot-plate of the stirrups. The use of hard-soled footwear must have just begun to spread to Hungary, obviously inspired by Western fashion, at the time of the Conquest, as examples of flat-plated stirrups have been uncovered, albeit rather seldom.

So much for female dress, though it is worth repeating an observation made earlier in the book, namely, there is reason to believe that the burial costume was the same as the bridal dress, or at least the woman took to the grave the ornate garments that made up her trousseau.

HORSE TRAPPINGS. An account of the construction of the saddle and harness used by the Árpádian Magyars was given in the previous chapter, so my comments here will be limited to the decorative motifs that were employed on them. Animal forms (dog or stag) were rarely employed; most ornamental mounts carry a design in relief consisting of what are usually described as four 'leaf' shapes around a central circle, though it seems obvious that this may, in fact, represent a four-petalled flower. The mounts are either disc-shaped or square, where a small eyelet is attached to the lower side it was to allow

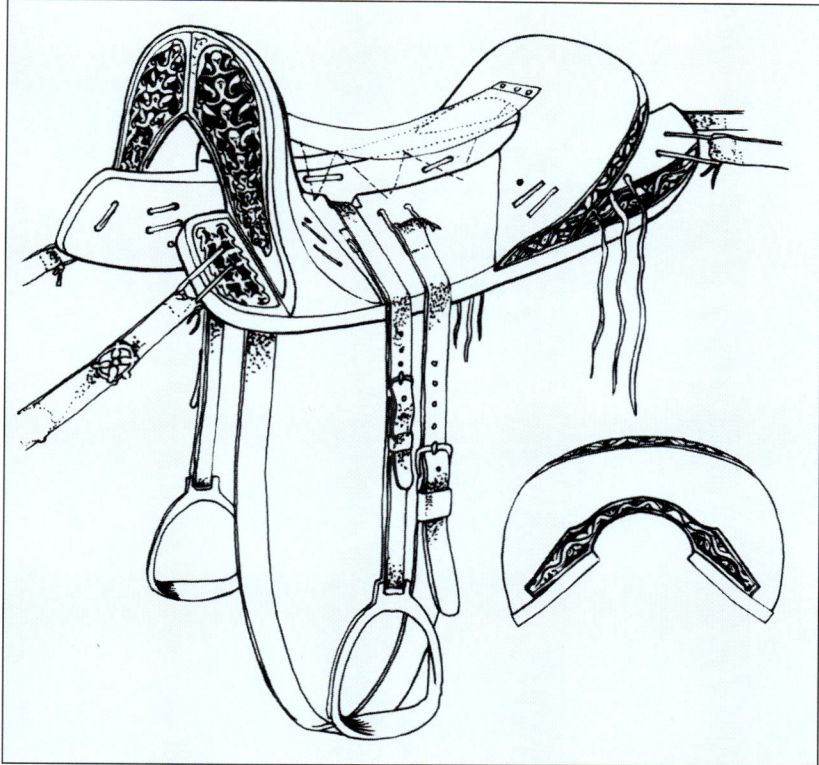

coloured tassels to be threaded on. This suggests that we should visualize the horse trappings as intended to be eye-catching and gaudy. Another kind of mount was a pendant made up of large, leaf-shaped silver plates with a gilded boss or appliqué ornamental casting at the centre.

Larger mounts might also be attached to the breast and crupper bands, but never to the reins, as this would have interfered with the transmission of the rider's wishes from hands to bit. Webbed crupper bands of the type used by the Avars have not been seen in Conquest-period Magyar burials, so it is all the more surprising to find these shown, richly embellished, in medieval miniatures depicting the Legend of St Ladislas.[83] The back of the cantle on the saddle carried a 'blood collar' which was for attaching prey that had been killed in the hunt.

WARFARE

The Árpádian Magyars used the same tactics in warfare as other nomadic horse peoples from the East. The highly complex movements of different squadrons that were employed – whether by the Magyars, as described by Emperor Leo the Wise, or by the hordes of Chingis Khan, as recounted in *The Secret History of the Mongolians*, or by the later Mongolian forces of Kubilai Khan, as related by Marco Polo – as well as the necessary skills in use of weapons demanded prolonged, intensive drilling of warriors practically from boyhood onwards. These manoeuvres were traditionally tested and coordinated by large-scale 'exercises' linked with a great hunt.

The description of a clash between the Byzantines and a joint Pecheneg-Turk army, as supplied by the Arab geographer Mas'udi, writing between 943 and 947, will serve to illustrate the efficacy of the tactics:[84]

When dawn had broken, the Pecheneg king ordered many cavalry detachments, each detachment numbering one thousand horsemen, to join the right flank, and likewise on the left flank. After the battle-lines had been drawn up, the cavalry detachments of the right wing broke upon the main body of the Byzantine army and unleashed a hail of arrows upon them, meanwhile crossing over to the left flank. The cavalry detachments of the left wing thereupon advanced likewise and set loose their arrows on the main body of the Byzantines, meanwhile proceeding to the place whence the right-wing detachments had started. In this way a continual stream of arrows was kept up… But when the formerly Mohammedan Christian converts and the Byzantines saw how their ranks were falling apart, and how the storm of arrows constantly returned upon them, they switched to an offensive with their disorganized ranks and fell upon the Turkish [main] force that had till then stood without moving. Thereupon the [Turkish] cavalry opened the way for them but then deluged them with a massive burst of arrows. This arrow-storm was the occasion for the Byzantines to turn to flight… The swords too were now unsheathed; the horizon grew dark and the cries of the horsemen came thick and fast.

That the Byzantine sources take cognizance only of the Turkic element within the ethnic patchwork that made up the Magyars is well known. Mas'üdi's description above conveys a sense of the imposing discipline, the unerring precision of drill, of such forces, reflected not least in the fact that the battle was decided by arrow-fire alone, before sabres were drawn for the close combat that finished it off.

The introduction of the 'modern' double-edged sword, the Westerners' successful weapon, into the Hungarian royal army was one of the initiatives of Géza and King

53. "The Siege of Aquileia" from *The Picture Chronicle*.

54. Scene of the Conquest from *The Picture Chronicle*.
55. Golden decoration from the sabre of Geszteréd.

Stephen. The new sword was certainly capable of inflicting more severe wounds than the light sabre, but its introduction had unforeseeable consequences for everyday life. Up until then, the Magyar cavalry, with their sabres, had been able to scurry across the face of enemy armies, always a step ahead when the latter tried to strike back. Now they were obliged to acquire the skills of man-to-man fighting, an essentially static mode of combat. Whereas a warrior could use the back edge of his sabre to slash with when withdrawing the blade after a blow, he found that with the double-edged sword a pause was needed after each thrust until the weapon could be raised again to strike another blow. The whole basis of a soldier's training, from boyhood on, had to be radically revised.

The use of the spear is given particular emphasis by Emperor Leo in his description of 'Turkic' warfare, but it should be noted that this weapon is seldom found amongst the relics of the Árpádian Magyars, whilst the mace, another nomad weapon, does not figure at all.

THE CYCLE OF LIFE

BIRTH. From our knowledge of later folk customs, it seems likely that a couple in Árpádian Hungary would have tried to determine the gender of their future offspring at the time of conception. If the man approached his wife from her left side, then a daughter would be expected, if from the right side, a son. The birth itself most likely took place beside the domestic hearth, with invocations being offered to the Blessed Virgin for an easy labour. After delivery, the mother would have had to refrain from sexual relations for a certain period. Every effort would have been made to protect mother and child from harm by the use of assorted magical spells.

NAME-GIVING. A child was usually named by the mother. Bálint Hóman noticed that within the Árpád dynasty, it was the practice for the child to take its name in accordance with the mother's nationality.[85] Thus, King Stephen I's wife, Gisella, was German, and their sons were called Henrik and Otto. Of the two sons of Stephen's uncle, Michael, one was 'Zar' Ladislas (the 'Zar' indicates that he had a shaven scalp and pigtail in the Magyar style and thus meant 'pagan'), who had a Ruthenian wife and a son named Bonuslo, whilst his elder brother, Vazul, took a pagan Magyar wife and had three sons by her: Levente, who himself remained pagan, Andrew (a second, Christian name, obviously assumed at a later date), and 'Zar' Béla. The same 'Zar' Béla's eldest son also bore a pagan name, Géza, but his Polish wife named their second son Ladislas.

Anonymus's chronicle records how Álmos came to be named:

But it was as the result of a miraculous event that he received the name Álmos, for when his mother was pregnant, a divine vision appeared to her as she was sleeping; it was in the form of a hawk which seemed to light upon her and made her pregnant... Now since in the Hungarian language the word for 'dream' is álom, and his birth was foretold in a dream, he was called Álmos.

[trans. G. F. Cushing]

Following the discovery by Dezső Pais that certain Árpádian-era names were prophylactic, being given to an infant to ward off harmful spirits, it was noticed that the Volga Bulgars, early in the tenth century, had had a prince who was also called Almys. This prompted the idea that the derivation of *Álmos* should be sought in the Turkish language, which led to a suggested interpretation of 'bought at the bazaar'; such a name would have been intended to confuse the evil spirits into thinking that the no doubt cherished offspring was not worth bothering about. The classical philologist Károly Kerényi, on the other hand, recalled that women who had regarded themselves as barren used to give an unexpected child the name of the fruit or grain to which they attributed their pregnancy; in this case, he suggested, *Álmos* might derive from the Hungarian *almás* 'connected with apples'. In other chronicles the name was translated as 'saint' on the basis of the Latin almus, and a similar reading as a eulogistic epithet, was proposed by László Rásonyi, though he posited a Turkic provenance.[86] So just this one name has inspired a whole series of more or less ingenious interpretations.

It is indeed the case that prophylactic names were current in older times, and are still sporadically encountered in Hungary to this day. Péter Bornemisza, the eminent Lutheran preacher and poet of sixteenth-century Hungary, wrote in his *Temptations of the Devil* that 'If your children before this one have died, then he should have the name Farkas ['Wolf'].' In other words, *Farkas* was a name given by families that had suffered a high rate of infant mortality thought to be due to an evil taint. Names of this kind appear in early documents of the Árpádian period, among them *Nemvaló* 'Unsuitable' *Nemvagy,* 'Are-not', *Mavagy* 'Here-today', *Nemél* 'Not-living', *Haláli* 'Deathly', *Csunya* 'Ugly', *Szennyes* 'Polluted', and *Szemét* 'Filth'. Ordinal and cardinal numbers *Előd* 'Primus', *Kettüd* 'Secundus', *Négy* 'Quartus', *Öt* 'Quintus', etc. – were also used. In my earlier book on the life of the Magyars in the Conquest era, I gave an example of the survival of this practice into the twentieth century: the nickname *Te-bárnevóna* 'You-would-it-weren't' was bestowed on a friend of mine by his dry-nurse because he had been such a sickly, pale child.

In the families of notabilities there was a preference for animal and bird names. It would seem that each family had, so to speak, its own descent myth according to which the clan ancestor was reborn in the infants, rather like Álmos in Emese's dream. Examples of such appellations are the Turkic names *Kaplony* 'Tiger', *Kurd* 'Wolf' and *Thonuzaba* 'Wild-pig-father', or the Hungarian names *Emese* 'Wild-pig-mother', *Héja* 'Goshawk', *Karvaly* 'Sparrow-hawk', *Kánya* 'Kite', *Sas* 'Eagle', *Ölyv* 'Buzzard', *Sólyom* 'Falcon', etc. A name like the Turkic *Tas* 'Stone' relects the custom of calling a child after the first object that the mother saw after giving birth – a widespread practice amongst Oriental peoples.

The reason for dwelling on the subject of name-giving is that in older times a person's name was equated with his or her character, or at least soul. In certain less-developed societies it is still the practice to change one's name after suffering a serious illness as a way of banishing the illness by attaching it to the former name.

Lastly, in a related vein, mention should be made of the Magyar designations of rank. Thus *Vajk,* the name used by King Stephen before his conversion to Christianity, had the meaning 'prince regent' (naturally he would have changed this when he acceded to the senior kingship). Similarly, the supreme ruler amongst the Magyars was the *Kende*, deriving from Turkic *kün* 'sun', whilst the *Gyula*, meaning 'torch' or 'moon', was the subordinate king. This was the same as the arrangement amongst the Khazars, whose supreme kagan was always preceded by a disc symbolizing the sun, which his subjects were not permitted to gaze upon, whereas the warlord's symbol was a torch signifying the moon.

CHILDREN'S GAMES. The rearing of children meant preparing them for the future. In Árpádian Hungary the children appear not to have had their own special games (at least there is no evidence of them from grave finds), unless they made these for themselves from pieces of bone, hollowed-out stems of elderwood, and the like. When still small they no doubt aped the various daily activities of the grown-ups and the singing and dancing of their festivities. Elements of old pagan religious ceremonies, for instance, are apparently preserved in certain children's songs and games that are still known in Hungary today. Géza Roheim pointed out that the following well-known Hungarian children's verse may recall an old shamanistic procedure for expelling evil spirits by shouting and raising a great din:[87]

> *Stork, oh stork, oh little stork,*
> *What has made your leg bleed so?*
> *A Turkish child made the cut,*
> *A Magyar child will cure it*
> *With fife and drum and a reed violin.*

The refrain of another children's song, in which the days of the week are called out in reverse order, is thought to preserve the memory of an old belief that the afterlife was a mirror image of this world:

> *A sieve, a sieve on Friday,*
> *Love it will be on Thursday,*
> *A drum on Wednesday…*

This concept of the afterlife belonged to the sphere of magic ceremonies. In medieval Hungarian witch trials, recitation of the Lord's Prayer backwards was the greatest crime of which one could be accused. This is just a tiny fraction of the huge store of ancient folklore that has been passed down in children's games, but it will have to suffice here.

MARRIAGE. Interestingly, we possess a relatively wide range of contemporary sources on the subject of wedlock due, no doubt, partly to the enduring fascination with tracing descents, partly to the need of traders to know what kinds of goods might be of interest for such occasions.

Let us examine first the episode relating to the abduction of brides which is included in the *Legend of the Wonder Stag*. As may be recalled, Hunor and Magyar, who had settled down in the Maeotid marshes around the Sea of Azov:

… came upon the wives and children of the sons of Belar [the Bulgar king] … seized them and made off with them as fast as they could. Now among the children they captured there happened to be two daughters of Dula, King of the Alans. One of them Hunor took as his wife, the other became the wife of Magyar.

From these two women all the Huns and Magyars were held to have descended. It should be noted that it was the island milieu of the Maeotis that attracted the two sons and hunting party, and that Magyar contacts with Bulgars and Alans are both historically and linguistically document facts.

There was, however, a second way in which marriageable women were abducted, as is attested by Article 25 of St Stephen's Second Decree. This prescribed that if any warrior shoud be so base and impudent as to take a girl without her parent's consent, then such and such a punishment would be meted out. Here the parental consent is the main thing, recalling as it does one of the ceremonies of Oriental marriage rituals in which the bridegroom carries off an unprotesting bride and is then pursued by a gang of unmarried men attending the wedding. Many variants of this custom, in more restrained form, continued to live on in Hungarian marriage traditions.

The Hungarian word for 'bridegroom', *vőlegény*, which is a corruption of the expression *vevő legény* 'purchasing lad', and also its counterpart, *eladó lány* 'bartered bride', are reminders that marriage had a strictly contractual aspect. The Persian Gardìzi tells more precisely what was involved among the Árpádian Magyars when he relates what kind of bride-price a man seeking marriage would have to pay for the woman, and what kind of dowry the bride's father would have to provide for his daughter. The groom's payment was primarily in cattle, though animal furs and skins might also be included, whilst the father of the bride gave horses, money and other goods. The couple would maintain separate reckonings of these 'purchase prices' for a while so that they could retrieve their respective portions should the marriage break up. Generally, seven years was regarded as the trial period for a good marriage, after which the woman's dowry would be incorporated with the property of her husband's family or clan.

Parallels to all these customs are found among various Oriental peoples, some related to the Magyars, but I shall pass over them here as they are dealt with at length in my *Life of the Conquest-period Magyars*.

DEATH. Conquest-period funerary rites were considered earlier in connection with the cemeteries of Árpádian Hungary, so my remarks here will be confined to a few supplementary remarks. The ceremonies that surrounded birth, marriage and death were broadly similar, and in each case horse-racing was the most important event. For the Magyars, as for their kinsfolk still living in the East, death was the focus for a great number of customs and rituals. We know that the deceased's steed was sacrificed, but as only the skin, together with the skull and lower legs, was actually placed in the grave to provide transport for the journey to the other-world, we may assume that the horse's flesh was eaten at a burial feast.

Rather than refer here to the wealth of anthropological data on such customs, let me instead pose the question: What was the fate in the afterlife of those who did not merit a horse burial? Among these were the great majority of women and also the 'poorer' male clan members, those without the right to even a single arrow. Did the clan, then, split up in the afterlife? István Dienes has put forward the intriguing idea that the clan chief was not given eight arrows but only seven (he thought that earlier excavators might have mistaken part of a quiver frame for an arrow), and that each arrow represented the key for entry into one of the seven layers of the after-world. Thus a dead man who received fewer arrows reached a correspondingly lower level in the heavens. It is difficult to give this much credence as I believe that the clan was intended to stay together in the next world as it did in life. Neverthless, how those who were buried without a mount were supposed to make that journey is not known. One possibility, though there are as yet no archaeological data to support it, is that they may have been provided with a symbolic horse, cut out of birch-bark, rather like those observed by Radloff in graves on the Barabinskaya Steppe of south-west Siberia.

We also do not know what happened to the personal belongings, or inheritance, of the dead. There may have been, a prohibition on passing on such belongings, or they may have been given away to a *táltos*, or medicine man. When the medieval Church eventually forbade the practice of horse burial, the prohibition was evaded by giving a dead man's horse to the Church, as the representative of the afterlife in this world. From those cases of partial horsebrial where it appears that the horse-skin was hung over the grave for a time before being interred at the foot of the grave we can deduce that certain Magyar clans or groups believed that a person's soul continued to sojourn on Earth for a short while (forty days is the rule) after death. Only after the elapse of this period did the deceased have need of a mount.

56. Gyula Rudnay: *The National Assembly at Pusztaszer.*

RELIGION, BELIEFS, AND CULTURE

A distinguished series of scholars, from Arnold Ipolyi and Ferenc Kállay in the last century to Géza Róheim and Vilmos Diószegi in this, studied the beliefs and primitive religion of the Magyars. All took as their tacit starting-point the idea that the Magyars had a concept of the universe that was similar in structure, if not in content, to that of Christianity. Their aim was to seek out what remnants of those beliefs had survived and thereby reconstruct the layout of the heavenly spheres in the dominion of the Magyars' Creator.

It is impossible for us nowadays to evoke that ancient religion in the wealth of detail that Ipolyi could muster, but I sense that his conception was essentially correct and that the belief-world of the old Magyars should not be reduced to the stammering chants of shamans who whipped themselves into a stupefied frenzy to the sound of drumbeats.

Historiography has tended to draw a sharp dividing line between Magyars of the 'pagan' era and those of the Christian era, between the Estern and Western heritages of Hungarian culture. However, the boundaries were never as distinct as this implies; indeed in many aspects of life the one heritage co-existed with and passed smoothly across into the other. To take just one example, the adoption of Christianity did nothing to shake belief in bewitchment by an 'evil eye', or the steps to be taken to guard against it, for these things lay outside the province of the Christian faith. So it is that in the small Romanesque church of Magyarszentpál (now Sinpaul near Cluj in Transylvania) the sanctity of the altar-table is protected by a carving set on a pilaster at the left of the chancel arch, which presents the shockingly profane image of a woman displaying her buttocks and pointing quite unashamedly at her pudenda.[88] It should be added, moreover, that the relief was polychromed in its original state. The only way that one can account for the creation of such an image, a good two to three centuries after Christianity had been introduced into Hungary, is by reference to belief in the 'evil eye', which survives to the present day in the country's peasant communities. Evidently, the preachers, too, must have either shared the belief, or at least felt that it was not incompatible with the tenets of the faith they promulgated, to allow an image of that kind to be carved and painted in the church. In this connection we might note that there is a record of a Hungarian witch using exactly the same sort of gesture to cast a spell upon an attacking Byzantine army around the middle of the twelfth century.

SHAMAN OR TÁLTOS? In recent decades, ever-wider currency has been given to the view that the primitive religion of the Magyars was a form of shamanism, and that the so-called *táltos*, or cunning folk, were none other than Magyar shamans. The proposition that a *táltos* should be regarded as the direct descendant of the Siberian shamans was put most cogently by the late Vilmos Diószegi,[89] one of the towering figures of Hungarian ethnology and the study of primitive religions, and instigator of a unique collection of shaman-related materials. Admittedly, the two do share a number of characteristics, such as the belief that their respective practitioners are born with a surplus bone and have to take part in a heavenly struggle in the form of a bull, as well as other less essential details. Nevertheless, there are many more differences: for instance, *táltos* do not travel through different levels in the heavens, do not cast spells at night, do not practice curative medicine, etc.

Not long ago, one of our well-known Hungarian poets made an experiment, under medical supervision, to experience for himself the mood alterations that certain Surrealist poets had achieved by the use of narcotic and hallucinogenic drugs. His recollections of his drugged state[90] read very much like accounts of the initiation rites of shamans, the core of which is the sundering of the body into pieces and its subsequent reassembly. For me this prompts the question whether the likenesses between shaman and *táltos* might have more to do with similar ways of attaining the trance-state, though admittedly there is no evidence of the use of drugs by Hungarian *táltos* for this purpose.

A greater obstacle to accepting that shamanism was part of Magyar religious beliefs is that its various purported relics have been collected separately in different Hungarian-speaking areas. Thus observations among the Csángó people of Moldavia and in the Palots area of northern Hungary have been collated with information from individuals who claim to have the *táltos* gift, and a composite picture has been built up of some archetypal *táltos* with attributes that were never observed together in a single subject. The same is true of the picture of Asian shamanism, into which elements collected from a diversity of peoples, from the Ghukchi to the Ob-Ugrians, from the Goldi to Turkic groups, have been telescoped to produce a unified phenomenon called 'shamanism', which was actually unknown in this concentrated form. In my opinion, *táltos* – or shamans, if it comes to that – were no more than people with the misfortune to suffer from certain nervous diseases and to whom ordinary people superstitiously turned for help. They no doubt had a knowledge of natural cures and the powers of various herbs and juices, but their role was probably little different from that of the 'wise women' who still operate in modern-day Hungarian villages.

It is likely that princely courts had their resident soothsayer, or fortune-teller, like the Avar Bokolabra, whose story has been told with great insight by István Dienes.[91]

A PAGAN ANTECEDENT OF THE LEGEND OF ST LADISLAS.
My suspicions about the complexity of Árpádian Magyar religious beliefs were fully roused by a series of frescoes depicting the Legend of St Ladislas that can be found in a string of medieval churches along the former frontiers of Hungary.[92] I was the first to realize the 'pagan' significance of these paintings, but this intuition has since been enriched by a splendid body of relevant folk-poetry material from Asia that Lajos Vargyas has identified.

The Legend of St Ladislas took shape long before the historical king of Hungary was alive and had nothing to do with Christianity, but was a pagan creation-myth. Dim memories of the myth have survived to posterity only in the texts of the chronicles and certain Hungarian folk ballads (e.g. *Anna Molnár, Kerekes Izsák*) and, of course, the official Church versions of the legend.

According to the most intact of the ecclesiastical versions, the one preserved in the so-called *Cronicon Pictum Vindobonense*, or Painted Chronicle, Ladislas set off from the stronghold of Nagyvárad (now Oradea) in Transylvania in order to fight the Cumans who were threatening to irrupt into Hungary. In the midst of the battle Ladislas noticed that a Cuman warrior was galloping away with a Magyar maiden who, he discerned, was none other than the bishop of Várad's daughter. Ladislas gave hot pursuit to the Cuman and tried, in vain, to stop the warrior with his spear (the frescoes show the Cuman as being hit but taking no notice of his wound), whilst the arrow-fire returned by the Cuman equally missed the Hungarian king. As the chase proceeded, the king called out to the maiden to pull the Cuman off his horse and on to the ground, which she duly did. The two weaponless heroes then continued their struggle on foot, grappling at one another's belt and throat, until the maiden picked up a battle-axe or sword and severed the Cuman's Achilles tendon. The heathen thereupon fell to the ground, but as he continued to grasp the king's hair, the girl finally decapitated him. The last scene of the series usually depicts Ladislas at the foot of a tree, with his weapons suspended from its branches, as he rests his weary head in the girl's lap whilst she runs her hand through his hair.

What has any of this to do with ancient religious beliefs? To start with, Géza Nagy, one of Hungary's eminent archaeologists and historians, spotted that the last scene had an almost exact counterpart in a golden buckle-plate, dating from around the beginning of the Christian era, which is now in the Hermitage collection.[93] The tree, the king and the 'combing' through his hair are seen here just as in the Transylvanian wallpaintings, except that the buckle shows two horses (those would be the mounts of the king and Cuman in the legend) with their reins held by a groom. I myself, whilst working on the frescoes, came across an exact equivalent of the fight on bronze plaques from the Ordos region of Mongolia, which depict a tethered horse on either side of two unarmed combatants, and the same scene can also be seen on silver plat-

ters from Persia. It was these parallels which induced me to try and follow the trail of the ancient myth.

The main clue came from a closer scrutiny of the wall-paintings, for what they presented were two heroes locked in mortal combat (an almost universal appurtenance of mythology), one of whom has a vulnerable spot at his heel. A Hungarian *táltos* legend provides an explanation. This tells of a cosmic struggle between two *táltos* who took the forms of a black and a white bull. The black bull could only be defeated if hamstrung, for when in human form, a falling leaf had touched his shoulder and heel whilst he was bathing in a magical potion, and these became his vulnerable points (the very expression 'Achilles heel' is a reminder that this element, too, is international). In different tellings of the legend the protagonists' steeds usually struggle with one another, too. Again, the horses of champions are well known in epic verse, but for this and all the other elements, including the role of the maiden, to be interwoven in a single story is peculiar to the Hungarian version of the legend.

The original legend was clearly an account of divine intervention in a battle between two cosmic heroes. When we add that everything about the figure of St Ladislas in the wall-paintings, including his steed and weapons, is white and shining, whereas everything about the Cuman is black and from his mouth a searing flame billows at the saintly king, then we have the archetypal myth of a struggle between forces of lightness and dark, which Christianity transformed into a struggle between good and evil. This mythological view of the world as a battleground of opposing forces is known in many forms throughout Europe and Asia. In Pahlavi, for instance, it is the struggle of Ormazd and Ahriman, whilst in Serbian and Russian accounts the role of the unnamed Cuman warrior of the Hungarian legend is filled by the fearsome leader of the Mongolian Golden Horde, Batu khan himself, and in the Vatican *Legendarium* of one of the Angevin princes the maiden who tends the king is the Virgin Mary herself. In medieval Hungary, especially in frontier areas (St Ladislas was a tutelary saint of borders), the legend was no doubt reinforced by the fact that enemy forces invading the country would frequently make off with the prettier young women. It is mainly in these areas – the Székely country of eastern Transylvania, the Szepes (Spis) and Gömör regions (now in eastern Slovakia), the Mura valley in the south-west – but also in certain localities on the Alföld plain and the village of Ócsa on the outskirts of Pest, that the legend survived in Hungary, most notably in the series of church paintings that I have been referring to.

Taking these various factors together, it is evident that the belief-world of the Árpádian Magyars stood on a par with the major contemporary religions, and it is misleading to think that primitive shamans were their only intermediaries with the divine world. The Magyar conceptions

57–62. Counter-clockwise: Szabolcs, Kund, Örs, Gyula, Hunor and Magyar. Figures from the Buzád clan from *The Picture Chronicle*.

of an afterlife and the rituals surrounding death an integral part of any religious teaching – have already been discussed in some depth. Further evidence for the relative sophistication of the pagan Magyar belief-world can be seen in the way that, following the official conversion of Hungary to Christianity, the newly introduced Church could call on an almost complete vocabulary in the Hungarian vernacular. As I have already noted, the whole of the Bible could have been translated with the stock of words already in existence before the eleventh century (e.g. *lélek* 'soul', *Isten* 'God', *hagymáz* 'demon of disease, fever', *ördög* 'devil', *bölcs* 'wise man', *koporsó* 'coffin', etc.). This is another area where the mistaken belief has arisen that Slavs brought the word of Christ to Hungary, despite the fact that the liturgical language for Slavs as for other peoples was then, of course, Latin and that such Hungarian words as are of Slavonic derivation relate primarily to aspects of ecclesiastical organization (e.g. *apát* 'abbot', *apáca* 'nun', *bérmál* 'confirm', *eretnek* 'heretic', *husvét* 'Easter', *parázna* 'fornicator', *pilis* 'tonsure', etc.) rather than to tenets of belief as such.

TOTEMISM.

It has often been argued that both the *Legend of the Wonder Stag* and the *Turul* (hawk) legend are totemistic in concept, whilst the various other animals that were incorporated as heraldic devices into the shields of Magyar clans in the Middle Ages are also reminiscent of totemic ancestors. Granted there is some truth in this, one must nevertheless point out that the era when those totemistic beliefs were alive had already long passed by the time of the Conquest; they persisted amongst the Conquest-period Magyars merely as so many fables or stories. This is evident from the manner in which the legends were recorded, with no reference to re-birth of the ancestors, nor even any suggestion that the clan ancestors were ever hawks, stags, or other noble beasts. The legends were preserved in the same way as happened, for example, when the history of Chingis's clan was set down in *The Secret History of the Mongols*,[94] in which Chingis's birth is described as resulting from the coupling of a wolf with a deer, despite the fact that Chingis's parentage was perfectly well known to his chroniclers.

Evidence attested for the existence of totemistic beliefs includes the habitual use of circumlocutions to refer to certain animals, on the grounds that it was taboo to utter the actual name of the totem animal. Examples of this would be the phrases 'long-tailed one' for 'wolf', or 'large-antlered one' for 'stag', or the replacement of the original Hungarian word for 'bear' by a Slav loan-word. However, the latter example is inherently implausible because the first Magyar contact with the Slavs can only have come at most a few centuries before their entry into Hungary, by which period totemistic beliefs were no longer prevalent. Why the Magyars should have borrowed the Slavonic *medved* (Hu. *medve*) for 'bear' is now as obscure as their adoption of southern Slav *zobálo* (Hu. *zabla*) for 'horse-bit' when it was the Magyars who were the nomadic horse-people. The vagaries of lexical history are so little understood that it would be wrong to deduce that the absence of a term from a language means the object or concept in question was unknown to speakers of the language; likewise the borrowing of a term from another language does not necessarily mean that the object or concept referred to did not exist previously in the culture but was taken over at the same time. By this token, the work of converting the Hungarian people to Christianity was undertaken by German and Italian priests but the Hungarian language shows practically no trace of this, perhaps precisely because the vocabulary already existed with which to designate the tenets of the new faith.

TREPANATION OF THE SKULL.

A number of linguists have followed Dezsó Pais in erroneously ascribing to shamanism the practice of symbolic wounding of the cranium, which is known to have occurred among Árpádian-era Magyars, whilst cases of actual trepanation are explained as connected with the expulsion of evil spirits. Among the data cited in support of this is the Hungarian word *agyafúrt*, now meaning 'cunning', but derived from *agy* 'brain' + *fúr* 'drill, bore'. However, though surgical opening of the skull by means of a 'drill', or trepan, was known to Arab physicians by the time of Árpád, it was practised elsewhere only later in the Middle Ages. Moreover, in Conquest-period Hungary the cranial wall was operated on either by chiselling through the bone or, in the symbolic operation, by incising a symbol (usually an oval or circle) on the skull.[95] For a while it was considered that the human operation might have been a legacy of the use of trepanation by Conquest-period shepherds to cure sheep suffering from the parasitic disease gid or sturdy, which causes staggering or circling movements, until it was pointed out that the disease was first known only much later on, amongst Merino sheep that had been imported from the west, and thus a method for treating it would hardly have preceded it.

The reasons for performing the two types of trepanation were clearly different. The full surgical operation may have been indicated when a person received a severe head wound, for instance from a sword blow, in which case, as can be seen on one of the skulls excavated at Benepuszta (Bács-Kiskun County), the wound was evidently carefully débrided, any bone-splinters removed, and the wound closed with a sheet of silver, which was either sutured to the surrounding scalp or stitched to the lining of a close-lyfitting cap.

Symbolic marking of the skull presents more of a puzzle as there is no way in which this procedure could have served as a means of artificially inducing, for instance, the 'softwittedness' that might turn someone into a shaman. It must have had some other purpose. In fact, most of the marks are found on those parts of the scalp which the Árpádian Magyars regularly shaved, so that the indented outline of the incision would still have been visible even after the wound had healed. In my view, the marks had the function of a talisman such as a cross or small reliquary suspended on the chest. The circle was possibly incised on the skull as a solar symbol (oval shapes may simply reflect lack of skill in executing a circular design). How such 'talismans' were made visible in life for women who underwent the operation is not known (perhaps their

scalp, too, was shaved). At all events, whether the purpose was protective or not, nobody could have submitted himself or herself on a mere whim to what must have been an excruciatingly painful operation, involving as it did raising a large skin flap.

ANCIENT HUNGARIAN POETRY AND THE 'LOST' NAIVE EPIC.

A recurrent source of sadness for Hungarian poets of the last century was the idea that their country had once possessed its own national saga, comparable to the *Niebelunglied*, the Finnish *Kalevala,* or the great classical epics of Homer and the *Aeneid*, but that this had been forgotten with the passage of time. This imagined loss spurred many attempts to fill the gap with 'reconstructed' epics, among them János Arany's *Death of Buda and Csaba* trilogy. There were, in fact, two distinct strands of Hungarian poetry with presumably ancient roots, one a type of bardic poetry, the other the *regös* songs or lays.

There is a reference to the first in the chronicles, which mention seven survivors of the Battle of the Lechfeld, near Augsburg, where the German king, Otto I, routed a Magyar army in A.D. 955. On their return to Hungary, the seven Magyars were humiliated by being forced to wander from place to place singing heroic songs in a first person narrative, as if the events they were relating had happened to themselves or, more precisely, as if they were narrating on the champion's behalf his vicissitudes, heroic deeds, and adventures. Songs of this kind are known to have been performed for entertainment at banquets at the court of King Matthias. However, unlike the *regös* songs, the texts of these heroic songs have been lost and so cannot be studied.

REGÖS SONGS.

Long sequences of these songs have been collected by folklorists in the Dunántúl (Transdanubia) and, to some extent, among the Székely people of eastern Transylvania. Chanted at the time of the winter solstice, the songs functioned as fertility spells.[96] A few lines from one will serve as an illustration:

Here we come, here we come,
Servants of St Stephen.
Following old custom
That we wish to observe.
Sej, regőrejte, sej regőrejte…
Over there approaches
A threatening black cloud;
Inside, preening himself,
Is a wondrous boy-stag.
The wondrous boy-stag has
A thousand antler-tines.
Let a thousand candles
Burn without being lit,
Go out without being snuffed.
Sej, regőrejte, sej regőrejte…

Plainly, elements from various cultural traditions have become interwoven in these songs, just as they have in the Székely ballad of *Fair Julia,* which contains the following image:

Over there a fine footpath descends,
Down the path steps a fluffy white lamb,
With sun and moon caught between its horns,
Carrying a shining star on its front;
For every hair of its fleece, a star shines out upon it…

Leaving comparative ethnographical considerations aside, let us simply picture for ourselves the captivating sight of that stag or lamb, for in antiquity there were indeed animals that appeared in trappings every bit as gorgeous as these. We have only to recall the horse ornaments excavated at Pazyryk, in the Altai mountains of Siberia, where animal heads, claws, and fighting animals swarm over the plaques that were attached to harness and saddle-cloths. Or, to take an example from the opposite end of Eurasia, the Scythiantype bronze matrix that was found at Garchinova, north-eastern Bulgaria, which shows a stag in attempted flight, with the head of a ram or raptorial bird on each branch of its antlers, a lion on its haunches, and further bird-of-prey heads on its flank and on each hoof. This was how horse trappings of those periods must have appeared, covered in mounts depicting stag's heads, animal limbs, bird's claws and eagle's heads, so the poetic image had some basis in reality, even if only in prehistorical times.

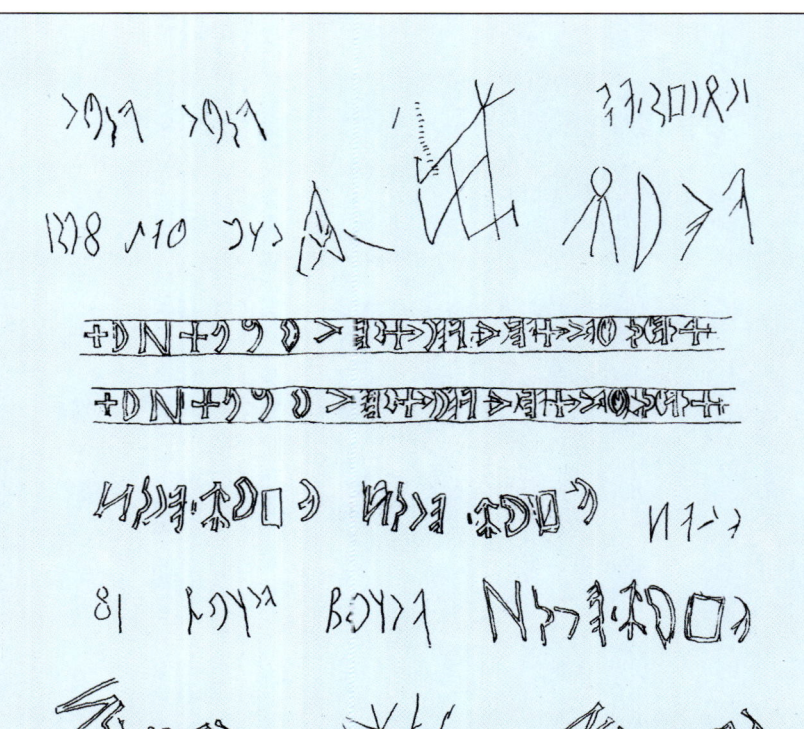

commented, there is nothing, apart from the linguistic link, to tie the Magyars to the Ob-Ugrians, and without the promptings of the linguists archaeologists would have had no reason to search for connections in this direction.

We all look to our own particular areas of expertise, but on this subject those best qualified to guide us are the more scholarly poets who, by virtue of their great familiarity with, and sensitivity to, linguistic usages, are able to discern minute inflections to which the rest of us are deaf. Géza Képes is one such poet, and his expositions on ancient Hungarian poetry are, for me, highly persuasive.[97]

Alliteration, it seems, was an important feature of ancient Hungarian verse, though not so much due to the workings of any specific poetic tradition as to the nature of the Hungarian language itself. I sometimes joke that for the finest relics of the ancient poetic heritage we owe our greatest debt to schoolchildren's tongue-twisters of the Peter-Piper-picked-a-peck-of-pickled-pepper kind. What emerges most clearly from Géza Képes's analysis, however, is that the rich Hungarian verse traditions are rooted much more in Turkic than in Finno-Ugrian poetry. In particular, the use of four-line stanzas and natural imagery and the intertwining of the various facets of the human condition which characterize Hungarian folk poetry all favour Turkic-Tatar sources of the tradition – broadly the direction that is also signposted by ethnomusicological researches, as we shall see in the next section.

FOLK MUSIC. Hungarian peasant song has been one of the great revelations of this century. After its discovery by Béla Vikár, who also produced a fine Hungarian translation of the *Kalevala*, the task of collecting Hungary's folk-song repertory was continued by Bartók, Kodály, László Lajtha, Sándor Veress and their latter-day pupils.[98] The main fruit of this work was the identification of a group of 'old-style' songs, manifestly Oriental in origin, that had pentatonic schemes and 'fifth-shifted' melodies, in which the second half of the melody repeats the first half at the fifth below. This type of melodic construction may well preserve some of the most primitive features of musical language as studies by Péter Szőke[99] suggest that pentatonality is the substratum of all music, whether birdsong or tunes from human lips. The models for this style were sought initially in Mari (Cheremis) folk song and later more widely in the pentatonic scales of various other Eurasian peoples. However, the researches carried out by Lajos Vargyas have led him to the startling conclusion that, far from the Hungarian 'old-style' pattern deriving from Mari tradition, precisely the reverse holds: the Mari tunes derive from the Hungarian tradition.

Whatever the truth about their developmental history, 'old-style' melodies were undoubtedly in existence by the time of the Conquest and, indeed, had already been fully assimilated by the Magyars before then. Of course, the tunes did not stand alone but had their associated texts; however, because a given melody could be used with dif-

Thus the Árpádian Magyars inherited a certain Scythian influence that may also be discerned, for instance, in their horse-bits or bone carvings. We should not think of this as having been some form of direct heritage but rather as a connection of the type whereby the deer was once a sacred animal for the Magyars, in their distant past, just as it had been for the Scythians. My grounds for drawing this parallel are by no means impeccable in strictly 'scientific' terms; I simply find it implausible that human imagination would have produced the fantastic images of the *regös* song or the *Fair Julia* ballad without some cue from the real world.

A few words should also be said about the bands or 'waits' of singers of these regös songs. By modern times, of course, they no longer had a role as rural fertility magicians but had become minstrels, evocators of the past, who wandered from fair to fair, from one settlement to the next. Their order was probably already on the decline during the Árpádian era, slowly degenerating into little more than wassailing companies or bibulous guilds. However, a glimpse into their original status may, perhaps, be gained from the life of the sixteenth-century poet-noble, Sebestyén Tinódi.

ANCIENT POETRY. Scholars have searched high and low for a Finno-Ugrian heritage in Hungarian folk poetry, but without conspicuous success. It seems possible that the incantations of traditional village mourners conceal a legacy of this sort; however, it is deceptively easy to read ancient heritages into texts like these when they are not fixed. Thus the pronouncements which have been made about 'Finno-Ugrian affinities' on this basis, in my opinion, would have emerged from comparison of material from any two 'primitive' peoples. As I have already

65. Ferenc Paczka: *Emese's Dream* (sketch).

ferent song-texts it is not possible to piece together the original verse from extant texts. We can nevertheless be confident in stating that the folk songs, in agreement with the findings of physical anthropology, provide a definite pointer back into Eurasian prehistory.

LITERACY. Though writing is, for us, one of the most important marks of civilization, it also brings a measure of impoverishment. Victor Hugo brilliantly hints at this in his *Notre-Dame de Paris*, in a scene where archdeacon Frollo converses with two visitors to his cloister-cell. As he contemplates the silhouette of the great cathedral, Frollo stretches out his hand towards a printed book lying open on his table and declares 'This will kill that… The book will kill the building.' In this sense, printing, or writing, is a sign of the weakening of a secure sense of community.

Literacy quite certainly penetrated to the courts of the Árpádian rulers, as the inscriptions on the Nagyszentmiklós Treasure attest. By similar token, we can deduce that at least some commoners must have known how to write from the finding of an inscription on an Onogur needle-case excavated at Szarvas and from the adoption of runic writing by the Székely of Transylvania. Early documents confirm the existence of a Hungarian alphabet that differed from Latin script. Thus Kézai, writing in the thirteenth century, comments that the Székely 'having mingled with Vlachs [i.e., Wallachians],… also make use of their letters.' And some two centuries later Antonio Bonfini, chronicler to King Matthias, recorded that 'they [the Székely] have Scythian letters by which they can express much meaning with few signs.' It is our good fortune that several documents which set out this runic alphabet have been preserved, among them the 'Nikolsburg ABC' included in Bartholomeus Angelicus's *De proprietate rerum*

of 1483, a 1589 primer prepared by János Telegdy and János Décsi, two schoolmasters at Marosvásárhely [now Tirgu Mures], and a copy of a runic calendar made by the naval architect Luigi Fernando Marsigli in 1690. In addition, a whole series of objects with short runic inscriptions have come to light in eastern Transylvania, the best known of which is one from the Unitarian church at Énlaka. More recently, possible evidence of use of the script has been found in the Felvidék region (formerly northern Hungary).

Thanks to this abundance of material, deciphering of the script presents no particular difficulties, though we are still left with the considerable problem of where the runic script came from. Kézai's reference to a connection with the Vlachs, who were originally a splinter group of Turkic Qarluqs (Karluks), directs our attention towards Turkish runic writing. Early in this century Gyula Sebestyén, later followed by Gyula Németh, made comparative studies of the Transylvanian relics and runic material from Central Asia, but their conclusions did not unequivocally corroborate such a link (for instance, they traced the signs for 'E' and 'O' to Glagolithic script, those for 'A', 'F' and 'H' to the Greek alphabet). More recently, in an effort to clear up this impression of eclecticism, some scholars have suggested that the Hungarian runes may derive from the most antique alphabetic writing systems or are a legacy of peoples like the Székely who already inhabited Hungarian territory before the Magyar conquest.[100] Though there have been a few attempts, mainly in artistic circles, to revive the use of runic script in the present century, these have remained isolated.

EPILOGUE

I have written several books about the Magyars and the Onogur Magyars, and I asked myself when I was commissioned to write the present volume, will I be able to say something new, because I didn't see much point in repeating myself. However, I found hope in the feeling that I have not said everything there was to say, which nagged me while I was writting my last book, and which offered a glimmer of hope. And I feel that I have been able to pose new questions after all, perhaps even offer new answers. Of course, sometimes a good question is worth more than the answer, for it can serve as a guide line for future research. A first-rate generation of new archaeologists has come to the fore in the past forty years, and I feel privileged to have had a share in pointing the way. The work they do is of such quality that I feel I am no longer needed. I have two more books to write, after which I will turn to painting, carving, and etching. Of course, I will never forget that for more than fifty years I lived, worked and thought as an archaeologists. And I am grateful to fate, for I have always worked on topics that are close to my heart. Though I agree with the poet János Arany that "there is more fame than merit" in all this, as I approach the end of my career, I hope I have "done right by my country. "

March 14, 1986   *Gyula László*

66. György Zala: Bronze statues of the Millennial Monument.

NOTES

By way of a prefatory remark, since I have already written copiously about the Conquest period, I have been unable to avoid making use here of some lines and paragraphs from earlier works, notably: Gy. László, 'A koroncói lelet és a honfoglaló magyarok nyerge' [The Koronco find and the saddle of the conquering Magyars]', *Arch. Hung.*, XXVIII, 1943; *A honfoglaló magyar nép élete* [Life of the Conquest-period Magyars], Budapest, 1944 – hereafter László, HMNÉ; *Őstörténetünk legkorábbi szakaszi. A finnugor őstörténet régészeti emlékei a Szovjetföldben* [The earliest phases of Magyar prehistory, Archaeological relics of Finno-Ugrian prehistory in the Soviet Union], Budapest, 1962 & 1971; *A honfoglalókról* [The conquering Magyars], Budapest, 1973; *A kettős honfoglalásról* [The double conquest of Hungary], Budapest, 1980; *Őstörténetünk* [Prehistory of Hungary], Budapest, 1981; *50 rajz a honfoglalásról* [50 pictures of the conquering Magyars], Budapest, 1982 – hereafter László, *50 rajz*; *Árpád népe* [Árpád's people], in press; and numerous shorter studies. The present book nevertheless stands in its own right, containing fresh material not published before.

1. Gy. Györffy, 'A honfoglalás és megtelepedés' [The conquest and settlement of Hungary], in: *Magyarország története* [History of Hungary], vol. I/1, ed. A. Bartha, Budapest, 1984, hereafter Györffy, *MT*. In English, see Gy. Györffy, *The Original Landtaking of the Hungarians*, Budapest, 1975.
2. I. Dienes, *A honfoglaló magyarok*, Budapest, 1972; English edition: *The Hungarians Cross the Carphatians*, Budapest, 1972. Also A. Bartha, *Hungarian Society in the 9th and 10th Centuries*, Budapest, 1975.
3. For literature on the archaeology of the Conquest era, see J. Banner & I. Jakabffy, *A közép-Dunamedence régészeti bibliográfiája* [Bibliography on the archaeology of the Middle Danubian Basin], Budapest, vol. I 1954, vol. II 1961, vol III 1968, vol IV 1981.

For written sources relating to the period: *A magyarok elődeiről és a honfoglalásról* [The forebears of the Magyars and the conquest of Hungary], ed. Gy. Györffy, Budapest, 1975 (2nd ed) – hereafter Györffy, *MEH*. Indispensable source-books on Hungarian prehistory and Árpádian Magyars are the volumes in the series prepared by the Szeged Working Group on Prehistory: *Bevezetés a magyar őstörténet kutatásainak forrásaiba* [Introduction to sources for research into Hungarian prehistory]. eds. P. Hajdú, Gy. Kristó & A. Róna-Tas, Budapest, vols. I–IV, 1977–1982. These bibliographies are the work of younger generations of Hungarian archaeologists, notably: Kornél Bakay, István Bóna, Csanád Bálint, István Dienes, István Erdelyi, Itsván Fodor, László Kovács, Béla Kürti, Károly Mesterházy, the late János Győző Szabó, and Péter Tomka.

4. See the summary in Gy. László, *Emlékezzünk régiekről* [Let us recall olden days], Budapest, 1978.
5. B. Hóman, *Magyar Történet* [Hungarian history], Budapest, 1935, vol. I, p. 124 (3rd ed); I. Györffy, L. Makkai, 'A honfoglaló magyar nemzetségek Erdélyben [Conquest-period Magyar clans in Transylvania]', *Századok*, 1944, 1–13; László *HMNÉ*, p. 222.
6. Gy. Almásy, *Vándorútam Ázsia szívébe* [My wandering in the heart of Asia], Budapest, 1903, p. 685.
7. A Hungarian tranlation (by D. Pais) of Anonymus's *Gesta Hungarorum* is in Györffy, *MEH*, pp. 133–181.
8. I. Szamota, *Régi utazások Magyarországon és a Balkán félszigeten* [Old journeys in Hungary and the Balkan peninsula], Budapest, 1981, pp. 16–17.
9. A Hungarian translation (by I. Juhász) of Oláh's *Hungaria* was published in 1938.
10. I. Szamota, *op. cit.*, pp. 91–92.
11. M. Pécsi & B. Sárfalvi, *Magyarország földrajza*, Budapest, 1960, pp. 7, 8, 17, 75, etc.; English edition – *The Geography of Hungary*, Budapest, 1964. See also S. Somogyi, 'Történeti földrajzi bevezető' [Geo-historical introduction], in: *Magyarország Története* [History of Hungary], vol. I/1, ed. A. Bartha, Budapest, 1984, pp. 25–68.
12. I. Györffy, *Nagykunsági krónika* [Chronicle of Greater Cumania], Karcag, 1922. Also the works of S. Szűcs, notably: *A régi Sárrét világa* [The old world of the Sárrét], Bólyai Akadémia, Budapest, n.d.; *Pusztai szabadok, Rajzok a régi Alföld életéből* [Free on the plains. Sketches of old Alföld life], Budapest, 1957; *A régi magyar vízivilág* [The water-world of old Hungary], Budapest, 1977.
13. J. Matolcsi, *Állattartás őseink korában* [Animal raising in the days of our ancestors], Budapest, 1982.
14. J. Nemeskéri, 'Az embertan és a magyar őstörténet' [Anthropology and Hungarian prehistory], in: *A magyarság őstörténete* [Prehistory of the Magyars], ed. L. Ligeti, Budapest, 1943 [reprinted 1986], pp. 223–239; K. K. Éry, 'Regionális különbségek a magyarság X. századi embertani anyagában' [Regional difference in the anthropological material on the 10th-century Magyars], *Anthropologiai Közlemények*, 1978, 77–86; P. Lipták, *Avars and Ancient Hungarians*, Budapest, 1983, and other works by the same author.
15. O. Herman, *A magyar nép arca és jelleme* [Physiognomy and character of the Hungarian people], Budapest, 1902.
16. On Romantic approaches to research on Hungary's prehistory: M. Zsirai, 'Őstörténeti csodabogarak' [Prehistorical curiosities], in: *A magyarság őstörténete* [Prehistory of the Magyars], ed. L. Ligeti, Budapest, 1943 [reprinted 1986], pp. 266–289; also the chapter 'Más megoldás is elképzelhető' [Other explanations are feasible] in my own *Őstörténetünk* [Our prehistory], Budapest, 1981.
17. A more detailed exposition is given in Gy. László, *Őstörténetünk*, Budapest, 1981.
18. A Hungarian translation (by Gy. Györffy) of Kézai's *Gesta Hungarorum* is from the English translation by G. F. Cushing in *Old Hungarian Literary Reader: 11th–18th centuries*, ed. T. Klaniczay, Budapest, 1985, pp. 51–54.
19. J. Pusztay, *Az 'Ugor-török háború' után* [After the 'War of the Ugrians and Turks'], Budapest, 1977.
20. See Note 17.
21. The origin of the Ugrians is a concern of almost the entire oeuvre of V. N. Chernetsov; e.g. his article in *Sovyetskaya Etnografiya*, n.d., 158–163. I have also taken up the question in *Őstörténetünk*, Budapest, 1981.
22. From a paper read at the Finno–Ugrian Congress, Syktyvkar: 'Zur Vorgeschichte der Finnisch–ugrischen Völker', *Studia Hungarica*, Syktyvkar, 1985, pp. 1–5.
23. The hypothesis of a proto–Magyar 'Urheimat' along the Kama valley was proposed by Zoltán Gombócz, Irén N. Sebestyén, Miklós Zsirai and Péter Hajdú.
24. P. Hajdú, 'A rokonság nyelvi háttere', in: *Az uráli népek. Nyelvrokonaink kultúrája és hagyományai*, ed. P. Hajdú, Budapest, 1975, esp. p. 32 *et seq.*; English edition – 'Linguistic Backround of Generic Relationships', in: *Ancient Cultures of the Uralian Peoples*, Budapest, 1976, esp. pp. 33–37.
25. György Györffy's most recent evaluation of Anonymus appeared in Györffy, *MT*.
26. *A magyar honfoglalás kútfői* [Major sources of the Magyar conquest], ed. Gy. Pavler and S. Szilágyi, Budapest, 1900. Györffy, *MEH*; I use this edition for the quotations here and elsewhere in the book. English translations of the relevant passages from the main Oriental sources, including Ibn Rusta and Gardîzi (trans. M. Smith), and from Constantine

VII's *De Administrando Imperio* are given in C. A. Macartney, *The Magyars in the Ninth Century*, Cambridge, 1930 [repr. 1968].

27. A. Hodinka, *Az orosz évkönyvek magyar vonatkozásai* [Hungarian references in the Russian chronicles], Budapest, 1916, p. 51.

28. The most recent discussion is by P. Király, 'A magyarok említése a Konstantin és Metód legendában' [Mention of the Hungarians in the Legend of Constantine (Cyril) and Methodius], *Nyelvtudományi Tanulmányok*, 1974, pp. 1–69.

29. A Hungarian translation (by J. Horváth) of the relevant passages from the *Casus Sancti Galli* is in: Györffy, *MEH*, pp. 234, 243. A shorter excerpt of the story, in English translation, is in G. G. Coulton, *Life in the Middle Ages. Part IV. Monks, Friars and Nuns,* Cambridge, 1967 (2nd ed), pp. 74–78.

30. Hungarian translations (by J. Horváth) of the pertinent entries from Regino of Prüm's *Chronicon* and Widukind's *Rerum gesta-um Saxonicarum* are given in: Györffy, *MEH*, pp. 204–209 and 246–255, respectively.

31. S. Nagy, *A magyar nép kialakulásának története* [History of the development of the Hungarian people], Buenos Aires, 1968, p. 240. Nagy takes a Sumerian origin as his basic thesis.

32. D. Csallány. 'Avar törzsszervezet' [Avar tribal organization], *Jósa Andrcs Múzeum Évkönyve*, VIII–IX (1965–66), Budapest, 1967, pp. 35–56.

33. *The Secret History of the Mongols*, Budapest, 1961.

34. G. Bárczi, *Régi magyar nyelvjárások* [Old Hungarian dialects], Néptudományi Intézet, Budapest, 1947.

35. G. Ferenczy & I. Ferenczy, 'Székelyföldi gyepük' [The Székely marshlands], *Korunk*, (Kolozsvár), 1972/2, 305.

36. See I. Dienes, *A honfoglaló magyarok*, Budapest, 1972, p. 22; English edition – *The Hungarians Cross the Carpathians,* Budapest, 1972.

37. G. Heckenast, *Fejedelmi (királyi) szolgálónépek a korai Árpád-korban* [Royal 'service' peoples in the early Árpádian era], Budapest, 1970, pp. 103–105.

38. H. G. Göckenjan, *Hilfsvölker und Grenzwächter in Mittelaltlerichen Ungarn,* Wiesbaden, 1972.

39. B. Hóman, 'Adalék X–XI. századi pénztörténetünkhöz' [Contribution to the history of Hungary's 10th–11th century coinage], *Századok*, 1918: 161–167. An English translation of this report was published by S. Rapaport, 'On the Early Slavs. The Narrative of Ibrahim-ibn-Yakub', *Slavonic Review,* VIII (1929): 331–341.

40. Györffy, *MT,* p. 623

41. László, *HMNÉ,* pp. 216–217.

42. For the etymology of Hungarian words relating to domestic life see the appropriate headings in: G. Bárczi, *Magyar szó-fejtő szótár* [Hungarian etymological dictionary], Budapest, 1941.

43. The material from Felgyő has not yet been fully worked up; the statements here are based on my own observations during the excavation. A brief report has been prepared by Gy. László, Tary & Nagyistók, *Régmúlt és jelen a Vidre parton* [Antiquity and present on the banks of the Vidre], Felgyő, n.d.

44. J. Kovalovszki, *Szentes környékének régészeti lelőhelyei* [Archaeological sites in the Szentes district], *Rég. Füz.* I/5:1955.

45. *Hódmezővásárhely története* [History of Hódmezővásárhely], Hódmezővásárhely, Vol. I, 1984.

46. Hungarian translations of the Latin texts of decrees of the Árpádian dynasty kings are included in: *Szöveggyűjtemény Magyarország történetének tanulmányozásához. I. 1000–1526* [Collected texts for study of the history of Hungary], ed. E. Lederer (trans. L. Szilágyi), Budapest, 1964.

47. B. Szőke, 'A honfoglaló és kora Árpád-kori magyarság régészeti emlékei' [Archaeological relics of the Conquest-period and early Árpádian Magyars], *Régészeti tanulmányok I,* Budapest, 1962.

48. N. Fettich, 'A honfoglaló magyarság fémművességének kialakulása' [The development of metalworking crafts among the Conquest-period Magyars], *Arch. Hung.,* XXI (1937), *passim*.

49. On horse burials see László, *Arch. Hung.,* XXVII (1943).

50. N. Fettich, *op. cit.,* pp. 105–110.

51. A. Jósa, *Arch. Ért.,* 1896: 385–412.

52. For an analysis of Bezdéd cemetery see László, *HMNÉ,* pp. 128–134.

53. The significance of left-right positionings is discussed more fully in László, *HMNÉ,* pp. 174–189.

54. V. Budinsky´–Kric̆ka & N. Fettich, *Das alt-ungarische Fürstengrab von Zemplin,* Bratislava, 1973. For a rebuttal of the hypothesis that this is Árpád's grave and for further literature, see Gy. László, 'A zempléni honfoglaláskori vezérsír-ról' [The Conquest-period chieftain's grave at Zemplén], *Arch. Ért.* (1976): 79–85.

55. J. Nemeskéri, P. Lipták & B. Szőke, 'Le cimetière du XI- siècle de Kérpuszta', *Acta Arch. ASH,* 1953/54: 205–370.

56. Gy. Török, *Die Bewohner in Halimba-Cseres nach der Landnahme,* Leipzig, 1959. For my own view see Gy. László, *Századok* (1964): 804–806.

57. K. Mesterházy, ' Régészeti adatok Hajdú-Bihar megye IX–XIII. századi településtörténetéhez' [Archaeological data related to the 9th to 13th century settlement-history of Hajdú-Bihar county], *Jósa András Múzeum Évkönyve,* 1974: 95–174.

58. S. Tettamanti, 'Temetkezési szokások a Kárpátmedencében a X–XI. században' [Funerary customs in the Carphatian basin in the 10th–11th centuries], in: *Előmunkálatok a Magyarság Néprajzához* [Preparatory work towards an Ethnography of the Hungarians], Vol. 10, Budapest, 1982, p. 87 *et seq.*

59. B. Kürti, 'Honfoglaláskori temető Szeged-Algyőn' [Conquest-period cemetery at Szeged-Algyő], *Móra Ferenc Múzeum Évkönyve,* 1971/1, 323–343.

60. For a more detailed treatment see Gy. László, 'A honfoglaló magyar nép élete' [History of the conquering Magyars], Budapest, 1944, pp. 166–219.

61. K. Tagányi, 'A földközösség története Magyarországon' [History of land-communities in Hungary], *Gazdaságtörténeti Szemle,* 1894: 199–238.

62. F. Gönczi, *Göcsej,* Kaposvár, 1914, pp. 136, 157 *et seq.*

63. Zs. Szendrey, 'A varázslócselekvések személye, ideje és helye' [The persons, time and the place of magical acts], *Ethnographia,* 48 (19?): 13 f.

64. I. Balassa, *Az eke és a szántás története Magyarországon* [History of the plough and ploughing in Hungary], Budapest, 1973.

65. B. P. Hartányi, Gy. Nováki & A. Patay, *Növényi mag- és termésleletek Magyarországon az újkőkortól a XVIII. századig* [Finds of plant seeds and fruits in Hungary from the Neolithic age to the 18th century], Magyar Mezőgazdasági Múzeum, Budapest, 1967–68, pp. 5–84.

66. Gy. Pauler, *A magyar nemzet története Szent Istvánig* [History of the Hungarian nation till St István], Budapest, 1900.

67. The description is the same as in *50 Drawings.*

68. O. Herman, *Halászat, pásztorkodás* [Fishing life and pastoral nomadism], Budapest, 1980, p. 103 *et seq.*

69. K. Gaál, 'Auswirkung der mittelalterichen Fischereiwirtschaft auf die tradizionelle Fischerei', in: *Festschrift F. C. Lipp,* Wien, 1978.

70. K. Sebestyén, 'Rejtelmes csontok népvándorláskori sírokban' [Mysterious bones in graves of the Migration period], Szeged, 1930; A magyarok íja és nyila [The bow and arrow of the Magyars], *Dolg.,* 8, 1932.

71. Gy. Fábian, 'Újabb adatok a honfoglaláskori íjászat kérdéséhez' [New data on the archery of the Conquest-period], *MFMÉ,* Szeged, 1980–81, pp. 63–76.

72. K. U. Kőhalmi, *A steppék nomádjai lóháton, fegyverben* [Mounted, armoured nomads of the steppes], Budapest, 1972. Also L. Révész, *Acta Antiqua and Arch.* XXVI. Suppl. V, Szeged, 1985, pp. 35–53.

73. The find at Koroncó is described in Gy. László, 'A koroncói lelet és a honfoglaló magyarok nyerge' [The Koroncó find and the saddle of the Conquest-era Magyars], *Arch. Hung.,* XXVII. (1943).

74. Gy. Szabó, 'A falusi kovács a XV–XVI. században' [Village blacksmiths in the 15th–16th centuries], *Folia Arch.,* (1954): 123–145.

75. J. Gömöri, *Jelentés a nyugat-magyarországi vasvidék Győr-Sopron megyei lelőhelyeinek kutatásáról. I Arrabona* [Report on exploration of sites of the N. W. Hungarian iron district in Győr-Sopron county. I. Arrabona], Győr, p. 138 *et seq.*

76. W. Radloff, *Aus Sibirien*, Leipzig, 1884, vol. 1, p. 469 *et seq.*

77. I. Dienes, 'Honfoglaláskori veretes tarsoly Budapest-Farkasrétről' [Conquest-period sabretache mount from Budapest-Farkasrét], *Folia Arch.*, (1973): 177–217.

78. Gy. László & I. Rácz, *The Treasure of Nagyszentmiklós*, Budapest, 1984.

79. N. Parádi, *Technikai vizsgálatok népvándorláskori és Árpád-kori edényeken* [Scientific analysis of pottery from the Migration period and Árpádian age], Budapest, 1959.

80. Veronika Gervers-Molnár, *The Hungarian Szűr: an Archaic Mantle of Eurasian Origin*, Toronto, 1973.

81. See the heading in G. Bárczi, *Magyar szófejtő szótár* [Hungarian etymological dictionary], Budapest, 1941; also the text and picture in László, *50 rajz*.

82. J. Balogh, 'A portyázó magyarok kucsmája és a német püspökök süvege' [The fur cap of Magyar raiders and the mitre of German bishops], *Ethnographia* 38 (1927): 42.

83. Gy. László, *A honfoglaló magyarok művészete Erdélyben* [Art of the conquering Magyars in Transylvania], Kolozsvár, 1943.

84. The original Arabic text of Mas'üdi's *Meadows of Gold* and a parallel French translation by C. B. de Meynard & P. de Courteille, 9 vols., Paris, 1861–77; a Hungarian translation (by K. Czeglédy) of the excerpt including this incident is in: Györffy, *MEH*, pp. 100–103.

85. B. Hóman, *A Szent László-kori Gesta Hungarorum és XII–XIII. századi leszármazói* [The Gesta Hungarorum of St Ladislas' reign and its 12th–13th century derivatives], Budapest, 1925.

86. L. Rásonyi, 'Török eredetű magyar személynevek' [Hungarian personal names of Turkish origin], *Forrás (Kecskemét)*, July 1983: 78–83; D. Pais, 'Az óvó és sorsirányító nevek' [Names that safeguard and point your way], *A magyar ősvallás nyelvi emlékeiből* [Linguistic Archaeology of the ancient religion of the Magyars], Budapest, 1975, p. 318. *et seq.* K. Kerényi, 'Árpád és a növényi termést jelentő magyar személynevek' [Árpád and Magyar personal names with plant-meanings], *MNy*, 1931. pp. 94–106.

87. G. Róheim, 'Sámánkodó gyógyítás nyoma egy gyermekversben' [Traces of shamanistic healing in a children's poem], *Ethn.*, 23: 336–337.

88. Gy. László, *Varázslat egy középkori falusi templomban* [White magic in a medieval village church], *Erdélyi Tudományos Intézet*, Kolozsvár, 1974, pp. 3–22.

89. V. Diószegi, *A sámánhit emlékei a magyar népi műveltségben* [Relics of shamanistic beliefs in Hungarian folk culture], Budapest, 1958. For a more recent English-language discussion of the question, see: T. Dömötör, *Hungarian Folk Beliefs*, Budapest, 1982, pp. 21–42 and *passim.*

90. F. Juhász, *Mit tehet a költő* [What poets can do], Budapest, 1967, p. 133 *et seq.*

91. I. Dienes, ' A sámánok társadalmi szerepe a nomád államokban' [The social function of shamans in nomadic states], in: *Az őshazától a Kárpátokig* [From ancient homeland to the Carpathians], ed. V. Szombathy, Budapest, 1985, pp. 375–387.

92. László, *HMNÉ*, p. 416 *et seq.* My monograph on the wall paintings is currently in press; L. Vatgyas, 'Honfoglalás előtti hagyományok Szent László legendájában' [Pre-conquest traditions in the Legend of St Stephen], *Athlete Patriae*, Budapest, 1980, p. 9 *et seq.*

93. G. Nagy, 'Magyar viseletek története: Népvándorláskori turán viselet' [History of Hungarian dress: 'Turanian' costume during the Migration period], *Arch. Ért.*, (1901): 318–323.

94. German translation by E. Haenisch, *Die geheime Geschichte der Mongolen*, 2nd ed., Leipzig, 1948.

95. For the literature on trepanation and symbolic marking of the skull see J. Nemeskéri, K. K. Éry & A. Kralovánszky, *Athropologiai Közlemények*, (1978).

96. Gy. Sebestyén, *A regősénekek* [Regős-songs], Budapest, 1902; L. Vargyas, 'A regősénekek problémájának újabb, zenei megközelítése [A new, musical approach to the problem of the regős-songs]', *Ethnographia*, (1979): 163–191.

97. G. Képes, 'A magyar ősköltészet nyomairól' [Traces of ancient Hungarian poetry], *Irodalmtörténeti Közlemények*, (1964): 1–44.

98. L. Vikár, 'The Music of the Finno-Ugrian Peoples', in: *Ancient Cultures of the Uralian Peoples*, ed. P. Hajdú, Budapest, 1976, pp. 319–336.

99. P. Szőke, *A zene eredete és három világa* [Music – its origins and three realms], Budapest, 1982.

100. A full historical survey and balanced analysis is given by Vásáry, 'A magyar rovásírás' [Hungarian runic script], *Keletkutatás 1974*, Budapest, 1975, pp. 159–171. For new attempts at resolving the problems: P. P. Péter & P. Simon, *Magyar Herold*, I, 1984: 7–71.

LIST OF ILLUSTRATION

1. Route followed by the Magyar tribes on their way to the Carpathian Basin (by Ágoston Dékány).
2. Antal Szécsi: *Árpád*, 1895. Guilt and painted statue on a pillar in the great hall of the Hungarian Parliament, Budapest (photo: János Pelbárt).
3-4. Árpád Feszty, Ignác Ujváry, Pál Vágó: *The Magyar Conquest* (details from the *Feszti Panorama*) – *Árpád and his Chieftains, Attacking Magyar Horsemen*. The reconstruction of the oroginal panorama, finished in 1895 and damaged during World War II, is from 1995. National Memorial Park (photo: Mihály Dömötör).
5. Bertalan Székely: *Blood Contract*, 1896-97. Mural from the assembly hall of the Town Hall of Kecskemét photo: Mihály Dömötör).
6-7. The sabretache from Galgóc with detail. Silver, 11.3 cm. Inv. no. 42/1871.3. Hungarian National Museum, Budapest (photo: János Pelbárt).
8. The sabretache from Rakamaz. Guilt, silver, 11.3-12.7 cm. Jósa András Museum, Nyíregyháza (photo: János Pelbárt).
9. The sabretache from Szolnok-Strázsahalom. Silver with embossed decoration. 14.3-12.2 cm. Inv. no. 58/1912.1. Hungarian National Museum, Budapest (photo: János Pelbárt).
10-11-12. Drawings from excavations: protective ditch around a yuhrt after excavation; cross-section from the excavations at Felgyi; ground-plan of the church of Geda-Halom (by Gyula László and István Méri).
13. The sabretache from the grave of a chieftain from the graveyard of Bezdéd. Guilt copper, 13.2 cm. Inv. no.: 86/1895.235.a. Hungarian National Museum, Budapest (photo: János Pelbárt).
14. The gold coin of Constantine "the Red", obverse and reverse sides. Inv. no. 64/1858.1. Hungarian National Museum, Budapest (photo: János Perlbárt).
15. The gold coin of Leo "the Wise", obverse and reverse sides. Inv. no. 170/1936.1. Hungarian National Museum, Budapest (photo: János Perlbárt).
16. Western coins from Conquest-period graves. Inv. no. 21.1853.17. Hungarian National Museum, Budapest (photo: Janos Perlbárt).
17. László Hegedűs: *Blood Contract*, 1908. Oil on canvas, 129x250 cm. Inv. no. F.K.683. Hungarian National Museum. Budapest (photo: János Perlbárt).
18. Mór Than: *Attila's Feast*, 1865. Oil on canvas, 68x89 cm. Hungarian National Gallery, Budapest (photo: Levente Szepsi Szűcs).
19. Caftan ornaments from Szeged-Bojárhalom. Guilt silver, 8.9 cm. Inv. no. 92.1.21. Móra Ferenc Museum, Szeged (photo: Mihály Dömötör).
20. Silver horse trapping decorations from grave #6 at Ártánd. Silver. Inv. no. IV.1970.2.63. Déri Museum, Debrecen (photo: János Perbált).
21. Guilt silver horse trapping from Pilin-Leshegy: chin-strap ornaments, diam.: 2.9 cm., Inv. no. 44/1898. 2385-96; chin-strap ends, 4-2.3 cm., Inv. no. 44/1898. 2399-2401; breast-plate ornaments, 5.1-5.5 cm., Inv. no. 44/1898.2377-81. Hungarian National Museum, Budapest (photo: János Perbált).
22. Bone mouthpiece from Tiszaderzs. 10.9-5.3 & 9.3-11.5 cm. Hungarian National Museum, Budapest (photo: János Perbált).
23. Carved bone mouthpiece with palmette design from Kiszombor. 8 cm. Inv. no. 53.7.52. Móra Ferenc Museum, Szeged (photo: Mihály Dömötör).
24. Iron bridles with silver inlay from Muszka. Diam.: 8 cm. Inv. no. 45/1898.9. Hungarian National Museum, Budapest (photo: János Perbált).
25. Hunting brothers from the drinking horn from Chernigov. 10th century. Drawing by Gyula László based on the original from the Historical Museum of Moscow.
26. Belt strap in the shape of a bird from Karos. Cast silver, 2-1.9 cm. Inv. no.: 5/1936.6. Hungarian National Museum, Budapest (photo: János Perbált).
27. Saddle ornament in the shape of a strap end from Törtel. Guilt and cast silver, 5.65-3.85 cm. Inv. no. 101/1895.42. Hungarian National Museum, Budapest (photo: János Perbált).
28. Arrow from the Conquest period in three states. (Drawing by István Ö. Dienes).
29. Inner carved bone plates from a saddle found at Soltszentimre. 18.8-7.2 & 9.8-4.2 cm. Inv. no. 61.14.1A. Hungarian National Museum, Budapest (photo: János Perbált).
30. Altaic "smithy" (drawing based on a book published by P.S. Pallas), (Puteshestvie po raznim provintsiam Rossiiskogo gosudarstva). 1-3,1773-1788.
31. "Winged" Carolingian spears from Szombathely and Kőszegszerdahely. Iron, 37.7-5.3 cm. Inv. no.: Fe 58.7551, ill. 40.3-5.9 cm. Inv. no.: Fe 58.7632. Hungarian National Museum, Budapest (photo: János Perbált).
32. Double-edged swords. 1. from Szentbékkálla, 64.4-4.2 cm. Inv. no. Fe 11/1905; 2. from grave #2 at Szob-Kiserdő, 70.4-4 cm. Inv. no. 2/1937.17; 3. from grave #18 at Szob-Kiserdı, 64.2 cm. Inv. no. 2/1937.20 Hungarian National Museum, Budapest (photo: János Perbált).
33. Hair ornaments from Nyíracsád. Silver, diam.: 4.7 cm. Inv. no. IV. 1977.157.1. Déri Museum, Debrecen (photo: János Perbált).
34. Open-work hair ornaments from Hencida with animal figures. Cast bronze, diam.: 5.6 cm. Inv. no.: 13/1933.1 Hungarian National Museum, Budapest (photo: János Perbált).
35. Hair ornaments with animal figures from Bashalom. Guilt and cast silver with bronze back, diam.: 5 cm; guilt and cast silver mountings, 1.6-1 cm., Inv. no. 60.175-8-9. Hungarian National Museum, Budapest (photo: János Perbárt).
36. The sabretache from grave # 3 at Eperjes. Silver with guilt background, 13-9 cm, Inv. no. 64.879.2. Józsa András Museum, Nyíregyháza (photo: János Perbált).
37. Silver sabretache with palmette ornamentation from Dunavecse-Fehéregyház. Silver with copper background, 13-12 cm, Inv. no. 55.41.588. Katona József Museum, Kecskemét (photo: Mihály Dömötör).
38. Belt ornaments from the Tarcal-Beregszász find. Suilt silver, 2.4-1.8 cm, 2.3-1.6 cm, 2.1-1.9 cm, diam. of guilt bronze "buttons": 1 cm, Inv. no. 8/1895. 42-46, 34-41; 51/1900. 4-8, 10-17. Hungarian National Museum, Budapest (photo: János Perbárt).

39-40-41. Pieces from the Tokaji Treasure. Silver shirt ornaments, 8.3-5 cm, Inv. no. 105/1896. 5-16; silver earrings, diam.: 5.2-6.5 cm, and 24/24/1897. 1-12, 1-2; silver half-moon charm, 4.3-5.9 cm, and 4.5-2.7 cm, Inv. no. 105/1896.17. and 1-2. Hungarian National Museum, Budapest (photo: János Perbárt).

42. Bracelets from Zsenye with animal heads. Silver and lectron, diam.: 7.1 and 7.9 cm, Inv. no. 2/1923. 1 and 3. Hungarian National Museum, Budapest (photo: János Perbárt).

43. The "ascension" scene from jug #2 of the Golden Treasure of Nagyszentmiklós. Gold, 22 cm. Kunsthistorisches Museum, Vienna.

44. Drinking cup with runic script (#8, 17.7 cm), drinking cup with ram's head (#13, 11-12.2 cm), and omphalos cup (#21, diam.: 12 cm). Kunsthistorisches Museum, Vienna.

45. Helmet tip with palette design from the Beregszász find. Silver plate with guilt background, 11.4-6.7 cm, Inv. no. 51/1900. 10-21. Hungarian National Museum, Budapest (photo: János Perbárt).

46. Pair of disks from Rakamaz. Silver plate with guilt background, diam.: 8.2-8.3 cm., Inv. no. 64.875.6-7. Jósa András Museum, Nyíregyháza (photo: János Perbárt).

47. Bronze belt-ends from the Vereb find, 5.1-1.9 cm, Inv. no. 21/1853.3 and 6.5-1.4 cm, Inv. no. 21/1853.4. Hungarian National Museum, Budapest (photo: János Perbárt).

48. Hair ornament with animal figures from Jánosszállás. Guilt silver, 5.6 cm, Inv. no. Jk-4. Móra Ferenc Museum, Szeged (photo: Mihály Dömötör).

49. Saltovo-type earrings from Szeged-Bojárhalom. Guilt silver, 8 cm, Inv. no. N.92.1.7. Móra Ferenc Museum, Szeged (photo: Mihály Dömötör).

50. The full saddle of a prince of Transylvania, later the ceremonial saddle of Francis Joseph. Wood, bone, leather, velvet, Inv. no. Fe. 57. 6702. Hungarian National Museum, Budapest (photo: János Perbárt).

51. Drawing of the bone plates of the saddle of Soltszentimre (drawing by Gyula László).

52. Reconstruction of the saddle of Soltszentimre (drawing by Gyula László).

53. "The Siege of Aquileia" from *The Picture Chronicle*. Facs. 1035. 7. National Széchényi Library, Budapest (photo: Csaba Gabler)

54. Scene of the Conquest from *The Picture Chronicle*. Clmae 404. Facs. 1038. 11.v. National Széchényi Library, Budapest (photo: Csaba Gabler)

55. The golden decoration from the sabre of Geszteréd. Gold treasury Inv. no. 68-69, 80, 89-90. Jósa András Museum, Nyíregyháza (photo: János Perbárt).

56. Gyula Rudnay: *The National Assembly at Pusztaszer.* Middle scene of a gobelin from the Gobelin Room of the Parliament, Budapest (photo: János Perbárt).

57-62. Counter-clockwise: Szabolcs, Kund, Örs, Gyula, Hunor and Magyar. Figures from the Buzád clan from *The Picture Chronicle*. Clmae. 404. Facs. 1041, 13v.; 1044. 13.v; 1040. 12.v.; 1042. 13.v.; 1043; 1053. 404.v. National Széchenyi Library, Budapest (photo: Csaba Gabler).

63. Árpád Feszty, Ignác Ujváry and Pál Vágó: *Horsemen in the Ancient Homeland around a Shaman*, detail from "The Magyar Conquest" section of the Feszty Panorama. The reconstruction of the painting finished in 1895 and destroyed during WW II is from 1995. National Memorial Park, Ópusztaszer (photo: Mihály Dömötör).

64. Runic scripts from the dishes of the Nagyszentmiklós Treasure (drawing by Gyula László).

65. Ferenc Paczka: *Emese's Dream* (sketch). Oil on canvas, 41-72 cm, Inv. no. 7739, Hungarian National Gallery, Budapest (photo: Levente Szepsi Szűcs).

66. György Zala: Bronze statues of the Millennial Monument, 1912. Heroes Square, Budapest (photo: János Perbárt).

On the cover: Árpád Feszty, Ignác Ujváry and Pál Vágó: *Árpád and his Chieftains*, detail from "The Magyar Conquest" section of the Feszty Panorama. The reconstruction of the painting finished in 1895 and destroyed during WW II is from 1995. National Memorial Park, Ópusztaszer (photo: Mihály Dömötör).

On the inside title page: Sabretache from Bodrogvécs. Silver on a bronze background, 14.3-11.7 cm, Inv. no. 63.2.A., Hungarian National Museum, Budapest (photo: János Perbárt).

On the back cover: Sabretache from the "horse grave" at Szolyva. Silver, 12-11.7 cm, Inv. no. 148/1870.5 Hungarian National Museum, Budapest (photo: Jánnos Perbárt).

A READER
ON THE
MAGYARS
OF CONQUEST
PERIOD
HUNGARY

This supplement is addressed to those who are interested in the contemporary sources and chronicles and the deductions that have been drawn from them during the last half-century. So it has been produced for general readers and it takes into account what it is they read. For the public has access not only to academic historical works and novels, but also to the writings of various Hungarian enthusiasts who, dazzled by nationalistic fervour, imagine the prehistory of our Hungarian people and its conquest of Hungary as consisting of one glorious episode after another. I, too, care passionately for my people and country, but in my researches I take my motto from the poet Endre Ady: 'their heart glowing, their brain ice-cold'. I do not intend to succumb to the seducements of illusions.

In accordance with these sentiments, this Reader is divided into two main parts:

1) Selected passages from the more or less contemporary records and chronicles, both Hungarian and foreign, that bear on our subject. Here I have aimed to acquaint readers with a range of Hungarian chronicles, besides the more familiar *Gesta* of Anonymous and Kézai. For this reason I have included extracts from the *Illuminated Chronicle*, Thuróczy's *Chronica Hungarorum*, Verancsics, and Heltai's *Chronica az Magyaroknac dolgairól* as additional flavour, even if they add little to those main accounts.

2) Modern interpretations of the old sources. Among these texts space has been given not only to history and linguistics, but also to archaeology, ethnography, anthropology, zoology, and, of course, geography. Due to the limitations of space, however, it has been necessary to omit mention of many distinguished researchers and works which undoubtedly belong here. In this part I have also given a platform for a few of our Hungarian poets and the folk memories of the Conquest that they articulate. Here a couple of those "enthusiasts" likewise get their opportunity to speak.

Wherever possible, I have deliberately slanted my selection at material originally published in the Hungarian language. Virtually all the authors who are quoted are Hungarian, which is hardly surprising given the subject. I have refrained from adding comments to the texts even in cases where the opinions expressed directly contradict my own. This was because, as a token of mutual respect, I wanted to give an opportunity to other authors to acquaint the reader directly with their views and findings, in their own words. With this supplement to my own text I hope to make the many different prospects that source-research opens up an enjoyable experience for the reader.

I must confess that it is precisely the decision to present divergent opinions without comment which reassures me that I have not taken unfair advantage of my critics by silencing them on this occasion. Naturally, I still believe that my own ideas and explanations provide a better solution than those advanced by my colleagues, both present and past. Quotations from my own earlier works have been restricted to a bare minimum because I did not intend to use this Reader as a forum for polemics but simply as a dispassionate information source. Of course, there will be many who will find deficiencies and, quite justifiably, will reproach me for including certain works but not others. However, I must plead that there was no option but to be selective, for any attempt to cover the literature dealing with the Magyar conquest of Hungary in a comprehensive manner would require a whole series of volumes rather than this short Reader.

I hope that my selection proves a trustworthy guide and that the reader will feel that he is able to become a participant in this "round-table" discussion on Hungary's prehistory.

Gyula László

I. CHRONICLES AND SOURCES

Most of the texts by Hungarian chroniclers which appear in this part of the Reader are quoted from in several places, with an abbreviated reference to their author. The following brief notes on the authors and the editions used in preparation of the English translations must suffice.

It is known that an early *Gesta Hungarorum*, or *Deeds of the Hungarians*, was written in the ninth century. Though this has long been lost, Anonymus and later chroniclers certainly drew on it and it has thus been at least partly reconstructible from the correspondences between the texts.

ANONYMUS

The author known as Anonymus is identified in the manuscript of his *Gesta Hungarorum* as "Master P., notary to the late, illustrious King Béla of Hungary of happy memory". Most researchers date the work to the reign of Béla III and hence to the turn of the eleventh and twelfth centuries. In content his *Gesta* is closer to that of a historical romance than a scholarly history based on authenticated data. Since the manuscript was first published in 1746 it has assumed a key role in shaping the historical consciousness of the Hungarian people.

Ref: P. Magister qui Anonymus dicitur, *Gesta Hungaro-rum. Praefatus est textumque recensuit Aemilius Jakubovich. Annotationes exegeticas adiecat Desiderius Pais*. In: *Scriptores Rerum hungaricarum tempore ducum regumque stirpis Arapdianae Gestarum*. I. Ed. E. Szentpétery, Budapest, 1937 (abbreviated *SRH* below).

KÉZAI

Simon Kézai, a priest at the court of King Ladislas IV "the Cuman", wrote his *Gesta Hungarorum* around the year 1283, basing it on earlier chronicle accounts. It is notable for laying unequivocal stress on the relationship of the Hungarians to the Huns.

Ref: Simonis de Keza, *Gesta Hungarorum. Praefatus est, textum recensuit, annotationibus instruxit Alexander Doma-novszky*. In: *SRH*.

ILLUMINATED CHRONICLE

The chronicle compiled by Canon Mark Kálti in the fourteenth century, dealing with events down to the reign of Charles Robert. It is famous chiefly for its beautiful illuminations: since the codex was kept for some three hundred years (until 1933) in Vienna, it was known as the *Chronicon pictum vindobonense*.

Ref: *Chronici Hungarici Compositio Saeculi XIV. Praefa-tus est, textum recensuit, annotationibus instruxit Alexander Domanovszky*. In: *SRH*.

THURÓCZY

János Thuróczy was a historian, jurist, and chief notary in the royal chancellary. His *Chronica Hungarorum*, which was published simultaneously at Augsburg and Brno in 1488, relates Hungarian history up to the time of King Matthias.

Ref: Johannes de Thurocz, *Chronica Hungarorum. I. Textus. Ediderunt Elisabeth Galántai et Julius Kristó. Bib-liotheca scriptorum medii recentisque aevorum 7*, Budapest, 1985.

VERANCSICS

Antonius Wrancius (1504-1574), or Antal Verancsics as he is known in Hungarian, was a prelate, diplomat and poet of Bosnian extraction who eventually became Archbishop of Esztergom.

Ref: Antonius Wrancius, *Sibenicensis Dalmata de situ Transylvaniae, Moldaviae et Transalpinae*. In: Verancsics Antal, *Összes Munkái*, ed. L. Szalay. Budapest, 1857, Vol. I. (*Monumenta Hungariae Historica, Ser. II: Irók. Vol. II.*).

HELTAI

Gáspár Heltai (1520-1575) was a historian, preacher and printer. His *Chronica az Magyaroknac dolgairól*, printed on his own presses, appeared just after his death. The only one of these sources to be written in Hungarian, it is largely an adaptation of Antonio Bonfini's Latin chronicle of 1568 (*Rerum hungaricarum decades*).

Ref: Magyar Helikon, Budapest, 1981. For convenience, the excerpts are identified by the chapter or section number of the passage in which they occur in the source work. Notes that may appear in the critical editions are omitted.

Prehistory

THURÓCZY

[1] [...] we have diverse views about the ancient history of the Hungarian nation and also about which part of the world gave birth to the Hungarians and how they flooded from there into this region, which was of old called Pannonia but is now Hungary after the Hungarians. In the end, we decided in the interest of our enquiry to con-

sult the historical works on this subject that were edited in earlier times […]

[2] […] every nation of the Christian faith accepts the view that after the punishment of the Flood all mortals were descended from Noah and his sons, Shem, Ham and Japheth […]

[3] The sons of Noah's second son, Ham, were: Cush… And again St Jerome here annotates: furthermore, Cush also begat Nimrod […]

[4] […] In the second of the two aforementioned volumes it is said that Hunor and Magor, the fathers of the Huns and the Hungarians, were not the sons of Nimrod… as the Holy Scriptures say, the Hungarians are descended from Magog, the son of Japheth… and his wife Enech begat the above mentioned Hunor and Magor, from whom the Huns and Hungarians originated and after whom they are named.

[5] [Anthoninus, archbishop of Florence] states that Silimer, king of the Goths, or Geths, and son of the great Gaderich who was their fifth ruler after their withdrawal from the Scythian island of Sycantia, when he marched into the Scythian land with his nation found amidst them certain women who in the Geth tongue were called 'Alirumnae'. Having suspicions of them, he drove them away and, chasing them far from his army, forced them to wander in the desert. When after that the men of the forest, whom some call the murdering fauns… saw these women wandering in the trackless desert, they embraced them and at once paired off with them. These women, then, gave birth to that wild, fearful and terrible race of men that first lived in the Maeotid marshes… From this stock, then, came forth the Huns: small in stature, to be sure, but cunning, free in their way of life, skilled at horse-riding, broad of shoulder for handling of the bow and arrows, stubborn by nature, and holding their heads high through pride; they strike fear and trembling in all the neighbouring peoples. Thus writes Anthoninus, Jordanes, on the other hand – and several other writers – states that the Huns take their origin from the demons that cause nightmares and from certain women… This view is also in conflict with the Scriptures… Diodorus Siculus, in the third book of his historical work, claims that the people of Scythia originated from beside the river Araxes and at first were few in number… It seems that the Scythians are the oldest of all the peoples in the world.

[6] […] Nor can the great king Attila be accused in any way of denying his birth. He avowed himself to be a grandson of the great Nimrod… and the Hungarians themselves trace their origin back to the line of the great Nimrod […]

Dealing with the Legend of the Wondrous Stag: […] they happened upon the wives and daughters of Bereka, who were camped in their tents without their husbands and just celebrating the feast of the horn and performing a choric dance […]

KÉZAI

[4] Prologue: The History of the Huns

[…] The giant [Menrot] moved to the land of Evilath after the confusion of languages, a country which in those days was called Persia. There his wife Eneth bore him two sons, Hunor and Magyar, from whom the Huns and Hungarians were descended. But the giant Menrot is said to have had other wives apart from Eneth, and begat many sons and daughters in addition to Hunor and Magyar. These sons and their descendants live in the country of Persia and are like the Huns in stature and colour but differ somewhat in speech, as the Saxons do from the Thuringians. But since Hunor and Magyar were the first-born sons of Menrot they lived in their own tents and not in that of their father.

[5] Now one day they happened to go out hunting, and in a desert place a stag leapt out before them. They gave chase, whereupon it fled before them into the marshes of the Maeotis. There it quickly vanished from their sight and although they searched for a long time they could find no trace of it. At length, having wandered through these marshes, they realized that the land there was very suitable for cattle-grazing. So they returned to their father and obtained his permission to migrate to the marshes of Maeotis with all their possessions and to settle there. Now the Maeotis region borders on the province of Persia, though apart from one small passage it is surrounded on all sides by sea. It has no rivers, but is rich in grass, wood, fowl, fish and game. It is difficult to approach and leave. Nevertheless they reached the marshes of the Maeotis and remained there for five years without stirring. In the sixth year they began to roam, and in a deserted spot they came upon the wives and children of the sons of Belar, who were living in tents, their husbands being away from home. They seized them and made off with them as fast as they could, together with all their possessions, to the marshes of the Maeotis. Now among the children they captured there happened to be two daughters of Dula, king of the Alans. One of them Hunor took as his wife, the other became the wife of Magyar. It is from these women that all the Huns are descended. After a long stay in the marshes of the Maeotis they began to grow into an exceedingly powerful tribe, so that the land there could no longer either contain or support them.

[6] They therefore sent out scouts from here into Scythia, and after these had reconnoitred the territory of Scythia, they moved with their children and cattle into that homeland in order to settle there. When they arrived in that country they came upon Alplozur inhabitants, who are nowadays called Pruthenes. These they annihilated, drove out or massacred and, as we know, against the wishes of their neighbours, they are still peacefully in possession of this land to the present day. […] The Don has its source in Scythia, and the Hungarians call it the Etül;

but where it flows forth to cut across the Rifei Mountains its name is the Don, and finally, on reaching the plains, it runs on the land of the Alans and then, splitting into three branches, it discharges into the Kerek [Caspian] Sea. [...]

The country of Scythia comprises a single territory, but it is divided into three provinces, namely, Bashkiria, Dentiria and Mogoriara. It has one hundred and eight districts for the one hundred and eight clans into which it was divided by Hunor and Magyar at the time they occupied Scythia. For Hungary has just one hundred and eight pure clans, and no more. And if there are others who have joined them, they are newcomers or are descended from captives; since, apart from any upstarts, one hundred and eight clans descended from Hunor and Magyar in the marshes of the Maeotis.

[7] In the sixth century, however, the Huns living in Scythia proliferated like the very grass, and in the year of our Lord 700, on assembling together, they elected captains, leaders and princes from amongst themselves in order collectively, as with one heart and soul, to occupy the countries of the West. [...]

THURÓCY

[7] Description of Scythia according to the older histories of the Hungarians

Early authors of the history of the Hungarians placed this Scythia in Europe, and they wrote that it extended towards the east... they say that the people live in pagan sinfulness, are fond of idleness, partial to sensual delights and love to plunder, and they are generally more dark in colour than white. Moreover, they also say that the name Scythia is a collective term, but it is divided into three countries, namely, Bostardia [Baskardia], Dentia and Magaria, and it has one hundred and eight provinces, which were divided so by the sons of Hunor and Magor in olden times when they entered among the marshes of the Maeotis for one hundred and eight clans stemmed from their loins [...]

[10] Concerning blood pacts among the Scythians:

[...] It is said that they solemnize peace pacts and treaties by drinking the mixed blood of each other... Nobody doubts that Scythia was the motherland of the Huns, which is to say the Hungarians [...]

ILLUMINATED CHRONICLE

[4] The Origins of the Magyars according to the Holy Scriptures

[...] From this it is manifest to all that the truth is [N.B. word 'not' clearly omitted in the original text] told by those who state that Hunor and Magor, the ancestors of the Hungarians, were the sons of Nemproth, who was the son of Chus, the son of Ham, who was reviled by Noah. Because, on the one hand, the Hungarians would not then be descended from the line of Japhet, as St Jerome asserts, whilst, on the other hand, Nemproth never lived

near the river Thanais, which is in the east, but by the ocean sea. Thus, as the Holy Scriptures and holy teachers say, the Hungarians are descended from Magor, son of Japhet, who, in the fifty-eighth year after the Flood, as St Sigilbert, bishop of Antioch, relates in his chronicle of the eastern peoples, entered the land of Evilath and by his wife Ene begat Magor and Hunor, after whom the Magyars and the Huns are named.

[5] The start of the Hungarian's expansion in eastern Scythia

It came to pass one day that they went out to hunt and in the desert they came upon a deer, which fled before them and they followed it into the marshes of Maeotis. There it vanished completely from before them, and although they sought it for a long while, they were not able to come upon it in any way. They roamed about the said marshes and perceived that they were suitable for rearing their cattle. Then returning to their father, they obtained his permission to go into the marshes of the Maeotis with all their effects and linger there to feed their livestock. The Maeotis region is in the neighbourhood of the land of Persia. Apart from one shallow place, it is surrounded on all sides by sea; it lacks rivers but has an abundance of herbage, woods, fish, birds and beasts; it is difficult both to enter and to leave. So having gone into the marshes of Maeotis, they stayed in the same place for five years without moving. And going out in the sixth year, in a deserted place, they came by chance upon the wives and children of the sons of Bereka [Belar = Alans] who were abiding in tents without their menfolk and were celebrating the feast of the horn and were dancing together to the sound of music, Quickly carrying them off, they took them and their effects away to the marshes of the Maeotis. This was the first booty after the Flood. It happened, however, that among those children seized in that battle there were two daughters of Dula, ruler of the Alans, one of whom was taken as a wife by Hunor, the other by Magor. From these women all the Huns or the Hungarians took their descent. It happened, however, that after they had lived for a long while in the marshes of the Maeotis, they began to increase in number into a very mighty people, and this region was able neither to accomodate them, nor to sustain them.

[6] [...] The Don is a great river which has its source in Scythia and is called Etul by the Hungarians; it flows across the alps surrounding Scythia, then its name changes and it is called the Don. To the south of its banks live the race of the Kitai and the Alans... [...]

[25] Here begins the prologue concerning the second entry of the Hungarians and the fortunate and unfortunate events that befell them.

Having disposed of the lineage of the Huns, their sucesses and misfortunes in war, and how often they had changed their abodes, let us now see when they returned again to

Pannonia, who were the captains of those that returned, and how great was the number of warriors in the army – these things I reckoned to be worthy to set out in the present little work.

[26] In the six hundred and seventy-seventh year after the birth of our Lord, one hundred and four years after the death of King Attila, in the time of Emperor Constantine III and Pope Zacharias, as it is written in the chronicle of the Romans, the Hungarians came out of Scythia for the second time in the following manner:

In Scythia, Eleud [Előd], son of Ugeg [Ügyek], begat of Eunodbilia's daughter a son who was called Almus on account of the fact that whilst his mother was pregnant, there appeared to her in a dream a bird in the form of a hawk and she was made aware that from her womb would come forth a torrent and it would multiply in a land that was not her own. This was because renowned kings stemmed from her loins. Since the word for 'dream' in our [Hungarian] language is 'alm' [*álom*], and his birth was foretold in a dream, this is why he was called Almus, who was son of Eleud, and he of Ugeg, he of Ede, he of Chaba, he of Ethele, he of Bendekus, he of Turda, he of Scemen, he of Ethei, he of Opus, he of Kadicha, he of Berend, he of Zulta, he of Bulchu, he of Bolug, he of Zambur, he of Zamur, he of Leel, he of Leuente, he of Kulche, he of Ompud, he of Miske, he of Mike, he of Beztur, he of Budli, he of Chanad, he of Buken, he of Bondofard, he of Farkas, he of Othmar, he of Kadar, he of Beler, he of Kear, he of Keue, he of Keled, he of Dama, he of Bor, he of Hunor, he of Nemproth, he of Thana, he of Japhet, he of Noah. Almus begat Arpad, Arpad begat Zoltan, and Zoltan begat Toxun. [...]

The Székely
Illuminated Chronicle

[21] However, three thousand men from among the Huns remained who saved their own skins by fleeing from the battle of Krimhilda and they managed to assemble on the field of Chiglameze [Csiglamező]. As they feared a sudden attack by the western peoples, they withdrew into Erdély [Transylvania], and they did not call themselves Hungarians but by another name, Zekul [Székely]. For even in the life of Attila the Huns had been hostile to the western nations. These Zekuli, then, are the remnants of the Huns and until the return of the rest of the Hungarians they dwelt on the previously mentioned field. When they got to know that the Hungarians were returning once more to Pannonia, they hurried to meet them in Ruthenia [Russia] and together they conquered the region of Pannonia. After this conquest they [the Zekuli] were entitled to a share in it but, as the Hungarians wished it, they took a portion, not of the Pannonian plain, but of the mountains in the border area, together with the Vlachs. They intermingled with the Vlachs and it is adduced that this is why they use their lettering.

And these Zekuli considered that Chaba died in Greece and that is why to this day it is proverbial among the people to say "Come back again when Chaba returns from Greece!"

THURÓCZY

[26] Apart from those Huns who accompanied Chaba, another three thousand men from the same nation who retreated fought their way out of the aforesaid conflict to stay behind in Pannonia; and at first they made headquarters for themselves in a camp called Czyglamezew. Fearful of the western nations that had been disturbed by Attila in his life, they moved to Erdély, that is, the border area of the Pannonian region, and they called themselves, not Huns or Hungarians, but Siculi, or by their own word Zekel [Székely], so that it should not be known that they were the remnants of those peoples [i.e. Huns and Hungarians]. In our times nobody doubts that the Siculi are the remnants of those Huns who first entered Pannonia, and because their people have not commingled since then with foreign blood, they are strict in their morals and they also differ from other Hungarians in the division of their fields. They have not yet forgotten the Scythian letters: they do not commit these to paper in ink but deftly incise them on sticks in the manner of runes... When the Hungarians were coming back again to Pannonia from Scythia, they [the Siculi] went with great joy to meet them in Ruthenia as soon as the news of their arrival reached them. After the Hungarians had once more taken possession of Pannonia and it came to the apportioning of the country, these Siculi, with the agreement of the Hungarians, received as their portion the same region as they had previously chosen for themselves as their abode [...]

VERANCSICS

Nobody disputes that the Siculi [Székely] are descendants of the Huns. Their origin is as follows: in the Hungarian chronicles it is held that King Attila, since he lived for 125 years, left more than sixty children behind him, among whom two were prominent, namely, Chaba and Aladár. They were mature in years, not unlike their father in intellectual vigour and gravity, and were judged to be more eminent than others. It was rightly decided that one of them should succeed their father in supreme power, and out of this arose furious discord between them as neither of them was willing to yield to the other. And in fact Chaba, supported by Honorius, the emperor of the Greeks, who was a grandson of his sister, and by the greater part of the Huns had ambitions to rule; Aladár could not count on many Huns but, because he was born of an Alemann mother, had the majority of the princes of Germany... and when they joined battle, there ensued enormous carnage... Defeated by the skills of Detric, Chaba, with the rest of his brothers and fifteen thousand men, set out to his uncle Honorius in Greece and thence to his uncle Bendeguz in Scythia. Now apart from them there were three thousand men who, fleeing from the battle, stayed in Pannonia, but fearing from the western nations that Attila had once greatly threatened, they moved northwards to the most distant corner of Transylvania, which is called Csíkmező... they named themselves Székely, which we now write in Latin as Siculi. After a long time had passed, when the Huns who had left with Chaba, having grown greatly in number, came back from Scythia, and news of this had already spread extensively to the Siculi, the latter went as far as Russia to meet them in order to regain their common native land. [...]

HELTAI

About the Székely, who are themselves Hungarian natives

When that Aladár was about to lose the combat under Scambria, three thousand Magyars ran away from the danger, and they set up camp on the soil of Cegléd. But since they were fearful of the might of Lord Dietrich and the other German lords, they set off from there and made their way with great haste to Transylvania. And because all the nations were attacking the Magyars, they disavowed themselves to be Magyars but called themselves Székely. Even now they live in Transylvania, and they have different laws and customs. They are divided into 'seats', the names of which are Csík, Gyirgyó, Kizdi, Szepsi, Orbai, etc. The heads of these were all freemen but because of their infidelities their freedoms had become restricted.

Reports of a Late 7th-century Magyar Occupation before the Árpádian Conquest

ANTAL HODINKA
[References to the Magyars in the Russian Chronicles]. Budapest, 1916, p. 33.

[...], whom they call Bulgars, and they settled along the Danube and became the settler descendants of the Slovenes. Then came the White Ugrians and they succeeded them on the land of the Slovenes. These Ugrians had appeared in the time of the emperor Heraclius, who attacked Chozdroy, emperor of Persia, with an army. In this time there were also the Obors... then later, in the time of Oleg, the Black Ugrians passed by Kiev.

WIDUKIND
Rerum gestarum Saxonicarum Libri Tres, in: Monumenta Germaniae Historia: Scriptores Rerum Germanicarum. Hannover, 1935.

Widukind (c. 925-1004), a monk in the monastery at Corvey, was a historian noted for his classical culture and knowledge of sources.

[I.17] [...] The Dalamanci were unable to hold back the attack by Henrik, duke of Saxony, and therefore they hired against him the Avars, a people exceedingly hard in war whom we now call Hungarians. [...]

[I.18] The Avars, however, as some believe, are the remnants of the Huns [...]

[I. 19] Charlemagne defeated them, however, and drove them beyond the Danube, and he encircled them with massive earthworks [...]

HELTAI

About Emperor Charlemagne; how he long fought with the Magyars, and how he defeated them

In that time the Roman Emperor was Charles, the king of France, who since then has been called Charlemagne, whom all the history books extol as a wise, good-hearted man, a distinguished warrior, and a devout and pious Roman Catholic. Charlemagne was unwilling to suffer the savage raids of the Magyars with which they had devastated their neighbours and the countries round about. For this reason he first dispatched his men to Tassilo, the duke of Bavaria, who had made an alliance with the Magyars, and he forced Tassilo to submit and render him homage. After that he conquered the Bohemians and made them too render him homage. After that he declared war on the Magyars.

Emperor Charlemagne's war against the Magyars lasted a long time, in point of fact for eight years. It proceeded with dreadful spilling of blood and with the wounding and loss of countless men. But the Emperor Charlemagne was victorious in this campaign too because he defeated the Magyars in many clashes. And because the Magyars would not surrender, but at all times heroically attacked him, almost all of the nobles amongst the Magyars were slain in the frequent encounters. The population, too, was greatly diminished and the great wealth that they had collected together in Hungary from so many countries with their many wanderings and pillages was all lost.

Because after the many struggles the Emperor Charlemagne laid siege to Scambria, where Duke Csaba was quartered, and after many assaults he took the town, where he found all the great treasures of the king. [...]

The Pre-conquest Period in the East

IBN RUSTA and GARDÌZÌ

Ibn Rusta, an Arab lexicographer and geographer who wrote around 930, and Gardìzì, a Persian historian from northern Afghanistan who worked around 1050-1053, both drew on an earlier, now lost, account written by Džaihànì, a statesman and scholar at Bokhara in the early tenth century. It is generally agreed that their descriptions report the state of affairs during the 870s, though according to other suggestions they could be contemporary and thus would relate to the Magyars at the time they entered their new homeland. The excerpts given here draw on the translation by M. Smith as published in C. A. Macartney, *The Magyars in the Ninth Century*, Cambridge, 1930 (Reprinted 1968), pp. 206–209. The main account is that by Ibn Rusta, with the additional information supplied by Gardizi interpolated thus:

THE MAGYARS

Between the country of the Bajanàkiyya [Pechenegs] and the country of the Askal [Szekely], who belong to the Balkariyya [Bulgars], is the first [outermost] of the Magyar boundaries.

The Magyars are a race of Turks and their king rides with horsemen to the number of 10,000 (their leader rides out with 20,000 horsemen) and this king is called Kanda and this name denotes their king, for the name of the man who is actually king over them is Jula [*gyula*] and all the Magyars accept the orders of their Jula in the matter of war and defence and the like).

They possess leather tents [yurts] and they travel in search of herbage and abundant pasturage. Their country is extensive (has an extent of 100 parsangs by 100) and one frontier extends to the sea of Rùm [Black Sea], and two rivers flow into that sea, one of them greater than Džaihùn [Amu Darya], and their dwellings are between these two rivers and in the winter they go to whichever river is nearest to them and settle there for the winter. They catch fish from it, and their abode for the winter is reserved to them there.

That is the Džaihùn which is on their left side [west]. Beside Saqlàb [Slavs] are a people of Rùm [Byzantines] who are all Christians and they are called Nandar [Danube Bulgars], and they are more numerous than the Magyars, but they are weaker. They call these two Džaihùns, the one Ìtìl [Don] and the other Dùbà. When the Magyars are on the bank of the river they see these Nandarin there.

Above the bank of the river is a great mountain [the Carpathians] and water flows out on to the side of the mountain, and behind that mountain are a people of the Christians whom they call Mirdàt [Moravians]: between them and the Nandar is a ten days' journey. They [the Moravians] are a numerous people and their dress resembles that of the Arabs, consisting of turban and shirt and overcoat. They have cultivated lands and seeds and vineyards, for with them the water runs over the surface of the land and has no canals for irrigation. They state that their number is greater than that of the Rùm and that they are a separate nation. The greater part of their trade is with Arabia. That river which is to the right [east] of the Magyars goes to Saqlàb and from there dwindles away in the district of Khazar and that river is [the bigger of] these two rivers.

The country of the Magyars contains many trees and much water and their ground is moist and they have many fields.

They exercise dominion over all of the Saqlàb, who are adjacent to them, and they put upon them heavy burdens, and they are in their hands in the position of captives.

The Magyars worship the sun and the moon. (The Magyars are fire worshippers.)

They are hostile to the Saqlàb (they go out to raid Saqlàb and Rùs) and they bring them as captives by the sea-coast until they come to the ascent of the country of the Greeks called Karàkh [Kerch], and it is said that Al-Khazar in former days was surrounded by a ditch as a defence against the Magyars and other nations adjacent to their country.

When the Magyars go with the captives to Karàkh, the Greeks come out to them and they trade there and deliver over to them the slaves and take Grecian brocades and carpets and other Greek goods.

These Magyars are a handsome people and of good appearance and their clothes are of silk brocade and their weapons are of silver and are encrusted with pearls.

They constantly plunder the Slavs and from the Magyars to the Slavs is a ten days' journey. Close to the border areas of Saqlàb is a city which they call Wàntìt.

It is a custom when marrying that when a woman is sought in marriage a dowry is appointed in accordance with the wealth in cattle less or more belonging to that man.

When they sit down to appoint that dowry, the father of the maiden brings the father of the son-in-law to his own house and whatever he has in the way of sable and ermine and grey squirrel and stoat and the belly of the fox and brocade, he collects all these skins together to the quantity of ten fur garments and folds them inside a carpet and fastens them on the horse of his son-in-law's father and speeds him to his house. Then whatever is necessary for the maiden's dowry which they have agreed upon such as animals and money and goods is all sent to him [the woman's father] and at that time they bring the woman to the house.

ANONYMUS

[1] [...] A long time afterwards, however, there stemmed from the progeny of this same king Magog Ugek [Ügyek], the father of duke Álmos, from whom the kings and dukes of Hungary are descended, as will be discussed in what follows. The Scythians, as we have said, are fairly ancient populaces about whom the historians who wrote about the deeds of the Romans speak this way: The Scythians were once an exceedingly wise and gentle people, who did not till the soil, and there was almost no sin amongst them. For they did not have homes built by craftsmen but only tents made of felt. They ate meat, fish, milk and honey and had plenteous spiced wine. They dressed in the skins of the pine-marten and other wild beasts. They had as much gold and silver and pearls as there are pebbles, since they can find all these in the rivers of their own land. They did not lust after what be-

longed to others since all of them were rich, owned many animals and had sufficient food. They were not promiscuous, but everyone had just a single wife. Nevertheless, of late the people in question, wearying of war, declined into such cruelty, or so say certain historians, that in their rage they ate human flesh and drank human blood. And I believe that it can be seen today in their progeny how tough a people they were. For the Scythian nation was not subjugated by any ruler… For the Scythian land, being so remote from the warmer climes, was all the more favourable for the multiplication of generations. And yet, despite its size being beyond measure, it was not enough to feed or accomodate the multitude of people born upon it. For this reason, the seven chief persons, who are called Hetumoger [the Seven Magyars], could tolerate the restricted space no longer and pondered how they might avert this.

Then these seven chief persons, conferring amongst themselves, agreed to occupy a land on which they would be able to dwell, and to this end they would leave their native land, as will be related in the following.

[2] Why they are called Hurgarians

It remains to be said why the people which left the Scythian land came to be called Hungarians. They are named Hungarians after Hungvar, the fortress of Hung, because after the conquest of the Slavs the seven chief persons stayed for quite a long time there after entering the land of Pannonia. Thence all the surrounding nations called Almus, son of Ugek, the leader of Hungvar and his soldiers they called Hungvari…

[3] Álmos, the first leader

In the nine hundred and nineteenth year after the birth of our Lord, Ügyek, as we have said before, was the most noble leader of Scythia. He was descended, after the passage of much time, from the line of King Magog and he took as his wife in Dentumoger the leader Eunedubelianus' daughter, who was called Emes. By her he had a son who was given the name Álmos. But it was as the result of a miraculous event that he received the name Álmos, for when his mother was pregnant, a divine vision appeared to her as she was sleeping; it was in the form of a hawk which seemed to light upon her and make her pregnant. It appeared to her that a torrent would issue from her womb and splendid kings would be descended from her and multiply, though not in their own country. Now since in the Hungarian language the word for 'dream' is *álom*, and his birth was foretold in a dream, he was called Álmos. Or he was called Almus, that is to say 'holy', in the Latin tongue, since holy kings and leaders were to arise from his descendants. But enough of this!

[5] The election of the leader Álmos

So the Hungarians, who were most valiant and mighty in war, as we have mentioned earlier, traced their origin to the Scythian people, whom in their own language they call Dentumoger. And that land became overcrowded with the multitude of people born there, so that it could neither feed nor sustain them, as we have said. So the seven chief persons, who even to this day are called Hetumoger [Seven Magyars], unable to bear the lack of land any longer, took counsel with each other and decided to leave their native soil, in order, by force of arms and battles, to look ceaselessly for territory that they might occupy. It was then that they chose to seek out the land of Pannonia, for rumour had it that this was the country of King Attila, from whose line Álmos, the father of Árpád, was descended. Then the seven chiefs realized with mutual and genuine understanding that they would be unable to reach the end of the route, once they had set out on it, unless they had a leader and commander over them. Therefore, of their own free will and by common consent, the seven men chose as their leader and commander Álmos, the son of Ügyek, and those descended from his tribe… Then with common consent they said to the leader Álmos, "From this day onwards we elect you to be our leader and commander, and whither your fortune leads you, we will follow you." Then the men we have mentioned all poured their blood into a single vessel, thus ratifying their oath to Álmos in the pagan manner. And although they were pagans, they remained loyal to the oath they had sworn amongst themselves to the day of their death. […]

[12] How they came into Pannonia

The leader Álmos and his chief men, accepting the advice of the Ruthenians [Russians], concluded an enduring pact with them. For the leaders of the Ruthenians, so that they should not be expelled from their settlements, gave their sons in marriage… together with innumerable gifts. Then the leader of Galich [Galícia] ordered that two thousand bowmen and three thousand peasants should go before them [i.e. the Magyars] and prepare a route for them through the Havas [Carpathian] forest to the boundary of Hung. At the same time he packed all their livestock with provisions and other necessities whilst he also presented countless beef-cattle in gift. Then the seven chief persons who are called the Hetumoger [Seven Magyars] and the seven leaders of the Cumanians… with their relatives and female servants, and with the advice and assistance of the Ruthenians, set out from Galich to the country of Pannonia. And so, passing through the Havas forest, they came down to the environs of Hung. When they arrived at the place they first occupied, they called it Muncas [Munkács], because they reached the land that they had chosen for themselves only with the greatest effort [*munka* 'work']. There, then, in order to rest from their exertions, they stayed for forty days, and they were delighted, more than can be expressed, with the land. But the Slavs, the 'inhabitants of the land', hearing of their arrival, feared greatly and of their own free will subjugated themselves to the leader Álmos, since they had heard that the leader Álmos was descended from the line of King Attila. And although they were the men of the leader Salan, they nevertheless served 'the leader Álmos with great honour and fear, offering him everything that was necessary for his sustenance, as is befitting to a master. And the same fear and trembling overcame the inhabitants of the country, and they tried to please the leader and his chief men, as servants will their own masters. They extolled to him the fertility of the soil, and they related to him in what manner, after the death of King Attila, the great Khan, who was ancestor of the leader Salan and who came from Bulgaria, had, with the help and advice of the Greeks, taken over that land, and also how they themselves, the Slavs, had been led out of the country of Bulgaria to the borders of the Ruthenians, and how their leader Salan treated them and theirs, and how much power he had over their neighbours all around.

[13] The fort of Hung

Thereupon the leader Álmos and his chief men, on hearing these things, were greatly heartened and rode over to the fort of Hung in order to capture it. And whilst they raised camp around the walls, the count of the fort, Laborc by name, who in their language is called a duke, took to flight and hurried towards the fort of Zemlum [Zemplén].

The leader's soldiers set off in pursuit, apprehended him next to a river, and hanged him on the spot, and from that day they call that river Laborc after his name. Then the leader Álmos and his men, proceeding into the fort of Hung, offered up great sacrifices to the immortal gods and they feasted for four days in celebration. But on the fourth day the leader Álmos, holding a counsel and swearing an oath with all of his people, whilst he was still alive made his son Árpád the leader and commander. And in foreign tongues Árpád was called the leader of Hungvaria whilst all his soldiers were called Hungvari, after Hung, and it is this name which survives up to the present throughout the whole world.

ILLUMINATED CHRONICLE

[26] [...] In the six hundredth or sixth hundred and seventy-seventh year after the birth of our Lord, the one hundredth year after the death of King Attila, in the time of Emperor Constantine III and Pope Zacharias, the Huns, commonly known as the Magyars, and in Latin as Hungarians, once more entered into Pannonia. They crossed the realms of the Bessi [Pechenegs] and White Cumans, Suzdal and the city which is called Kyo [Kiev], then passed over the snowy Alps into a province where they saw countless eagles. Due to those eagles they were not able to stay there, for the eagles swooped down from the trees like flies and devoured their cattle and horses. Because God so willed it that they should go down into Hungary as soon as possible. After that, in three months they descended from the mountains and arrived at the border of the kingdom of Hungary, or rather Erdelw [Transylvania], against the will of the previously mentioned peoples. Having made ready seven earthwork fortifications to guard their wives and their effects, they stayed here awhile. That is why the Teutons have, from that day, called this region Simberg [Siebenburg], which is to say 'Seven Castles'.

[27] Election of the seven captains

Whilst they dwelled in these fortresses, fearful that the neighbouring lords would fall upon them, by communal decision they chose seven captains from among themselves and divided into seven armies in such a way that each army had a single captain apart from squadrons and troops disposed in the usual manner. And in fact each army had three thousand men at arms, not counting the captains. From each of the one hundred and eight clans which departed from Scythia on this second occasion two thousand armed men went out, not counting the members of their families.

[28] The first captain

Among those captains the richest and most powerful was Arpad, the son of Almus, son of Eleud, son of Ugeg. His father Almus was murdered in the dwelling-place of Erdelw and so he was not able to enter into Pannonia. In Erdelw [Erdély = Transylvania], therefore, they rested and they allowed their cattle to revive. But when they heard from the inhabitants of the fertility of the soil, and how the Danube is the finest of rivers, and that there is no better land in the world than those parts, after holding common counsel they sent as an emissary Kund's son, Kusid, to go and spy out the land and get to know its inhabitants. Thus when Kusid arrived in the middle of Hungary and went down to the region of the Danube, he saw that the terrain was pleasing and that all around the soil was good and fertile, the river was good and banked by meadows, and he was satisfied. Next he went to the leader of the province, a man by the name of Zuatopolug [Svatopluk], who governed after Attila, and he greeted him in his people's name and disclosed why he had come. On hearing this, Zuatopolug rejoiced with great gladness, for he thought that they [the Magyars] were peasants who had come to cultivate his land; because of this, he graciously sent the emissary back. But Kusid, having filled a flask with water from the Danube and put some of the meadow-grass in his hide bag and collected a clod of the black soil from the land, returned to his people. And when he related everything that he had heard and seen, they were exceedingly pleased, and then he showed them the flask of water, the soil and the grass. And when they were acquainted with these, they were convinced that the soil was excellent and the water sweet, and the meadow-grass just as the emissary had told them. Arpad, indeed, filled his horn with the Danube water and on that horn, in front of all the Hungarians, called upon the mercy of almighty God that the Lord should grant them this land in perpetuity. When he had finished his words all the Hungarians cried out the name of their god three times. From this grew a custom which the Hungarians preserve even to the present. Then by common resolve they sent back the same emissary to the aforesaid leader [Svatopluk] and for his land they sent him a large, white horse with a saddle gilded in Arabian gold and a gilded bridle. On seeing this, the leader was even more delighted because he thought that they had sent it to him for land as guest settlers [hospitalari]. So the emissary requested land, pasture and water from the leader there and then. Smiling, the leader said: "In exchange for this gift you may take as much as you wish." The emissary therefore returned to his people. But in the meantime Arpad with the seven leaders had entered into Pannonia, though not as guests but as the owners of the land by hereditary right. Then they sent another emissary to the leader and he was to pass on these words: "Arpad and his people say to you that you shall in no way stay any longer on the land that they have procured from you, for they have purchased that land with the horse, the grass with the bridle, and the water with the saddle. And you, through want or avarice, have conceded them the land, pasture and water in perpetual tenure." And when the emissary had given this message to the leader, he [Svatopluk] smiled and said: "Strike that horse down with a mallet, throw the bridle away on the meadow, and cast the gilded saddle into the waters of the Danube!" To this the emissary responded: "And what harm will come us from this, Lord? If you kill the horse, you will give victuals to your dogs; if you have the bridle thrown out on the grass, your own men who reap the hay will find the gold of the bridle; and if you cast the saddle into the Danube, your fishermen will land it on the shore and carry it back home. So if they have the land, the grass and the water, they will have everything." On hearing this, then, the leader, fearful of the Hungarians, swiftly assembled an army and ordered help from his friends, and uniting with them all he came to face the Hungarians. They in the meantime had come up to near the Danube and at daybreak, in a most beautiful meadow, they set to battle. But the Lord was helping the Hungarians and the oft-mentioned leader retreated in flight before them. The Hungarians pursued him up to the Danube and he, in his fright, cast himself into the Danube and drowned on account of the fury of its waters. Thus the Lord restored Pannonia to the Hungarians, just as in the time of Moses he gave back the land of 'Seon [Sihon], king of the Amorites, and all the kingdoms of Canaan' to the sons of Israel as an inheritance. And since the captain Arpad enjoyed the special distinction in Scythia, and his own clan enjoyed it by the lawful and approved traditions of Scythia, that he must go ahead of expeditions that set out for war and bring up the rear on their return, for this reason he preceded the other captains on the entry into Pannonia. And for this reason, when Arpad, together with the other Hungarians, defeated and killed Zuatapolug, as is described above, he pitched camp on Noah's [Novaj] hill, near to Alba [Székesfehérvár]. This was the first place that Arpad chose for himself in Pannonia, and that is why the city of Alba was founded near there by King St Stephen, who was descended from him.

An excerpt from Demeter Csáti's narrative poem, *Conquest of Pannonia*, written in the early sixteenth century (from the translation by John Bowring in: *Poetry of the Magyars*, London, 1830, pp. 2–9):

> *For snow-white steed thou gav'st the land;*
> *For golden bit, the grass,*
> *For the rich saddle, Duna's stream*
> *Now bring the deed to pass.*

The prime source for the history of the Magyars under Árpád is the *De administrando imperio*, written by the Byzantine Emperor Constantine Porphyrogenitus between 948–952. He obtained his information about the Magyars from Bulcsú and crown-prince Tormás, the great-grandson of Árpád. The excerpts cited here are from the edition prepared by Gyula Moravcsik in the parallel translation by R. J. H. Jenkins (Budapest, 1949). The designation 'Turks', as used by Constantine, is here to be understood as meaning 'Magyars'.

From Chapter 37:

The Pechenegs fled and wandered round, casting about for a place for their settlement; and when they reached the land which they now possess and found the Turks living in it, they defeated them in battle and cast them out, and settled in it, and have been masters of this country, as has been said, for fifty-five years to this day."

Chapter 38. Of the genealogy of the nation of the Turks, and whence they are descended

The nation of the Turks had of old their dwelling next to Chazaria, in the place called Lebedia after the name of their first voivode, which voivode was called by the personal name of Lebedias, but in virtue of his rank was entitled voivode, as have been the rest after him. Now in this place, the aforesaid Lebedia, there runs a river Chidmas, also called Chingilous [location not identified]. They were not called Turks at that time, but had the name 'Sabartoi asphaloi', for some reason or other. The Turks were seven clans, and they had never had over them a prince, either native or foreign, but there were among them 'voivodes', of whom the first voivode was the aforesaid Lebedias. They lived together with the Chazars for three years, and fought in alliance with the Chazars in all their wars. Because of their courage and their alliance, the chagan-prince of Chazaria gave in marriage to the first voivode of the Turks, called Lebedias, a noble Chazar lady, because of the fame of his valour and the illustriousness of his race, so that she might have children by him; but, as it fell out, this Lebedias had no children by this same Chazar lady. Now, the Pechenegs who were previously called 'Kangar' (for this 'Kangar' was a name signifying nobility and valour among them), these, then, stirred up war against the Chazars and, being defeated, were forced to quit their own land and to settle in that of the Turks. And when battle was joined between the Turks and the Pechenegs who were at that time called 'Kangar', the army of the Turks was defeated and split into two parts. One part went eastwards and settled in the region of Persia, and they are to this day called by the ancient denomination of the Turks 'Sabartoi asphaloi'; but the other part, together with their voivode and chief Lebedias, settled in the western region, in places called Atelkouzou, in which places the nation of the Pechenegs now lives. A short while afterwards, that chagan-prince of Chazaria sent a message to the Turks, requiring that Lebedias, their first voivode, should be sent to him. Lebedias, therefore, came to the chagan of Chazaria and asked the reason why he had sent for him to come to him. The chagan said to him: "We have invited you upon this account, in order that, since you are noble and wise and valorous and first among the Turks, we may appoint you prince of your nation, and you may be obedient to our word and our command." But he, in reply, made answer to the chagan: "Your regard and purpose for me I highly esteem and express to you suitable thanks, but since I am not strong enough for this rule. I cannot obey you; on the other hand, however, there is a voivode other than me, called Almoutzis [Álmos], and he has a son called Arpad: let one of these, rather, either that Almoutzis or his son Arpad, be made prince, and be obedient to your word." That chagan was pleased at this saying, and gave some of his men to go with him, and sent them to the Turks, and after they had talked the matter over with the Turks, the Turks preferred that Arpad should be prince rather than Almoutzis his father, for he was of superior parts and greatly admired for wisdom and counsel and valour, and capable of this rule; and so they made him prince according to the custom, or 'zakanon', of the Chazars, by lifting him upon a shield. Before this Arpad the Turks had never at any time had any other prince, and so even to this day the prince of Turkey [i.e. Hungary] is from his family. Some years later, the Pechenegs fell upon the Turks and drove them out with their prince Arpad. The Turks, in flight and seeking a land to dwell in, came and in their turn expelled the inhabitants of Great Moravia and settled in their land, in which the Turks now live to this day. And since that time the Turks have not sustained any attack from the Pechenegs. To the aforesaid nation of the Turks that settled in the east, in the regions of Persia, these Turks aforesaid who live toward the west-

ern region still send merchants who look them up, and often bring them back official messages from them.

The place of the Pechenegs, in which at that the Turks lived, is called after the name of the local rivers. The rivers are these: the first river is that called Barouch [Dnieper], the second river that called Koubou [Bug], the third river that called Troullos [Dniester], the fourth river that called Brouos [Prút], the fifth river that called Seretos [Szeret].

Chapter 39. Of the nation of the Kabaroi

The so-called Kabaroi [Kavars] were of a race of the Chazars. Now, it fell out that a secession was made by them to their government, and when a civil war broke out their first government prevailed, and some of them were slain, but others escaped and came and settled with the Turks in the land of the Pechenegs, and they made friends with one another, and were called 'Kabaroi'. And so to these Turks they taught also the tongue of the Chazars, and to this day they have this same language, but they have also the other tongue of the Turks. And because in wars they show themselves strongest and most valorous of the eight clans, and are leaders in war, they have been promoted to be first clans. There is one prince among them, I mean, among the three clans of the Kabaroi, who survives to this day.

Chapter 40. Of the clans of the Kabaroi and the Turks

The first is this aforesaid clan of the Kabaroi which split off from the Chazars; the second, of Nekis [Nyék]: the third, of Megeris [Magyar]: the fourth, of Kourtougermatos [Kürt and Gyarmat]: the fifth, of Tarianos [Tarján]: the sixth, Genach [Jenő]: the seventh, Kari [Kér]: the eighth, Kasi [Keszi]. Having thus combined with one another, the Kabaroi dwelt with the Turks in the land of the Pechenegs. After this, at the invitation of Leo, the Christ-loving and glorious emperor, they crossed over and fought Symeon and totally defeated him, and drove on and penetrated as far as Preslav, having shut him up in the city called Moundraga; and they went back to their own country. At that time they had Liountikas, son of Arpad, for their prince. But after Symeon was once more at peace with the emperor of the Romans and was free to act, he sent to the Pechenegs and made an agreement with them to attack and destroy the Turks. And when the Turks had gone off on a military expedition, the Pechenegs with Symeon came against the Turks and completely destroyed their families and miserably expelled thence the Turks who were guarding their country. When the Turks came back and found their country thus desolate and utterly ruined, they settled in the land where they live today, which is called after the above names of the rivers, as has been said.

The place in which the Turks used formerly to be is called after the name of the river that runs through it, Etel and Kouzou, and in it the Pechengs live now. But the Turks, expelled by the Pechenegs, came and settled in the land which they now dwell in. In this place are various landmarks of the olden days: first, there is the bridge of the Emperor Trajan, where Turkey begins; then, a three days' journey from this same bridge, there is Belgrade, in which is the tower of the holy and great Constantine; then, again, at the running back of the river, is the renowned Sirmium [Szerém, now Mitrovica], a journey of two days from Belgrade; and beyond lies Great Moravia, the unbaptized, which the Turks have blotted out, but over which in former days Sphendoplokos [Svatopluk] used to rule.

Such are the landmarks and names along the Danube river: but the regions above these, which comprehend the whole settlement of Turkey, they now call after the names of the rivers that flow there. The rivers are these: the first river is the Timisis [Temes], the second river the Toutis [Béga], the third river the Morisis [Maros], the fourth river the Krisos [Körös], and again another river, the Titza [Tisza]. Neighbours of the Turks are, on the eastern side the Bulgarians, where the river Istros, also called Danube, runs between them; on the northern, the Pechenegs; on the western, the Franks: and on the southern, the Croats. These eight clans of the Turks do not obey their own particular princes, but have a joint agreement to fight together with all earnestness and zeal upon the rivers, wheresoever war breaks out. They have for their first chief the prince who comes by succession of Arpad's family, and two others, the gylas [*gyula*] and the karchas, who have the rank of judge: and each clan has a prince.

Gylas and karchas are not proper names, but dignities.

Arpad, the great prince of Turkey, had four sons: first, Tarkatzous [Tarkacsut]: second, Ielech [Jeleg]: third, Ioutotzas [Jutocsát]: fourth, Zaltas [Zoltán].

The eldest son of Arpad, Tarkatzous, had a son Tebelis [Teveli], and the second son Ielech had a son Ezelech [Ezeleg], and the third son Ioutotzas had a son Phalitzis [Falicsit], the present prince, and the fourth son Zaltas had a son Taxis [Taksony].

The Árpádian Conquest

HELTAI:

About the Magyars' second exodus from Scythia into Pannonia

After the Hungarians had entered into Scythia, for three hundred years there were many changes in Pannonia and many nations succeeded one another in the realm because one attacked, beat, killed and ousted the other. As so it came to pass that, when the seven hundred and forty-fourth year after the birth of Christ, our Lord, had been written in the books, the Hungarians again set out from Scythia in order to come once more to the good, fat and productive soil of Pannonia.

But after they had passed through several countries and had reached the cities of Suzdal and Rio, they rested

there. After the rest they came across a very large and high alp. And descending from there they reached an immense plain and there they settled. But suddenly a great many vultures came down on them, to circle there around all their cattle like flies, and they began to consume their cattle. Because of this they got up and hastened from there with all their cattle, and they went up again into the great mountains and it took three whole months until all of them were able to get across. Once they had crossed, they descended and in this way reached Russian soil, which lies next to Poland.

There were two matters which induced the Magyars to set out from Scythia: first of all, the testament of the captain Csaba, the son of Attila. For when Csaba was extremely advanced in years, after he had returned to his native land from Pannonia, and was by this time on his death-bed, he called to him the chief persons among the Magyars. He made them swear to their gods, to Damasek and the others, that when their number grew with time they would again wish to depart for the land of Pannonia and occupy it for themselves, and to undertake to revenge their good father, Duke Attila, on his enemies.

The second motivating reason was a dream that they would come out of Scythia. For when the lady Enodbil, the wife of Eleud, became pregnant in Scythian Hunnia, she had the following dream: A very fine falcon appeared before her and it placed its head close to hers. After that, in her woundrous sleep, a splendid running water bubbled forth from her womb, and this water swelled greatly and, streaming out from Scythia, it flowed to a foreign land and there began to spread until it had enclosed the entire country.

When the lady Enodbil related this dream, the magicians and dream-readers interpreted it as follows: that the lady Enodbil would give birth to a child from whom in the future a prince would be descended who was to bring a large population out of Scythia and conquer and take possession of another country.

When therefore the time had come for the lady Enodbil, she gave birth to a handsome male child. And his father named the child Álmos, after the dream that his wife, the lady Enodbil, had seen... It was from the descendants of this Álmos that a chief by the name of Árpád was to spring later on. And in his time the Magyars set off for the second time from Scythia, as I have already related above. [...]

REGINO, ABBOT OF PRÜM

From his Chronicon, completed in 908.

In the 889th year of the birth of our Lord the Hungarians, a most ferocious people more cruel than any monster, about whom earlier generations had not heard as they had no name, came out from the Scythian provinces and the marshes that the Thanais has spread over a vast area by its inundation. But before we follow the cruel deeds of this people with the pen, it does not seem superfluous for us to say a few things about the location of Scythia and the customs of the Scythians, following the accounts of the historians.

Scythia, as they say, lies in the east, being enclosed on one side by the Black Sea, on the other by the Riphei mountains, and at the rear by Asia and the River Ithais. It is large in extent both in length and breadth. For the men that live here there are no boundaries between themselves, for only rarely do they cultivate the land; they have neither homes, houses nor fixed abodes since they are always grazing their herds and flocks and wander on the uncultivated wildernesses. They take their wives and children with them in carts; because of the rain-showers and cold, they have roofs made from hide for their homes. There is no more serious crime amongst them than stealing: for if they were permitted to steal, what would remain in the desert for them when they keep their herds, flocks and food without the protection of a roof? They do not hunger after gold and silver like other mortals; they occupy themselves with hunting and fishing and feed on milk and honey. The use of wool and clothes is unknown to them, and although they continually suffer from the cold, they dress only in the skins of weasels and game… They are hardened to toil and to wars, their physical strength is prodigious…

The above-mentioned people, therefore, were driven out of the aforesaid place by a people neighbouring to them who are called Pecinaci [Pechenegs]… [the Hungarians] kill but few by the sword, but many thousands by arrows, which they direct so skilfully with their horn bows that it is scarcely possible to protect against their striking.

For they do not know how to fight close to the battlefront or capture cities. They fight on horseback either charging forward or falling back and they often simulate flight. Nor are they able to fight for long; otherwise they would be intolerable if their endurance were as great as the force of their attack. Often they will desist from fighting in the very heat of combat and a short time later return to battle from flight, so that just when you might think that you are winning you are placing yourself at gravest risk.

Their way of fighting is all the more perilous the more unusual it is for other peoples. The difference in combat between them and the Britons is that the latter use spears and they use arrows. They live in the manner, not of men, but of wild beasts. For it is rumoured that they eat raw flesh and drink blood; the hearts of the men that they capture are cut into pieces and devoured as if they were a medicine, they are unmoved by any plea for mercy and their hearts are impervious to feelings of pity. They crop their hair to the scalp with knives.

They are constantly on their horses, whether going standing, thinking or conversing on them. They diligently teach their children and servants to ride and to shoot with the bow. Their spirit is haughty, rebellious, deceitful and insolent for they instil the same ferocity in the women as in the men. They are always liable to stir up unrest whether abroad or at home; they are taciturn by nature and readier to act than talk […]

ANONYMUS

[8] […] and a great many among the Ruthenians [Russians] and Cumans were slain. But the leaders of the Ruthenians and Cumans, seeing that their men were getting the worst of the battle, turned in flight and in order to save their lives they hurriedly withdrew to the city of Kiev. The leader Álmos and his soldiers pursued the Ruthenians and Cumans right up to the city of Kiev and they split the shaven heads of the Cumans like so many uncooked pumpkins. The leaders of the Ruthenians and Cumans who had entered the city, however, when they saw the audacity of the Scythians, stayed quiet as mutes.

[9] Peace between the leader and the Ruthenians

After the victory, the leader Álmos and his soldiers took possession of the land of the Ruthenians and, seizing their goods, in the second week set about laying siege to the city of Kiev. And when they set about placing scaling ladders against the wall, the leaders of the Ruthenians and Cumans, seeing the boldness of the Scythians, began to fear greatly. And when they realized that they were unable to resist them, then the leader of Kiev and the other leaders of the Ruthenians, and likewise those of the Cumans who were there, sent emissaries, and they asked the leader Álmos and his chiefs to make peace with them. But when the emissaries came before Álmos and asked him that their masters should not be expelled from their quarters, then the leader Álmos, holding counsel with his men, sent the emissaries of the Ruthenians back [to say] that their leaders and nobles should give up their sons as hostages and pay an annual tribute of ten thousand marks and moreover food, clothing and other necessities. The leaders of the Ruthenians, albeit unwillingly, nevertheless conceded all this to the leader Álmos, but they asked Álmos that on leaving the land of Galich they should proceed westwards beyond the forest of Havas to the land of Pannonia, which had earlier been the land of King Attila, and they extolled to them how good beyond measure was the land of Pannonia. For they said that there was the confluence of the most magnificent sources of water, the Danube and the Tisza and other magnificent sources abounding in good fish, and that the land was inhabited by Slavs, Bulgars and Vlachs and the shepherds of the Romans. For after the death of King Attila the Romans had called the country of Pannonia pasture-land because their flocks grazed on the land of Pannonia. And it was rightly said of Pannonia that it was the pasture-land of the Romans, for even now the Romans graze on the fruits of Hungary. But enough of this!

In the eight hundred and eighty-fourth year after the incarnation of our Lord, as is written in the chronicles for that year, the seven chief persons who are called the Seven Magyars came out of the Scythian land towards the west. Among them also came the leader Álmos, son of Ügyek who was from the line of King Magog, a well remembered man, their master and their counsellor. And with him was his wife and his son Arpád and the two sons of his uncle Hülek, namely, Zuard [Szovárd] and Cadusa [Kadosa] as well as an innumerable great host of allied peoples from that same region. And for very many days they passed through deserted places; they swam across the River Etil [Volga or Don] in the pagan manner, seated on leather bags, and nowhere did they come across a road leading to a city or habitations. Neither did they eat of the fruits of human labour, as was their wont, but they fed on meat and fish until they came to that part of Russia which is called Suzdal. And their young men were out nearly every day hunting, and that is why from that day right up to the present the Hungarians are better hunters than other peoples. And in this way the leader Álmos, together with all his people, came to that part of Russia which is called Suzdal.

EMPEROR LEO VI THE WISE

Emperor Leo, who was born in 866 and ruled from 886 until his death in 912, to be succeeded by his son Constantine VII Porphyrogenitus, wrote his compilatory handbook on the arts of war, usually known as the *Taktiká*, early in the ninth century, soon after the Magyar conquest of Hungary. The parts dealing with the 'Turks', by which name he knew the Magyars, occur mainly in Chapter XVIII, 1. 40-77 (for a recent edition of this, as well as other Byzantine sources, see: Gyula MORAVC-SIK, *Az Árpád-kori magyar történet bizánci forrásai – Fontes byzantini historiae hungaricae aevo ducum et regum ex stirpe Árpád descendentium*, Budapest, 1984, pp. 14-23). In these passages Leo took over more or less literally the sections relating to the 'Scythians, which is to say Turks and Avars' that occur in the *Stratêgikhón* attributed to 'Mavríkios', a work written some three hundred years earlier, though there are significant additions. Here paragraphs 60-67 inclusive of the relevant chapter are translated: [60] If, however, any of their pursued enemies should flee to a fortified place, they do their best to spy out precisely what lack both horses and men are suffering from, and they go to all lengths, by denying them access to these things, to seize their opponents or to force them into a settlement to their liking. This is done in such a way that initially they dictate milder terms then, if the enemy accepts these, they put forward other, more important matters.

[61] These are the chief traits of the Turks, which differ from those of the Bulgars only in that when the latter made the Christian faith their own they changed slightly under the influence of the Romans' morals, when they divested themselves of their wildness and nomadic nature along with their infidelity.

[62] The lack of pasture-land is disadvantageous to our Turkish enemies in view of the great many horses that they take with them.

[63] At time of conflict it is chiefly the infantry formation in the battle order which will do them great damage, which is to the detriment of those who are cavalrymen and do not get down from their horses; for they are unable to stand their ground on foot since they grew up on horseback.

[64] Marshy and desert terrain is also to their disadvantage, as is a dense forward line of the cavalry which is ceaselessly at their heels.

[65] Hand-to-hand combat with weapons is also disadvantageous to them and night-time attacks, which will be certain of success in cases where one part of the attack takes its stand in battle order whereas the other part stays concealed.

[66] They are likewise put greatly out of humour if any among them crosses over to the Romans. For they know full well that their people is fickle-minded, and that they are profit-seekers and composed of many tribes, so precisely for these reasons they have no respect for relatives or for mutual understanding.

[67] Because if only a few of them begin to desert and enjoy a cordial reception from our side, whole masses will follow them; that is why they harbour such resentment against those who defect from their ranks. […]

The Double Conquest

KÉZAI

[25] Thus when Otto of Swabia was ruling in Germany and Italy, Louis, son of King Lothar, in France, and Antonius Durus, son of Theodore, in Greece, in the eight hundred and sixty-second year after the birth of Jesus Christ, the Huns, or more accurately the Hungarians, once more entered into Pannonia. They crossed the realms of the Pechenegs, the White Cumans and the city of Kiev, and then they settled down by the river called the Hung, where they built a fortified place. It is from that river, of course, that they are called Hungari by the western peoples. And since, apart from this, they established another six forts, they stayed in these parts for some time.

[26] When they had finally done away with Svatopluk, in the manner related above, they divided into seven armies in such a way that each army, apart from squadrons and troops of cavalry, had a single captain to whom, as to a leader, they were bound to render as of one mind their efforts and obedience. Each of these armies had thirty thousand armed men, not counting the commanders of the cavalry. So, setting off with raised standards, with their wives, children and cattle, they crossed the Danube

at Pest and at the ferry of Zub [Szob], where they captured a fort near the Danube in which Svatopluk's soldiers had gathered, having taken to flight when their ruler was killed. Here, however, one of Morot's very elderly kinsmen was killed, amongst others, and to the present day it is idly asserted that this was Morot himself.

[27] The wealthiest and most powerful of these captains was Árpád, the son of Álmos, son of Ügek's son, Előd, of the Turul clan. This Árpád, with his tribe, was the first to penetrate the Ruthenian Alps and the first to set up camp at the river Hung since his family had been invested with the distinction, before the other tribes of Scythia, of heading the army when it advanced and bringing up the rear when it retreated. And when, having crossed the Danube, they entered into Pannonia, Árpád himself set his tent on the place where the city of Albana [Székesfehérvár] was to be founded. And this place was the first that the leader Árpád made his quarters.

[28] Now the second captain was called Zobol [Szabolcs], who set up his camp in the place where Csákvár now lies in ruins. The Csák clan is descended from this Zobol.

[29] Gyula was the captain of the third army; he, though he entered Pannonia along with the others, later on lived in Erdély [Transylvania].

[30] The fourth captain is called Urs [Örs]; he, it is said, made his camp around the River Sajó.

[31] Now the captain of the fifth army was Cund. He lived around Nyír and his sons were called Cusid and Cupian.

[32] Lel was the commander of the sixth army. At first he lived around Galgóc, after he had rooted out the Messiani and the Bohemians, but finally he moved to settle in the Nyitra region. From him is descended the clan and kindred of Zovárd.

[33] The leader of the seventh army is called Werbulchu [Vérbulcsú]. It is said that he settled down at Zala, near Lake Balaton. He was called Werbulchu because his grandfather was slain by the Germans in the battle of Crimhild. As this was certainly known to him, he wanted revenge on them, and he roasted many Germans on the spit; and he raged with such cruelty against them that he also drank their blood as if it were wine. These captains, then, picked out for themselves the aforesaid places and encampments, and the other clans likewise chose the places that were agreeable to them. [...]

ANONYMUS

The leader Árpád

[14] In the nine hundred and thirtieth year after the birth of our Lord, the leader Árpád, dispatching his armies, occupied the entire land which lies between the Tisza and the Bodrog up to Ugocsa, together with all its inhabitants. He laid siege to the fortress of Borsova and took it by storm on the third day: he raised it walls and the soldiers of the leader Salan whom he found there he had led in chains to the fort of Hung. And whilst they were staying there for a number of days, the leader and his men saw the fertility of the soil and the abundancy of all kinds of game as well as the great quantities of fish in the Tisza and Bodrog, and they were delighted beyond words with the land. And when the leader Salan heard about everything that had been going on from his men who had taken to flight, he did not dare to raise a hand but, sending his emissaries in the Bulgarian manner, he began to make threats. And he greated Árpád derisively as the leader of Hungary and mockingly called his men Hungvari: and he was beginning to wonder greatly who they were and whence they came that they should be so bold as to do such things. And he sent word that they should put right the ills that they had done and in no way should they dare to cross the river Bodrog, otherwise he himself would set forth with the help of the Greeks and the Bulgars and, to redeem the ills that they had done, he would scarcely leave one of them to return home and announce his joy at being saved. The emissaries of the leader Salan, coming to the fort of Zemplén, crossed the River Bodrog and the next day reached the leader Árpád. On the third day, however, they greeted the leader Árpád in the name of their master, and they relayed to Árpád what he had bid. On hearing the emissary of the arrogant leader Salan, however, Árpád the leader replied, not with arrogance but with humility, saying: "Although the land which lies between the Danube and Tisza up to the borders of the Bulgars, and which now belongs to him, once belonged to my forefather, the almighty King Attila, and it is not for fear of the Greeks or Bulgars that I am not persuaded to rise up against them, but because of friendship for your leader Salan I seek a small part of my own right for my cattle, namely, the land up to the River Sajó. Furthermore, I ask from your leader that he sends me out of his own goodwill two pitchers full of water from the Danube and a clod of grass from the sands of Alpár." [...]

THURÓCZY

[26] [...] When the Hungarians had returned again to Pannonia, they found here a ruler, Polish by nation, who was by name Swathepolug [Svatopluk], the son of Maroth ...By the donation of various gifts, the Hungarians – as the story written below plainly expresses – deceived him and at the same time they reconnoitred and suddenly irrupted upon a town near the bridge of Ban [Báhida], the ruins of which survive to this day; they surrounded it and with all their military might destroyed it [...]

[28] [...] Thus in the year of seven hundred and forty-four from the birth of the Lord Jesus Christ, and the three hundredth year from the death of King Attila, the people who in the vernacular are called Magyars or Huns, and in Latin the Hungarians, once again entered into Pannonia in the time of Emperor Constantine V and Pope Zacharias... they came within the borders of the Pannonian region to the land that is now called Erdel. [...]

The Incursions on the West

HELTAI

The campaigns of the Magyars

After the Magyars had occupied Pannonia and had settled in it, they rested for six years. In the seventh year after that they set off on a campaign. First of all they went to Bohemia and Moravia. And, having plundered these two, they returned to Pannonia, where they laid up for a year.

Setting off again after that, they clashed with the dukes of Carinthia, Carniola, Styria and Merania and the Magyars were victorious against these. And when they had plundered eveything from their lands, they again returned to Pannonia and once more rested.

Three years later they once again set out to war and, plundering the whole of Bulgaria, they went back to Hungary with a large booty.

After that they went to Lombardy and they captured and sacked Padua. And when they had stripped the entire province they returned home to Hungary. They rested then for ten whole years.

In the eleventh year after that they once more set forth on a campaign and went to Germany. And when they had plundered all of Syonia, Thuringia, Swabia, Franconia and Burgundy, they returned to Hungary and rested for sixteen years.

After that they set forth for Italy and going by way of Iulius Vasar […] they laid waste to everything. And they again entered Lombardy and ransacked them of all their goods, and they destroyed many monasteries. There they killed Bishop Luther, the emperor's counsellor, and they took away innumerable treasures from his church. Then, burdened with their great booty, they came back to Hungary and again they rested for ten years.

After that they went to Bavaria. But when they reached the fortress of Abach, beside the Danube, and had laid waste to the land everywhere around and they were just about to set off home, the Germans confronted them. And the Germans joined battle with them in good order and they defeated the Magyars and cut down a great many from among their ranks. And those who managed to escape hurried back empty-handed to Hungary.

THURÓCZY

The defeat of a Magyar army by the Prince of Saxony at Eisenach

[36] […] At the city of Thuringia, he put all the Hungarians to the sword except for seven. These seven he spared and he sent them to Pannonia with their ears severed, saying: "Go to your Hungarians and tell them thus, that they should never again come to this place of toments."…

Since they returned alive, and were not content to share the death of their companions, these seven Hungarians without ears were sentenced thus by the community: they were stripped of everything that they possessed, whether in fixed or moveable property, they were separated from their wives and children, and were not permitted to have any belongings. Moreover, they were compelled to go begging from camp to camp, for as long as they lived… these seven captains composed songs about themselves and they sung these among themselves for the sake of worldly praise and the spreading of their own names […]

After the failed siege of Augsburg; the legend of Lehel

[52] At this place the illustrious captains Leel and Bulchu were taken prisoner and were led before the emperor. When the emperor enquired why they were so cruel to the Christians, they replied: "We are the wrath of God on high, he sent us as a whip upon you." At this the emperor said: "Choose for yourselves whatever death you wish." To this Leel declared: "Bring me my horn so that first I may blow it." And they brought the horn to him and he, approaching the emperor as if he were just about to start playing, struck the emperor on the brow with such force that the emperor dropped down dead from this one blow. And Leel said to him: "You will go before me and you will serve me in the other world." For it is the belief of the Scythians that whomsoever they kill in their lives is obliged to serve them in the next world. […]

[KÉZAI on this same episode: Some contend, in a manner befitting legends, that when they were brought in front of the emperor, one of them smote the emperor on the head so hard that he was killed on the spot. This hearsay is contrary to probability, because prisoners are led before leaders with their hands in fetters…]

The legend of Botond [53]: […] they laid seige to Constantinople. Whilst the Hungarians were going about placing the aforementioned city under seige, the Greeks sent out a Grecian giant from the city to engage in combat. He challenged two Hungarians together to do battle with him, saying that if he did not defeat both of them, the emperor of the Greeks would bind himself to pay tribute to the Hungarians. Since he spoke out in so exceedingly a pugnacious manner against the Hungarians, they searched for an opponent for him, and he, going out before the Greek, said: "I," quoth he, "am Botond, a true Hungarian and the smallest of the Hungarians. Place beside yourself two more Greeks, one of them to grasp your soul as it exits, the other to bury your body, for I certainly shall make the emperor of the Greeks a tribute-payer to my people." The captain of the Hungarians, one Opour [Apor] by name, ordered Botond to go with his axe to the city gate which was made of metal and to demonstrate his strength with the axe on the gate. He thus came up to the gate and delivered such a blow on the gate, that it was large enough for a boy of five years to be able to walk in and out through the gap. And when the time came for the tourney of the Hungarians and the Greeks, they prepared an arena for combat in front of the city gate and they struggled fiercely with one another for a bare hour, when the Greek was thrown so violently to the ground by the Hungarian that his soul immediately exited from him.

II. ANCESTRAL HOME, ANCESTRAL CULTURE

MIHÁLY BABITS
'Mi a magyar?'
[What is Hungarian?],
Arcképek és tanulmányok, Budapest, 1977.

It is the essence of Hungarianness that interests me – that which is distinctive and unmistakeable, that which differentiates it from all else.

Might this be a racial trait, then? Not exactly, or indeed not at all. It is certainly not some bodily or tribal characteristic that is physically inheritable. I do not expect to learn much from anthropological researches about what I am seeking. Petőfi, who was not himself of pure Hungarian stock, says more to me in this respect than the brains of all the anthropologists put together. The Hungarianness of which I seek the essence is a historical phenomenon; and the manner in which it evolved historically is not a physical but an intellectual phenomenon. The inheritance which ensures its continuity is not physical, but intellectual. Here the effect of physical inheritance, if anything, is the opposite, leading to more colour, more variety. For the Hungarians have been a mixed and constantly mixing people since the time of St Stephen and quite certainly from even before that. So what, then, might we justifiably point to as the primary colour, the oldest stratum, the 'prototype' Hungarian? And is that the same as what we would today recognize as Hungarian? [p. 157]

ZOLTÁN GOMBOCZ
'Életföldrajz és a magyar őshaza'
[Physiological geography and the Magyars'
ancient homeland],
Természettudományi Közlemények, LVII (1925).

One of the crucial, most disputed problems of palaeo-linguistics, from its very beginning, has been the question of the ancient homeland. It is here that physiological geography, dealing with the geographical distribution of animals and plants, links in with prehistorical and linguistic researches.

The methodological principle can be put briefly as follows. If in some of the languages of a language-family certain plants and animals have common names, that is, names deriving from the period of linguistic unity, then one should search for the original homeland of that language-family in the place where the plants and animals in question co-occur. Of course, one must be extremely cautious when it comes to applying the principle in practice... in not a few cases the distribution ranges of plants and animals have shifted significantly even within recent millennia... The first serious attempt to apply data supplied primarily by physiological geography to the question of the ancient homeland of the Finno-Ugrians (and naturally, at the same time, the Magyars) was made in 1890. That was when the Russian natural scientist Fyodor Petrovich Keppen published his celebrated article, 'Zoo-geographical contribution to the question of the Indo-European and Finno-Ugrian homeland', in the journal *Ausland*. Keppen started out from the fact that the honey bee (*Apis mellifica*) occurs naturally in Asia only within a narrow band that stretches across Asia Minor, Syria, Persia, Afghanistan and the Himalayas to Tibet and China, whereas it was originally unknown in Siberia, Mongolia and Turkestan... Now this can can be compared with the linguistic fact that the words *méh* 'bee' and *méz* 'honey' are common denominators for all the Finno-Ugrian languages and thus originate from the time of the primordial language. It follows of necessity that the original Finno-Ugrian people must have had a knowledge of bees and honey, so that we should not seek the ancient homeland of the Finno-Ugrians in Asia, but in Europe... The northerly limit of the bee's range in East Europe broadly coincides with the northerly limit of the oak, along latitude 57-58°, to the south of Perm, Vyatka and Vologda. The original abodes of the Finno-Ugrians must have been situated south of this line, probably in the well-watered, richly forested region stretching between the Volga bend and the Ural mountains. [p.309]

After considering the distribution of the reindeer, pine and Arolla pine (*Pinus cembra*), Gombocz goes on to conclude:

Thus the data supplied by physiological geography, some examples of which I have set out here, point fairly unequivocally to a region lying along the Kama, Oka and Belaya rivers, from the Volga bend to the Urals: in all probability this area was the original dwelling-place of the still unified Finno-Ugrian people. The Ugrian-Magyars, i. e., the Finno-Ugrian tribe from which the Magyars were later to emerge, inhabited the most easterly flank from the very beginning... at all events, the Magyars were the first tribe to pass over the eastern slopes of the Urals and move to the forest-steppe boundary region, thereby becoming swept up in the maelstrom of Turkic ethnic movements in the early centuries of our own era... The Magyars were an organized equestrian nomadic people by the time they reached their second homeland – one that is also confirmed by historical sources – of Levedia, which should be sought on the plain lying to the north of the Caucasus, in the region of the Don and Kuban rivers. [pp. 369-74]

The Earliest Periods of Prehistory

In my book *Budapest*, 1961, I utilized the results of Soviet pollen analyses in an attempt to fix the boundary of the forest zone during the Finno-Ugrian prehistorical era, and I concluded that the *Urheimat* of the Uralic or Finno-Ugrian people was located somewhere between central Poland and the Ural mountains. Péter Hajdú, also drawing on pollen analysis data but taking into account additional tree species, has reached the following conclusions:

... the ancient habitat of the Uralic people must have been situated north of the Central Urals, from the beginning well into the middle of the Middle Holocene period, along the lower and middle reaches of the Ob and in the northern regions of the Ural Mountains, including the source of the Pechora; for the most part, however, it was situated on the Siberian side of the area thus delimited. In terms of time-scale, this means the sixth to fourth millennia B.C." (Péter Hajdú, 'Linguistic Background of Genetic Relationships', in: *Ancient Cultures of the Uralian Peoples*, ed. P. Hajdú, Budapest, 1976, pp. 11-46, esp. p. 36). In other words, he places the location of the ancestral homeland in the *taiga*.

PÉTER T. VERES
'A szovjet etnogenetikai kutatás és a magyar őstörténet'
[Soviet ethnogenetic research and Hungarian prehistory],
Magyar tudomány, 1980/5.

Anthropological research utilizing the methods of population genetics, both in the Soviet Union and here in Hungary, has come to the conclusion that the so-called Andronovo type can be regarded as a determining factor in the evolution of the anthropological features of the proto-Magyars. The localization of the settlement area of the nomadic Magyars to the regions north of the Caspian Sea thereby obtained is also in accord with the palaeo-linguistic evidence. A. A. Chigureva has shown that, besides birch, hazel and lime, pollen remains of the elm (*Ulmus*) as well as oak can be found in the lower Volga basin. The word for elm in Hungarian – *szil* – is of Finno-Ugrian origin and can be dated to the Uralic period. [pp. 379-380]

LÁSZLÓ SZABÓ
A Magyar rokonsági rendszer
[The Magyar kinship system],
Debrecen, 1980.

Hungarian kinship terms that can be dated to the Finno-Ugrian period are *hölgy* 'woman, female', *atya* 'father, father-in-law, grandfather', *ipa* 'father-in-law or

wife's elder brother', *atval* 'step-father' (obsolete), *úr* 'man, hero, warrior', *fiú* 'male descendant', *öcs* 'younger brother or sister', whilst at the end of this period, or possibly in the Ugrian period, *ara* appears as a collective noun for (younger) male members in the female line. It is striking that only one of the terms that originated in the Finno-Ugrian period, the word *hölgy*, refers to females... In the proto-Magyar period it is not so much that the number of terms denoting males grows, as that the system relating partly to females, partly to children and youngsters gains in refinement... [p. 30]

The leading role of males within society continued to grow in the Ugrian period (*had* 'clan', *hím* 'man'), and this is also reflected in the terminology. [p. 36]

Foreign words rarely entered Hungarian kinship terminology before the end of the proto-Magyar period, which indicates that the Magyars, despite all their contacts and co-habitation with others, preserved their integrity – at least in the stratum of commoners – and barely established any marital links with speakers of other languages. It is therefore noteworthy that after the Magyar conquest, if we ignore the few Latin or Latin-mediated words that entered Hungarian from the official language, the only influence which can be said to have been significant is Slavonic... [p. 114]

LAJOS LIGETI
'Az uráli magyar őshaza'
[The Magyars' ancient Uralian homeland].
In: A magyarság őstörténete [Prehistory of the Magyars], ed. L. Ligeti, Budapest, 1943 [Reprinted 1986], pp. 36-69.

... The move out of the forest region on to the steppe, the switch from a hunter-fisher to an equestrian nomadic lifestyle, has been thought somehow to be near impossible. Somehow, everyone has envisaged both lifestyles in idealized forms that recognize no transition, as though forest-dwellers would never have ventured out from the depths of the forest, or as though a people which did not have herds of ten or a hundred thousand horses could not be equestrian nomads. The belief has also become rooted among Hungarian prehistorians that a people of Finno-Ugrian origin could not have gone anywhere near the Turks of its own free will since the Finno-Ugrians were forest-dwellers whilst the Turks, along with the Mongols, had been the equestrian nomads of the steppe from the beginning of the world...

If we examine the history of Central Asia more closely, however, we find that the picture is far from being as inflexible as that...

It should be remarked that our sources note about several tribes, mentioned by name, that they carried on both economies simultaneously. Cases where a forest-dwelling hunting tribe later became a nomadic steppe people are very common, demonstrated by many examples. There are even examples, albeit much rarer, of weakened, impoverished nomadic tribes of animal breeders withdrawing to the wooded steppe and thence into the forest zone to adopt the tougher, humbler lifestyle of hunters.

Judging from the records derived from numerous Chinese and Turkic sources, it is also demonstrable that Turkic peoples did not all, or always, rank as steppe-dwelling equestrian nomads. [pp. 60-61]

DENIS SINOR
'Történelmi hipotézisek és a nyelvtudomány' [Historical hypotheses and linguistics].
In: A vízimadarak népe [The waterfowl folk], Budapest, 1975, pp. 325-338.

... The words *borjú* ['calf'], *ökör* ['ox'] and *bika* ['bull'] can equally, or even more plausibly, be derived from Mongolian as well as from Turkic languages. The scholars who deal with this question are influenced, consciously or subconsciously, by the historical – and not linguistic hypothesis that the Magyars had lived together with the Turks: consequently, the Hungarian loan-words had to derive from the Turkic language. If we take this a step further and pose the question as to how we know that the Magyars lived together with the Turks, then the main argument that we hear in response is that the Hungarian language contains many Turkic loan-words, such as *borjú*, *ökör*, *bika*... In other words, a classic case of circular argument. [p. 329]

BÁLINT HÓMAN
Ősemberek – Ősmagyarok – [Prehistoric man – prehistoric Magyars],
Budapest, 1944 [Reprinted Atlanta, Georgia, 1985].

...We must dispose, once and for all, of the hypothesis that the Magyars had contacts with Bulgar Turks in western Siberia and the Ural region and that a cultural transformation took place under Bulgar influence. There is no longer even a need to make such conjectures nowadays. The latest results from anthropological, ethnographic, archaeological and linguistic researches have rendered resort to any bridging theory quite superfluous.

The physical and mental endowments of the interrelated palaeo-Europid races, the Lapps, Ob-Ugrians and Samoyeds... are entirely different from those of the Magyars and other Finno-Ugrian peoples. The primitive conditions in which they live to the present day were unknown amongst even the ancestors of the latter peoples. Even in their original homeland, the ancient Finno-Magyar people enjoyed far more advanced lifestyles and a higher cultural level than their palaeo-Europid coevals. In contrast to those primitive peoples, living chiefly from fishing supplemented by hunting, the Finno-Magyars were forest hunters who were already rearing animals and cultivating the land in prehistoric times.

For this reason I feel obliged to exclude the Ob-Ugrians and Samoyeds from the circle of close kinsfolk of the proto-Magyars and am forced to conclude that earlier generations of Hungarians, reared in the knowledge of their Scythian-Hun origin, were right to recoil instinctively from the thought, educed from linguistic considerations, that they were related to the Lapps, Voguls, Ostyaks and Samoyeds... the Hungarian people can have no reason for spurning its Finno-Magyar ancestors, who were in no way inferior to the ancestors of western European peoples, who sprang from the same stock as they did. [p. 109]

After the long-abandoned theory of an original homeland in Asia, we must also consign the attractive theory of a homeland in the Urals to the ranks of erroneous scientific hypotheses.

Anthropological, linguistic, archaeological and historical data, both separately and combined, all go to show that the ancient Finno-Magyar people came from the west, from the vicinity of the Indo-German peoples, to the forest region lying to the north-east of the Bug-Dnieper region, above the Pontic steppe... The original homeland of the prehistoric ancestors of the Finno-Magyars should be sought in the locality where the progeny of the Continental prototype and its East European subtype had the opportunity to live in close community with the Northern type, namely, that area of Europe which lies to the north of the Alps and the Carpathians. The homeland of the Finno-Magyars themselves, on the other hand, should be sought where, after parting company with their Indo-German coevals, they would have been able to come into proximity with the Ugrian-Samoyed peoples of Sibirid type, namely, the Russian forest zone... In interpreting these [views]... we must get away from the doctrines of those linguists and archaeologists who seek a nonexistent "proto-Uralic" people, and also a "proto-Finno-Ugrian" people supposedly originating from them, in the Ural region. [p.124]

The classical site of stone Battle-axe culture and Fatyanovo culture is the section of the Russian forest zone from the Dnieper to the Oka. In this same area, and to its north, we also encounter Corded Ware culture. This, therefore, was the Finno-Magyar homeland where, in the third to second millennia B.C., the proto-Finno-Magyars, parting from their Indo-German neighbours and moving eastwards, settled and united into a Finno-Ugrian socio-linguistic community with the palaeo-European ethnic elements whom they found there, later to split into several branches that scattered towards the north-east and north-west. [p. 125]

However, the Magyar myth of origin which had sustained the idea of a Hun-Magyar identity, or rather awareness of the Hun origins of the royal house, had already moved from oral tradition into the original, 11th-century source [*Gesta Hungarorum*] and from there into the later chronicles... [p. 151]

ERIK MOLNÁR
A magyar társadalom története az őskortól az Árpád-korig
[**Magyar social history from prehistoric times to the Árpádian age**],
2nd ed., Budapest, 1949.

As a broad generalization, therefore, the decisive arena for Magyar prehistory can be traced to the territory which is bordered on the west by the Volga and Kama rivers, on the east by the Ural mountains, on the north by a line through Tyumen, Sverdlovsk and Molotov, and in the south by the segment of the Ural river between Chkalov and Uralsk. [p. 15]

Above all, it is erroneous to surmise that the predecessors of the modern Finno-Ugrian peoples at some time spoke a common language and constituted a single people. It is impossible to reconcile this surmise with social relations in the prehistorical era... [pp. 7-8]

Molnár later went on to suggest possible locations for the original homeland beside the Aral Sea and, later still, the Altai.

JÁNOS HORVÁTH
'A hun történet és szerzője'
[**The history of the Huns and its authorship**],
Irodalomtörténeti Közlemények, (1963): 446-476.

Dealing with Kézai's authorship, Horváth follows Anonymus in making a distinction between the Székely, as remnants of the Huns, and the other the Magyars:

"But whilst the Hun Legend acknowledged the stag merely as a 'leading animal', the Magyar people's myth of origin honoured the hind as its totemistic ancestress."

An animal ancestor, however, was unacceptable to Kézai, because man could only be descended from man, hence "the Magyars, like other peoples, sprang from man and woman." [p. 455]

Anonymus was also aware of this myth, and not from written sources but from folk legends. [p. 457]

"... Despite all the misgivings, it must be said that the descent from the hind is the ancient Magyar myth of origin, and since the Huns also had a legend (though not a myth of origin) about the hind which lead them into their new homeland, this apparent concordance became, for Kézai, incontrovertible evidence of the identity of the two peoples. [p. 458]

... Amongst both Turkic and Finno-Ugrian peoples a substantial portion of the myths of origin talk about only one clan-founding ancestor, *i.e.* either an ancestral mother or an ancestral father." [p. 459]

The kindred peoples which stayed in Persia "were similar in build and colour to the Huns and differed from them somewat only in language, rather like the Saxons from the Thuringians". Kézai must have had specific information about them, but beyond this he also knew of a fragment "which lives on Scythian land right up to present day". [p. 462]

The linguistic evidence concealed in the name 'Hunor' cannot throw any light on historical contacts of the Huns and Magyars but only on the one-time existence of Magyar-Onogur connections. [p. 464]

Kézai introduces Magyar historical elements into the history of the Huns. [p. 466]

MIKLÓS ZSIRAI
'Őstörténeti csodabogarak'
[**Prehistorical curiosities**].
In: A magyarság őstörténete [Prehistory of the Magyars], ed. L. Ligeti, Budapest, 1943 [Reprinted 1986], p. 269.

... Apart from the Finno-Ugrian, or Uralo-Altaic, languages, Hungarian has been shown to have concordances with the following more important languages or language groups, with corresponding inferences for prehistory being drawn from each of the concordances: Hebrew, Egyptian, Sumerian, Etruscan, Hittite, Basque, Persian, Pelasgian, Greek, Chinese, Sanskrit, English, Tibetan, Tamil, Koryak, Kamchadal, Yukagir, Japanese, Ainu, Dravidian, Maori, Magari, Chin, Lepchà, Dafla, Abor-Miri, Khasi, Mikir, Munda, Gondi, Armenian, Bodo, Koch, Garo, Kachari, Manipur, Teluga, Mèkhalì, Brahui, Takpa, Manyak, Sok, Horpa, Serhta, Sunwar, Gyarung, Rodong, Chaurasyà, Kulung, Bàhing, Lohorong, Sangpang, Dumi, Bhutan, Kham, Khumi, etc. [p. 269]

JÓZSEF DEÉR
Pogány magyarság, keresztény magyarság
[**Pagan Magyars, Christians Magyars**],
Budapest, 1938.

The ancient Magyar culture was, therefore, identical to the culture of those Voguls and Ostyaks who, in the reports of the travellers who went amongst them, from the sixteenth century onwards, feature as primitively organized peoples living predominantly from hunting and fishing, i.e. hunter-gatherers. However, this undeniably logical deduction from the linguistic evidence cannot be squared immediately with historically authenticated facts, which confront us with a picture of the Conquest-period Magyars, in the last decades of the ninth century, as a dominant people of nomadic warriors, How timid forest-dwellers could become an equestrian people with a characteristically Turkic culture is the question to which we must give an answer... [p. 35]

Through the Bulgar-Turks the Magyars became associated with a people that reared all the pertinent domestic animal species, was familiar with the basic principles of agriculture, and besides which had a well developed political and military organization. This cultural influence is likewise reflected in the linguistic marks it left in the form of Bulgar-Turkic loan-words. [p. 42]

Ancient Magyar culture was thus only enhanced by the Bulgar-Turkic influence, gaining a harmonious adjunct without being fundamentally altered in nature. [p. 44]

ANDRÁS RÓNA-TAS
A nyelvrokonság
[Linguistic affiliation],
Budapest, 1978.

The question… arises as to when and how Hungarian separated from the original Ugrian language. Did the three sister-languages branch off at the same time, or did Hungarian become separately detached first whilst the other two continued for a long time together and only later separated? The general view is that the Ob-Ugrian languages remained together for a while, but there are other tenable opinions. It is also disputed whether there continued to be contact between Hungarian and the other two Ugrian languages after their separation: indeed, it does not seem entirely impossible that we should posit a relatively late contact, or renewed 'encounter', between the Magyars and at least some groups of Ob-Ugrians.

At the same time, it is virtually certain that in the course of their subsequent existence the Magyars did meet up with one or another of the groups speaking the Permian language…

Interestingly, little has been said about any late encounter the Hungarian language may have had with languages of the Volga Finns, the Cheremis and Mordvins. [p. 451]

Ancient Folk Music

BÉLA BARTÓK
'Miért és hogyan gyűjtsünk népzenét?'
[Why and how should folk music be collected?],
Budapest, 1936. Reprinted in: Válogatott zenei írásai [Selected writings on music], eds. A. Szőllőssy and B. Szabolcsi, Budapest, 1948, p. 46. (Also in Összegyűjtött írásai [Collected writings], vol. I., ed. A. Szőllőssy, Budapest, 1966, pp. 581-96.)

…We have known for a good 25 years that the chief characteristic of the oldest Magyar folk songs is a certain pentatonic system and a certain so-called 'descending' melodic structure… [in] most of the melodies of the Volga Cheremis… we find the same pentatonic system, the same descending melodic structure, and even variants of the Magyar tunes themselves. [p. 46]

ZOLTÁN KODÁLY
'Zenei néphagyomány'
[Folk musical tradition].
In: Magyarság Néprajza [Hungarian Ethnography], 3rd ed, Vol IV, Budapest, n.d.

The route along which Hungarian music evolved cannot have differed from that of the language or the people. Wherever the people went in the course of its growth, its music went with it: whatever acted on the language was able to act on the music, too. As there is no hope of obtaining contemporaneous data, we have to fall back on the music of related and neighbouring peoples or their

descendants… There is, however, one small kindred people, the Cheremis. What has come to light so far about their music displays such a surprising and profound similarity with one of the strata of Hungarian folk music that there can be scarcely any doubt today about their original connection. Time may have effaced the Oriental traits from the features of the Hungarians, but a bit of the ancient East still lives on in the depths of their souls, where music takes its source, and it links them with some peoples whose languages they have long ceased to understand and whom they are quite unlike in their overall spiritual disposition.

It is miraculous that, after so many foreign influences and so much racial intermixing, the ancient musical language of the Magyars should have been preserved almost intact in at least several hundred melodies. [p. 12]

BENCE SZABOLCSI
'A primitív dallamosság: a hanglejtéstől az ötfokúságig'
[Primitive melody, from cadence to pentatonality].
In: Emlékkönyv Kodály Zoltán hatvanadik születésnapjára [Memorial volume for Zoltán Kodály's sixtieth birthday], Budapest, 1943.

… Pentatony, which I am deeply convinced is a heritage of the most archaic high-cultures in all parts of the world. If what I once expounded years ago in this connection is still valid, pentatony displays a double articulation in cultural history. As a system of sounds it preserves the memory of an ancient community, or equivalent initiating focus, and, as an arsenal of melodic forms, points back to some ancient differentiation, a separation of parts of the world and cultural groups. The community which finds its reflection in the sound-system may still be part of the primitive world; the differentiation which is shown by the melodic forms is, at all events, linked with the emergence of the ancient high cultures… Pentatony, is a tree whose roots extend into the primitive world but whose foliage already belongs to the mature musical cultures… [pp. 28-29]

LÁSZLÓ VIKÁR
'The Music of the Finno-Ugrian Peoples'.
In: Ancient Cultures of the Uralian Peoples, ed. P. Hajdú, Budapest, 1976, pp. 319-336.

Just as there exists today no unified Finno-Ugrian basic language, it would likewise be a vain experiment to force the present-day music of the Finno-Ugrians into some sort of reconstructed unity. There is no Finno-Ugrian language; there are only various Finno-Ugrian languages displaying degrees of relationship. There is no expressly Finno-Ugrian music, but each people with a Finno-Ugrian language has its own musical tradition and the music of these peoples is related in some respects and distinctly individual in others, just like the languages. [p. 322]

In Cheremis folk music we can distinguish two basic types… The first type includes short, simple melodies with a relatively small range. The other type contains ornamented melodies with long lines and broader ranges and their main characteristic is that the first half of the melodies is then repeated a fifth lower. (Kodály compared this type with Hungarian melodies which likewise have an answer at the fifth.)…, and we can say that the characteristics of the Cheremis folk music alive today are closer to the Turkic [i.e., Chuvash, Tatar and Bashkirian – Gy. L.] than to the other Finno-Ugrian traditions. [p. 333]

LAJOS VARGYAS
'A magyar népzene tanúsága és a baskiriai őshaza'
[The testimony of Hungarian folk music and the ancient homeland in Bashkiria].
In: Keleti hagyományok – nyugati kultúra. Tanulmányok [Eastern traditions and western culture, Studies], Budapest, 1984, pp. 152-54.

But the flourishing style of repetition at the fifth and pentatony of that territory and its total lack of equivalents in Asia or in Europe, taken together with its complete concordance with the Hungarian style, which is made even more manifest and unquestionable by the further concordance of individual pieces within the style all this could only be the result of a direct link. This link in turn is only conceivable in terms of Magyars who stayed in the East and were gradually absorbed into the surrounding two kindred peoples. They transmitted the style to the two neighbouring peoples who survived them, whilst the main body of the Magyars took it with them into the Carpathian basin and preserve it to the present day. [p. 152]

What lessons does this outline of the development and geographical environment of Hungarian music hold for the 'Bashkirian homeland'? When and in which part of modern (or old) Bashkiria could the Magyars, or a section of them, have lived? My own view, based on the folk-music links, and balancing these against the sociological findings, is as follows:

The Magyars may initially have reached the middle part of the region between the Volga and the Urals, which corresponds with the earlier territory of Bashkiria, after their first association with a Turkic (Mongol?) people, and probably led by them. At that time there could have been no trace of the Bashkirs themselves in the region. From there the Magyars moved to the steppe, to the approaches of the Caucasus, which was then under Khazar dominion. Several of the musical types that link the Hungarians with the Cheremis – and only with the Cheremis – are relics of this 'first' sojourn between the Volga and the Urals. By the second occasion it was not the whole Magyar people which returned but only a separated splinter, the Magyars known to Julianus. [pp. 153-154]

History of the Magyars

ISTVÁN VÁSÁRY
'A magyar őstörténet kutatásának hagyományai'
[The traditions of research into Magyar prehistory],
Magyar Tudomány, 1980/5.

… Sadly, the old magic circles, now in new form, are still all around us. Here we have a new Sumerian theory of the 'Kuruc opposition, etc.' up against the 'official Labanc line' on the Finno-Ugrians. It is necessary to find a new type of national identity which at long last transcends these bogus Kuruc – Labanc, Finno-Ugrian – Sumerian and other tribal loyalties… Magyar prehistory will best serve the Hungarian national consciousness in the future if it strives to become an integral, but not dominant, part of it.

KÁROLY CZEGLÉDY
'Keleten maradt magyar töredékek'
[Magyar splinter groups that remained in the East].
In: A magyarság őstörténete [Prehistory of the Magyars], ed. L. Ligeti, Budapest, 1943, [Reprinted 1986], pp. 154-177.

It has been common for smaller groups to slip the ties of nomadic tribes that are forced into a change of place or set off on conquests and for them to either stay on their old pastures or migrate in another direction, along more peaceful ways, to a new homeland. It is less common for the memories of such broken tribal ties to be preserved in the sources. This is natural, of course, as their attention is primarily held by the larger tribal alliance as it forges ahead like a tornado, constantly sucking in defeated populations. Detached tribes, if they are small in size and weak, are soon absorbed into the more vigorous tribes of surrounding peoples. However, the knowledge of affiliation to the tribes that set off down the conquest route still survives in the souls of later generations.

In the course of the migrations of the Magyar tribes there were two occasions when larger groups split away – the Bashkirian Magyars and the Savards. The separation of the Bashkirian Magyars occurred in some little-known period of prehistory, but their sense of belonging was still alive at the time of the Árpáds, both amongst the Magyars who moved into the new homeland and amongst their Bashkirian brothers. We are able to gain a clearer picture of the detachment of the Savards from our sources. These relate that even decades after the Magyars had set off to conquer the new home, and with the increasing distance in space, they still maintained contacts. Their memory, however, faded more rapidly than that of the Bashkirian Magyars: scarcely any trace of them remained in the tradition of the Magyars who moved into the new homeland…

The earliest reports that relate to the Bashkirian Magyars are to be found in the works of Arab geographers.

However, since this information can often be interpreted in a number of ways, it would be more sensible to hear first what the western tradition has to say about the Bashkirian Magyars.

The first representative of the western tradition known to us today is Gottfried of Viterbo, who was priest to the court of Henry VI and compiled a world chronicle for his king. According to this chronicle there were two Hungaries – new and old (*nova, antiqua*). The Hungarians were the same as the Huns and their ancestors, under the leadership of two of the Trojan heroes, ended up in the marshes of Maeotis after the destruction of Troy.

This information dates from the second half of the twelfth century.

Another world chronicle also preserves a record of the old homeland of the Magyars. Its author was Vincent of Beauvais, contemporary and friend of Louis IX and the most diligent reader and most prolific writer of his own, and perhaps any, age.

His vast work [the *Speculum Maius* of c. 1264], at the end of its first part, speaks about Pannonia, which, according to him, was occupied by Huns who dwelt beyond the Maeotis marshes. They named their new homeland Hungaria. Vincent then continues: 'According to Orosius, there are two kinds of Hungaria, one larger and one smaller'. The Huns came into Pannonia on the occasion of a hunt after deer and other game. The Orosius to whom Vincent refers was a fifth century scribe of Spanish descent who wrote his world chronicle on the advice of Augustine. His work was continued by others after his death and we do not know who originally wrote the above sentence into the later chronicle.

The world chronicles were the precursors of world histories in the modern sense. Most of them can be traced back to the chronicle of Eusebius [*History of the Christian Church*]. This work of Eusebius included, in digest form, the rich material of the eastern and western Hellenistic literature that was still extant at the time. Its historical perspective is in keeping with that of the Book of Daniel in the Bible. Most of the post-Eusebian chronicles actually continue Eusebius' work. Their importance lies in the fact that we find in these world chronicles historical data relating to the various peoples of Europe right up to time when, modelled on the early gesta literature, the forerunners of European national history writing start to appear.

The above information on Hungary given by the two world chronicles probably must be connected with a Hungarian tradition about the original homeland. But whilst the data in the two world chronicles are from no later than the early thirteenth century, data on the Hungarian tradition relating to Magna Hungaria derive from later than the 1230s. The national tradition is contained first and foremost by the report about the journeys to Magna Hungaria of the Hungarian dominican friars that was prepared by an otherwise unknown priest, Richardus.

The mission to the Balkans and the East [the Cumans] was designated the principal task of the Hungarian Dominicans by the founder of the Order, St Dominican himself. The decision to organize in Hungary was made at the Order's Ghapter General in Bologna a few years after its first papal confirmation [at the end of 1216]. At this general assembly the world was divided into eight provinces. In two of these [one was Hungary] there was no monastery; nevertheless the Hungarian Order was very active and within just a few years already had a vigorous organization here too. The Dominicans were the first propagators of the new western, 'Gothic' culture in Hungary. From the very beginning, the Order set as a goal the most thoroughgoing scholarly training of its members. They did not reach the areas of their missionary activity haphazardly but by means of of methodical inquiry.

Hungarian Dominicans turned up in Magna Hungaria on several occasions. The first testimony of this is the already mentioned report by Richardus, which begins by briefly describing the events that led up to the journey: "It was found in the chronicles of the Christian Hungarians that there was another Ungaria Maior [greater or older Hungary], whence the Seven Chieftains had issued with their people to search for a dwelling-place for themselves, for because of the large numbers of the population their land was no longer able to support them. After they had passed through many countries and wrought much devastation, they finally reached the land which is now known as Hungary but was then called 'the pasture of the Romans.' Even from this quotation it is evident that the friars had first made a thorough study of the chronicles; at least this is what may be deduced from the evocation of Anonymus' words in the quoted passage. The expression 'Ungaria maior' can already be found in Vincent's work.

We then read: "When that aforementioned fact came to light from the chronicles, several of the Preaching Friars took pity on those Magyars, from whom they too were descended, that they were still living in a pagan state: and they sent out four friars to search for them and, wherever they might be, with God's help find them. They knew from the writings of the ancients that they were in the East, but where they were, they had not the slightest knowledge."

According to this, the Hungarian tradition supplied no information on the whereabouts of the eastern Magyars. Or do the last words of the quotation mean that the Dominicans had applied due criticism to the tradition which identified the Hungarians with the Huns and which placed their old homeland in the marshes of Maeotis? For nowhere in the reports of the journeys of the Dominicans do we read about the marshes of Maeotis.

Richardus' report next goes on to say that the four friars searched for three years for Magna Hungaria, but only one of them, a certain Otto, was able to gather more precise news of it. In one pagan country he met some people who spoke Hungarian and were able to give him information about the country they sought. He then returned to Hungary to make a fresh attempt to reach Magna Hungaria with other friars. Otto died shortly after arriving home, but not before he had told the Dominicans the route by which they coud find the place. With this a second group of four friars – Julian and three companions – was sent to look for Magna Hungaria.

The friars boarded a boat at Constantinople and set down at the Circassian city of Matrica [modern Taman], opposite the Kerch peninsula. Here they waited around for fifty days in the hope of finding travelling companions: then, with the backing of the ruling princess, they started out and after a journey of thirteen days reached Alania, situated on the northern slopes of the Caucasus. According to the report, the Mongols were by now very close and so they were able to make further progress only with difficulty. (This mention of the Mongols is hard to reconcile with information that we have from other sources.) At this point two of the friars returned to Hungary; the other two, Julian and an ill Gerard, made their way across the trackless steppe and on the thirty-seventh day arrived at the the city of Bunda[z] in the Saracens' [Mohammedans'] land of Vela. These place names have still not been identified so that the route they took cannot be established either. It seems likely, however, that the friars turned northwards out of Alania and at first headed towards the mouth of the River Don to somewhere east of the Don, in the area where the Don and Volga bend closer together. The following section of the journey took them to the Bulgarian empire besides the Volga and Kama rivers. The report does not mention that they crossed the Volga, thus they may have proceeded northwards to somewhere west of the Volga. Then follows a description of Magna Bulgaria. Here Julian came across a Magyar woman who gave him directions for reaching Magna Hungaria. "He found the Hungarians besides the great River Ethyl. When they saw him and learned that he was a Christian Hungarian, they were exceedingly pleased at his arrival. They showed him around their dwellings and settlements. They inquired diligently about the king and country of their Christian Hungarian brothers and gladly listered to all he had to say about religion and other matters, because they spoke entirely in Hungarian and they understood him and he them. They are pagans and know nothing of God, but nor do they worship idols. They live like beasts; they do not till the land. They eat the meat of horses, wolves and the like; they drink mare's milk and blood. They have many horses and weapons and are resolute in battle. They know from the stories of the ancients that those [Christian] Hungarians had gone away from them, but where they were, that they did not know." The report then refers to the relations of the Mongols and the Hungarians. The Hungarians were worthy opponents of the Mongols in battle: as allies now they were exceedingly strong and together had conquered fifteen countries. In Magna Hungaria Julian also met the Mongol ambassador, who, amongst other things, was able to speak both Hungarian and German. From him he learned that the Mongol army, which was encamped just five days' journey from there, was only awaiting the return of the armies that had been fighting in Persia before setting off to attack the Germans. Julian did not stay in Magna Hungaria for long. He considered that the countries lying between the Christian and the Bashkirian Hungarians would block the route between the two countries if they saw that the pagan Hungarians were to be converted to Christianity and join forces with the Christian Hungarians. But he also hastened back to give an account of his journey as soon as possible because he feared that he might die suddenly or fall ill, in which case his own efforts would have been in vain and others might not even find the way to Magna Hungaria. The report records precisely the day of his return: he started back on June 21st, 1236, taking the shorter route through Russia and Poland as he had been advised by the Bashkirian Hungarians. He arrived back on Hungarian soil on December 24th of the same year. [pp. 154-160]

East of the Carpathians

GÁBOR VÉKONY
'Levedia meg Atel és Kuzu'
[Levedia, Atel and Kuzu],
Magyar Nyelv, (1986).

It can be shown from several approaches, then, that Levedia lay to the east of the Volga, in the region of the River Emba, just as it can also be shown from several approaches that Atelkuzu was the territory between the Volga and Dnieper, with its central settlement area near to the Volga.

This picture throws new light on Magyar prehistory of the ninth century, and a goodly number of hitherto unexplained circumstances now become explicable... Around 840, and in the forties of the ninth century, the Magyars were still in Levedia – to be sure for a very short while only.

We should take the three years of living and fighting together literally... [pp. 51-52]

E. A. CHALIKOVA & A. H. CHALIKOV
Altungarn an der Kama und im Ural,
Budapest, Magyar Nemzeti Múzeum, 1981.

From the fact that remains characterized by pottery of the Kushnarenkovo type appear at the turn of the sixth and seventh centuries B.C. we can deduce that the early Magyar tribes moved over to the western side of the Urals following the events of 597-598, when the Ugrians (proto-Magyars) living in West Siberia and the southern Urals rose up against the Turks.

The following outline of the history of the pre- and proto-Magyars emerges from an examination of the data available to us:

1. The roots of early Magyar culture lead us back to the Sargatka archaeological culture of West Siberia from the fourth century B.C. to the fourth century A.D.
2. In the fourth century A.D., at the start of the Great Migration of Peoples, the early Magyars had formed ties with the nomads of the southern Urals and West Siberia.
3. In the second half of the sixth century the proto-Magyars were probably part of the framework of the western Turkish khaganate and their culture was exposed to strong Turkic, Sassanid-Iranian and Asian-Sogdian influences.
4. From the seventh century to the beginning of the ninth century the Magyars founded a strong, semi-nomadic state, known as Magna Hungaria, on the western side of the Urals, and this population left to us cemeteries similar to that at Bolshiye-tigani.
5. The Bolshiye-tigani and similar cemeteries were abandoned at the beginning of the ninth century, which is obviously explained by the fact that the early Magyar tribes then moved to the West.
6. The westward route of the Magyars is marked by graves at Vorobyevo by the Don, Voloshnoshtkoye in the Dnieper region and Krylosz in Galicia. [p. 95]

GYULA NÉMETH
A honfoglaló magyarság kialakulása
[The genesis of the Magyars of the Conquest],
Budapest, 1930.

Before they became attached to the cultural sphere of Central Europe, the Magyars had been together with Turkic peoples for a thousand years. [p. l]

The Magyars then became a people with a Turkic organization... Under no circumstances do I believe that the Magyars, in the Ugrian (Vogul-Ostyak-Magyar) period of their prehistory, would have been on the level of the modern Voguls and Ostyaks. These peoples have declined greatly in relation to their prehistoric conditions. I take as decisive proof of this the fact that whereas nowadays they tend to know about the horse from hearsay and legends, in their prehistoric state they were horse-breeding equestrian peoples. [p. 124]

After that, around the sixth, seventh and eighth centuries, the Magyars... are found in the Caucasus, in the vicinity of the Bulgar Turks, where, amongst other names, they bear the Bulgar Turkic name *ongur* (<*onugor*). [p. 125]

As I see it, the linguistic influence of the Bulgar Turks persisted even on the territory of modern Hungary. [p. 126]

Among the Byzantine sources, Emperor Leo the Wise (886-912) was the first to call the Magyars 'Turks', in Chapter XVII of his *Taktiká*, then his son, Constantine

Porphyrogenitus, and after them a whole series of Byzantine writers. [p. 198]

The name 'Turks' became attached to the Magyars as a result of Turkish conquest and their link with the Khazars. [p. 200]

This sudden disappearance of tribal names is natural since the tribe is a secondary formation founded on an arbitrarily created alliance... an artificial political structure, serving for purposes of legal protection but primarily military in its intention... [p. 226]

The word 'Magyar', as an ethnic name, does not occur before the ninth century, which can hardly be accidental but is much more likely to be due to the circumstance that up to the ninth century the Magyar-Megyer tribe, or group of tribes, participated in various tribal alliances and in these was equal in rank to other tribes or tribal groupings but did not belong to their leading, name-giving part... Then around the year 800 a situation arose in which the Magyars, who had already become the leading, name-giving tribe within a larger (Onogur, Sabirian, Khazar) tribal federation, together with their appendages, founded a state that was independent of all other tribal federations. [p. 272]

From these three elements emerged a people that was new in character and which cannot be identified either with the Finno-Ugrians, or with the Bulgars, or with the Turks. [p. 277]

This tribe [the Magyars], as its name and language attest, was a Finno-Ugrian tribe by origin... The remaining tribal names (Kavar, Kürt, Gyarmat, Tarján, Jenő, Kér, Keszi), as we have seen, were of Turkish origin... We are unable to say anything plausible... in respect of the Nyék. [p. 272]

COUNT ISTVÁN ZICHY
Magyar őstörténet
[Magyar prehistory],
Budapest, 1939.

They settled down in an area lying towards the Sea of Azov. We have plausible evidence of their presence there from as early as the beginning of the sixth century. Later, at the start of the seventh century, they were part of the 'Great Bulgarian' empire of Kouvrát (Krovát) and after its dissolution – when the Danube Bulgars migrated to the west – the Magyars evidently formed the core of Bayan's 'Bulgar' people, who were compelled to yield to the powerful Khazar empire that had arisen by then. They probably dwelt there, in the 'patria Onogoria', up to the beginning of the ninth century, when they transferred their camps to the region between the Don and the Dnieper. This was the territory that Ibn Rusta described as the second of the Magyar boundaries and it might have been the homeland of Levedia out of which the Pechenegs drove them into the Etelköz, the land between the Dnieper and the lower Danube. [p. 74]

MIKLÓS ZSIRAI
'A magyarság eredete'
[The origin of the Magyars].

In: A magyarság őstörténete [The prehistory of the Magyars], ed. L. Ligeti. Budapest, 1943 [Reprinted 1986], pp. 9-35.

Judging by the migrations of the Finno-Ugrian peoples and their subsequent locations, and indeed, according to the deductions of archaeologists, already during the period of Finno-Ugrian union, the Ugrians comprised the eastern flank of the Finno-Ugrians. Even after the break-up of the Finno-Ugrians the Ugrian group remained on the European slopes of the Ural mountains. By the time of this Ugrian period, if not earlier, they had probably begun to filter onto the forested ridges of the Urals and perhaps even onto the Siberian side. A hint supplied by archaeologists is particularly thought-provoking in this regard: the Ananyino bronze culture which is attributed to the Ugrians was also transmitted from East Russia to the eastern side of the Urals, to the region of the Iset, Tobol and Pysma rivers.

We can obtain some information from comparative linguistics about what sort of ethnic environment and external influences the Ugrian people were exposed to and what sort of cultural changes they underwent. In all probability, the numeral *hét* 'seven', of Aryan origin, and *tegez* 'quiver' are borrowings from the Ugrian period, as perhaps are *titok* 'secret', *holló* 'raven', *ara* 'maternal relative (now bride)' and possibly a number of other words. However, there seems to be no convincing proof for assertions that the proto-Ugrian people had significant contacts with other peoples besides the Aryans.

Relying on the inferences of linguistic palaeontology, we have been inclined to assume that a decisive change took place in the Ugrians' way of life, that the cultural level of the proto-Ugrians became much higher than it had been during the period of Finno-Ugrian unity. In particular, it has been usual to emphasize that where the Ugrians had formerly been almost exclusively occupied with hunting and fishing, they began to develop in part as an animal-rearing, and above all equestrian, people. The weightiest argument for this is that whilst there is no common appellation for the horse in Finno-Ugrian languages, and thus the proto-Finno-Ugrians could not have known this species, all the more important horse-breeding and -handling terms are found together in the Ugrian languages: Hu. *ló* ~ Vog. *lù*, *lùw*, Ost. *lau*, etc. 'horse': Hu. *másodfű-ló*, *harmadfű-ló* ~ Vog. *kit pum lùw* 'two-year-old horse': Hu. *nyereg* ~ Vog. *nayrä*, Ost. *noyär* 'saddle'; Hu. *fék* ~ Ost. *pèk* 'halter'. The words *ostor* 'whip' and *kengyel* 'stirrup' which have been drawn into this group of expressions without any misgivings should probably be interpreted somewhat differently: an *ostor* may have been a neutral ability that served to spur on or drive any kind of animal, whereas *kengyel* was originally an equestrian term that was produced after the Hungarian language had begun its separate existence. The latter word is an obscure compound: the first syllable is *kengy* and corresponding to it are Vogul *kéns*, Ostyak *kents*, *kes* 'chaps, leggings': the second syllable is the archaic *al*, *alj*. At any rate, as a result of the debates which have gone on around the equestrian culture of the Ugrians, we can conclude that the proto-Ugrian people migrated down from the former abode of the Finno-Ugrians in the northern forest zone to a region more suitable for breeding animals and keeping horses, in the more southerly wooded steppe. There they were introduced to horses and made use of them, even to some extent bred them, but it is not likely that they were true, out-and-out horse-breeders on a large scale. From the technical terms and expressions it is equally possible to draw the conclusion that the Ugrians gained their knowledge of the horse from one of their neighbours – a Caucasian people according to some, a Turkic people according to others. [p. 32]

ERIK MOLNÁR
A magyar társadalom története az őskortól az Árpád-korig
[Magyar social history from the prehistorical era to the Árpádian age],

2nd ed., Budapest, 1949.

Production: The Magyars' principal branch of production on the steppes of the Kuban region could only have been animal-breeding... [p. 45]

Society: During the initial period of pastoralism the Magyar clan may have been a settlement and migration unit... But with the growth in animal stocks the clans went their different ways because they needed separate grazing-grounds and drinking-places for their enlarged herds and flocks. From then onwards the clans had their winter camps apart from one another, and from spring until the autumn they moved about separately. The separation of clan life is borne out by the tiny communities of early Árpádian-age Hungary and the very small cemeteries of the Conquest period. [p. 62]

Contacts with Turks: The Magyar-Ugrian tribes acquired their knowledge of more advanced methods of animal breeding, as is manifest from the terms of Turkish origin in the Hungarian language, from elements of Turkic pastoral peoples. The Magyars made their appearance in history as an equestrian nomadic people of Turkic culture... The elements of Turkic extraction were distributed among the various social strata... [p....]

The social stratification of the Magyars as they entered into history was based on economic rather than ethno-political grounds. Their ruling caste was not composed of conquering Turks as against a mass of conquered Ugrians but of the wealthy as against a mass of poorer people, without ethnic differences at the same time separating richer and poorer strata. [p.]

ANDRÁS RÓNA-TAS
'A magyar őstörténetkutatásról'
[Research into Magyar prehistory],
Magyar Tudomány, 1980/5.

We are able to trace the history of the Magyars back to a community of fishermen and hunters pursuing a hunter-gatherer type of economy. This community switched to an arable-animal rearing economy and later on became pastoral nomads, rearing large animals. Having attained a distinctive type of nomadism which incorporated a relatively advanced form of agriculture, they arrived in the Carpathian basin. Here they were able to impose the early feudal relations of eastern Europe as the dominant principle within their own socio-economic system and to found a state without losing their ethnic identity by relinquishing their historical continuity. [p. 328]

J. A. HALIKOVA
'Volgai Bulgária és a X. századi Magyarország népessége etnikai rokonságának kérdéséhez'
[The ethnic affiliation of Volga Bulgaria and the population of tenth-century Hungary].
Offprint from Hajdúsági Múzeum Évkönyve, Hajdúböszörmény, 1973.

An interesting feature of early Bulgarian burial customs, parallels to which have been observed in Magyar cemeteries, was the practice of partially burying the horse as well... The presence of kindred clans within the populations of Volga Bulgaria and Hungary made relations between the two states possible throughout the tenth century and, indeed, beyond that right up to the Mongol onslaught... In Anonymus' chronicle (Chapter 57) we read that during the rule of Prince 'Toksun', around 970, two lords of the highest rank (*nobilissimi domini*), the brothers Billa and Bochu, came to Hungary from Bulgaria (*de terra Bular*) with a large retinue, who were already professing the Islamic faith. These lords received grants of property at various places in Hungary, among them the castle of Pest... We find an indirect reference to the fact that Muslims were still living in Hungary later on, in the twelfth century, and were maintaining contact with Volga Bulgaria, in the writings of the Spanish Arab, Abu-Hamid al-Garnati al-Andalusi. He visited the Volga Bulgars on several occasions from the 1230s to 1250s and from there came via Russia to Hungary, for that was where his eldest son, Hamid, lived after marrying the daughters of Hungarian Muslims... [p. 24]

JÁNOS MATOLCSI
'A közép Volga-vidéki finnugor népek állattartása a korai vaskorban'
[Animal rearing among Finno-Ugrian peoples of the mid-Volga region in the early Iron Age].
In: Magyar őstörténeti tanulmányok [Studies in Magyar prehistory], Budapest, 1977, pp. 243-65.

In summary, we may conclude that this examination of the bone material of Ananyino culture and its comparison with the pertinent data in the literature, have led to only partial elucidation of the economic background to the early phase of Magyar prehistory but have resulted in our posing questions that are new in many respects. The evidence of an overwhelming numerical superiority of certain domestic animals at some sites, and the relatively small numbers, or even absence, of the same species at other places, forces us to consider that a variety of economic formations may have existed alongside one another. It is possible, though it does not necessarily follow from our knowledge of the conditions, that the large variance between sites reflects diverse stages in a developmental process. This would provide reason enough for a coordinated study of how the appearance of domestic animals at different points in time, and the different degrees to which they were utilized, are related to other archaeological phenomena. Falling within this, I feel, would be a check on whether there might have been some kind of anthropological or ethnic dimension to the postulated economic formations which is demonstrable at the various sites within a chosen study area. The same question is also raised by the view of A. V. Zbruyeva that the population of Ananyino culture comprised both Mongolid and Europid elements, and that the inhabitants who dwelt there in the Iron Age were multilingual.

With regard to the economy, both forest and steppe elements were intermingled and thus the economic level of the peoples of Ananyino culture in respect of animal breeding was not below the general level of economic development for the region and the era; indeed, in respect of horse and cattle breeding it was even somewhat more advanced. A part in this was probably played by their amply demonstrated contacts with the peoples of the Black Sea region, the Scythians and the cities of antiquity in that locality. [p. 265]

ELEMÉR MOÓR
A honfoglaló magyarság megtelepülése és a székelyek eredete
[The settlement of the Conquest-period Magyars and the origin of the Székely],
Szeged, 1944.

In arguing for a connection between the Székely and the population of western Hungary, there is no way in which one can turn for evidence to certain similar or identical peculiarities of dialect because, as has already been mentioned in other contexts, the modern Hungarian dialects are far from ancient, even if we do not know much about their historical development. And this is despite the fact that in the Székely and western language districts, since they are marginal and isolated areas, it would have been easy for linguistic phenomena to be preserved that long became extinct in the central parts of the Hungarian-speaking area... There may be more significance in the homologies that can be demonstrated between the Hungarian populations of the eastern and western borderlands in respect of the folk custom of wassailing (*regölés*) and the folk texts associated with it. [p. 86]

J. BENZING
'Die angeblichen bolgar-türkischen Lehnwörter im Ungarischen',
Zeitschrift den Deutschen Morgenlandischen Gesellschaft, 98 (1944).

In his work on linguistics, the *Divàn lugat at Turk*, written in 1073, Mahmud of Kashgiria was still unaware of the Z→R and A→Y phonological shifts.

Since, on the basis of the above facts, we have every right to state that the Z→R and A→Y (I) phonological shifts did not occur in Bulgarian before the eleventh century, under no circumstances could the Magyars have borrowed from the Bulgars the loan-words which have hitherto been held to be Bulgarian, because already by then they had no connection of any sort with the Bulgars. [p.]

DEZSŐ DÜMMERTH
Az Árpádok nyomában
[On the trail of the Árpáds],
4th ed., Budapest, 1987.

The historian, if he wishes to penetrate deep into the nation's memory, and thereby that of its first ruling house, cannot avoid a study of the mythological tradition. Indeed, in the absence of other sources, he is compelled to take this as his starting point. [p. 24]

The guiding idea in the texts of the Hungarian chronicles is not just that Álmos' family was descended from Attila but also that the Magyar people itself was an offshoot and successor of the Huns... The chronicles, whose original wordings have been lost and whose 13th-14th century texts were reworked by the hands of rationalist editors, are obscure as to whether the Magyars were a kindred people of the Huns or identical to them. Simon Kézai, priest to the court of Ladislas IV, recognizing his king's sympathy for the nomadic equestrian peoples of the East, was responsible for implanting that sympathy into the public consciousness. He identified descent from the Huns with the nobility's past, with a free and independent life and a martial way of life. From him sprang the idea of a Hun tradition that became the ideology of the nobility up to János Thuróczy's chronicle, which in turn enduringly shaped the fifteenth-century Hungarian historical perceptions that were to form the basis of the later, strictly nobiliary standpoints of Werbőczy's *Tripartitum*. According to the latter, the Huns' descendants in Hungary were the ones who enjoyed noble privileges, whilst the feudal peasantry were descended from prisoners of war who had been captured outside the country, slaves who had submitted of their own accord, or 'cowards' who had disqualifed themselves by refusing to undertake military service. In the course of social development, naturally, this explanation lent itself not only to debarring from the body politic those who were already excluded from privileges, making the past a subject of no interest to them, but also, later on, to suspecting aristocratic sympathies in anyone who did not disabuse himself of the notion of a Hun kinship.

The confusion was further increased when, from the second half of the last century, and with some support from the Habsburg regime, the historical perspective began to change – in a typically Germanic fashion – into a linguistic and racial perspective with the discovery of the Finno-Ugrian origin of the Hungarian language. [p. 25-26]

Nowadays there can no longer be any question of a one-sidedly Hunnic or, for that matter, one-sidedly Finno-Ugrian, perspective. It would be a mistake to deny the Finno-Ugrian basis of Hungary's past, for the language is living proof of it, but mere linguistic researches cannot be made a vital part of our history, because there is nothing, beyond the language's character itself, to act as a memorial to this. It would be a great mistake to close one's eyes to the fact that the language was exchanged, or to the more recent social structure and lifestyle of the martial, equestrian Hun race, if only because they were distorted by the noble ideology in the past. But when the historian is forced to conclude that Hungary's intellectual traditions, and the motifs of the country's social evolution, have more in common with the Huns than with the Finno-Ugrian peoples, he must at the same time conclude that there can also be no question of linguistic and racial identity with the Huns. This is all the more so as in history the designation 'Hun' has a very broad range of connotations. The main evidence of an intellectual affiliation to them lies precisely in the fact that the Magyars of the Conquest period and Árpádian era thought no differently than had Attila's subjects in earlier times. Anyone – provided he was a freeman – who accepted the dynasty's supremacy, and was willing to take up arms to further its goals, counted as a 'Hun' or 'Magyar', whatever the blood in his veins and whatever his language. The free equestrian tribes that galloped across the plains, always ready to conquer but just as liable to fragment, were held together internally by consanguinity only within the framework of family and clan. The individual tribes, however, conglomerated without any reference to race or blood, and they named themselves variously as Huns, Avars, Turks or Magyars.

The historical distortion in the Hungarian nobility's perspective, incidentally, grew out out of this same notion of equating nobility and freedom. Kézai justifiably points out that, in the beginning, all Magyars were 'noble' in the sense of not being anybody's servants." [p. 27]

COUNT ISTVÁN ZICHY
Magyar őstörténet
[Magyar prehistory],
Budapest, 1939.

Summary from the chapter on 'The mental and physical endowments of the Magyars' [pp. 72-73]

Now that we have discussed the problems of Magyar prehistory in some detail, let me summarize briefly how I believe we should picture the evolution of our people, the course of its prehistorical existence.

The ancestors of the modern Voguls and Ostyaks – the Ob-Ugrians – inhabited the territory which was later to become known as Ugria: the upper Kama, the Chusovaya and upper Pechora region. The settlements of the Onogurs were to the south of this forest-clad territory, in the region of the Ufa and Byelaya rivers and on the farther side of the Urals, possibly as far as the Tobol-Ishim region – an area of wooded and open steppe country that was later to become Bashkiria. The forest-dwelling ancestors of the Ob-Ugrians were hunter-fishers, whilst the Onogurs, living on open ground, were animal breeders and arable farmers, although they still continued to trade in furs as well. The Onogurs, with their well-developed social structure, brought the scattered communities of their neighbours under their sway and thereby acquired fur goods from them in tribute. The memory of this rule, which extended ever further northwards with the decline in the populations of fur animals, is preserved in the place-name Ugria and the name 'Ugrian' given to the Voguls and Ostyaks.

The fur-trading tribes of the Onogurs, in the course of time, learned the tongue of their Finno-Ugrian subjects and this may have been transmitted from them to other tribes. These tribes also continued to speak their Turkic tongue for as long as they remained within the Ogur ethnic community, so they became bilingual. This bilingualism must already have been longstanding when the sudden advance of the Sabirs, around 460–65, precipitated the first known migration of Ogur-Turkic peoples. One segment of the Onogurs, among them the great mass of Magyars, moved to the lowlands lying north of the Caucasus, whilst the other – obviously smaller – segment stayed on in their abodes along the Ufa and Byelaya rivers. It was the descendants of these Onogur-Magyars, who already spoke a Finno-Ugrian tongue, whom Julian encountered in the thirteenth century in the region of the Ethil = Byelaya.

We must suppose, therefore, that the Magyars, speaking a Finno-Ugrian language and yet 'Turkic' not only in their culture but also in sharing the same mental complexion as the Turks, had essentially emerged before the fifth century A. D.

We must put this emergence to such an early date because, according to the Arabic and Persian sources and, later still, the evidence of Julian, the traditions of both branches of Magyars preserved the memory of a common origin, and thus this Magyar folk-consciousness must already have developed before their separation. [pp. 72-73]

GYULA KRISTÓ
Levedi törzsszövetségétől Szent István államáig
[From Levedi's tribal federation to St Stephen's state],
Budapest, 1980.

It seems that a portion of the 'Magyars' who migrated southwards out of Magna Hungaria was made up of Turkic-speaking peoples (Bashkirs, Volga Bulgars). This is

also borne out by place-names in the Carpathian basin. Since we know from Džaihàni that of the three 'classes' of Volga Bulgars one was the Barsul and a second the Bulgars themselves, the place-names Bercel and Bolgár which we come across in the old 13th-15th-century toponymics of the Carpathian basin may point to tribal fragments of Bulgars that had merged with the Magyars and came with them into the Carpathian basin. If it could be proved that the Székely were identical with the third population of Volga Bulgars, who were recorded by Dz`aihàni in the form 's. g. l.', then this would lend further support to our declared conjecture that part of the emigrants from Bashkiria were Turkic-speaking... The typical ethnicity of those who set out from Bashkiria to the south was Magyar. The population of the Nyék and Megyer tribes was certainly from the Volga region, as both tribes adverted to their Finno-Ugrian character in their names. The Nyék tribe took its name from the Hungarian word *nyék*, meaning 'enclosure, hedge', which is Ugrian in origin, whilst the Megyer tribal name contains a heritage of the Ugrian period in its first syllable (*magy* is the name for part of the later Magyar, Mansi and Hanti peoples) and of the Finno-Ugrian period in its second syllable {*ar* originally meant 'man'). Nor should we blind ourselves to the possibility that behind one or two other tribal names of Turkic origin may have lain Finno-Ugrian-speaking tribal populations who were pulled into a tribal framework by northwards-migrating Bulgars, whence their Turkic-sounding tribal names... In the ethnogenesis of the Magyars, then, we must also allow a role to certain tribes and tribal fragments which shared the fate of the Pontic Hun, Turkic, Khazar and Onogur empires in south-eastern Europe. These would have been purely Turkish-speaking elements whose names – Hun, *Savarto asphalo*, Turk and, most likely, Ungr (Onugor) – refer to their earlier imperial setting. It is not impossible that the destruction of the system of fortifications on the right bank of the Don which occurred in the 810s was carried out by these peoples, who, having been expelled from Khazaria on to the right bank of the Don as a result of their opposition to Khazar suzerainty, were cutting free altogether from the Khazar empire. These Turkish-speaking peoples may have joined with the tribal grouping of mixed Finno-Ugrian and Turkish speakers that came from the north under Levedi's leadership... [pp. 56-58]

Around 830 the Magyar tribal confederation was brought into being, in the Don region, out of two major ethnic components. The first branch had moved southwards from Bashkiria and in respect of its ethnicity and language was fundamentally Magyar (though with a not unimportant Onogur-Bulgar component); the second had newly detached itself from the Khazar khaganate, had shared the destinies of the peoples and political formations of South-east Europe – the Sabirs, the kindred Khazars, the Onogur empire that had succumbed to conquest by the Khazar khaganate – and in ethnicity and language was Turkic, bearing specific features of both the Common Turkish and Chuvash tongues in respect of its language. We may be sure that Levedi and his tribe came from Bashkiria and that the organization of the heterogeneous tribes and tribal fragments into a unified tribal confederation took place under the control of a Hungarian-speaking chieftain and a leading tribe that for the most part was Hungarian-speaking. [p. 137]

The Conquest

The following selection draws particularly on the works of József Deér, György Györffy and Gyula Kristó.

JÁNOS KARÁCSONYI
A magyar nemzet őstörténete 896-ig
[Prehistory of the Hungarian nation up to 896],
Nagyvárad, 1924.

… Contrary to older opinions and assertions, the truth is that:

1. the Magyars were not an Asian people and never even lived in Asia;
2. the Magyars were never part of the Turkic race and only loan-words from Turkish occur in their language;
3. the Magyars had nothing to do with the Hun nation (they may have been the Huns' subjects but had no linguistic or consanguineous ties with them);
4. the Magyars were only indirectly subjects of the Avars during the years 550-634 but otherwise were not linked with them either linguistically or racially;
5. the Magyars were direct subjects of the Onogur (= Ten Ugurs) Turkic nation from 453 to 710 but after 710 they assimilated the latter into their ranks and thus entered into a certain consanguinity with the western Turks whilst adopting some 200 Ugrian words into their language;
6. the Magyars paid tribute and supplied auxiliary forces as subjects of the Khazar khagan from 710 to 863 but otherwise were autonomous;
7. the Magyars never adopted the Jewish or Islamic faiths because they were obliged to flee from the Khazar empire before these religions had become widespread amongst the Khazars and thus before the Magyars could have been proselytized. [pp. 57-58]

JÓZSEF DEÉR
Pogány magyarság, keresztény magyarság
[Pagan Magyars, Christian Magyars],
Budapest, 1938.

Just as the Turkic khagan, in his speech from the throne, addressed his words first to his family, his clan and his chief notabilities, then to the Turkish beys and people, and last of all to the subject tribes, so too amongst the Magyars everything was now orientated towards the reigning prince, his clan and his tribe and led to the establishment of a hierarchy of distinctly aristocratic character.

The Magyars already possessed this organization when they accomplished the prodigious feat of the Conquest of Hungary, and the occupation of the new homeland took place fully in accordance with the principle of a gradated stratification from the top downwards. The leader, Árpád, was 'wealthier and more powerful' than the other tribal chieftains, and a whole series of privileges were the right of his family, clan and tribe. The leader's people acquired the economically most valuable, the most densely populated and at the same time the best-protected areas within the territory of the new homeland. The settlement pattern of the Magyars consisted of a series of concentric circles, with the individual circles expanding outwards from their centre. The core of this system was made up of the settlement areas of the reigning dynasty – the territories of the later counties of Pilis, Solt and Fejér, and Csepel Island, which had the defences of the Danube. Towards the east these settlement areas were surrounded, fan-like, by the properties of other clans belonging to the leading tribe, which were succeeded in turn by a living defensive screen, formed by the remaining tribes, as far as the marchlands and beyond those to the wild, uninhabited lands that extended up to the natural boundaries. The other tribes that took up positions around the leader's clan and tribe did not do so in a random manner, or by some accident of occupation, but in accordance with a definite plan and, indeed, order of precedence. The Nyék tribe, together with the Kavars, who had allied themselves to the Magyars immediately before the Conquest, and the Székely, who joined forces after the Magyars were already in the new homeland, took up positions as border guards on the peripheries of the country. Indeed, the Kavars, in accordance with the use that nomads customarily made of their tributaries, always provided the vanguard in battle, just as, in the time of the Christian kings, this role was later to fall to the Székely and the Pechenegs, who earned the epithets 'wicked and vile' as a mark of the contempt in which they were held by the Magyars.

All these tribes collectively comprised a political system the control of which lay in the hands of a leader wielding absolute power. He placed relatives and trusted intimates as his warlord at the head of each tribe, and he appointed the two chief dignitaries who ranked immediately below the leader. These two, the *gyula* and *horka*, held judicial posts but, besides that, each was also commander of a tribe which, due to the privileged position of the leader, counted as higher-ranking than the others. The existence of these two dignitaries alongside the reigning prince is evidence of a typically Turkic political organization amongst the Magyars, because the same duality in the chief offices was also observed amongst the Huns, the Turks and the Khazars, the Magyars' long-time rulers.

The *gyula*, who ranked more highly than the *horka*, occupied, with his people, the eastern part of Hungary, whilst the *horka* received the western and south-western parts. This stemmed from an orientation to the right flank, or east, that operated amongst the Turks and Khazars, as did the characteristic of the Conquest-period Magyar rite of interring their dead with the face turned towards the east, in the direction of the rising sun. Thus the Magyars, like the Turks and Khazars, had a cult based on a sun mythology, rather than the lunar cult of the Asian Huns. The sun symbolized their chief deity, who by those times rose as a figure of almost monotheistic purity above the colourful world of demons, a group of both benign and harmful natural spirits. Those few folk tales which have survived to our own day in their original purity, untouched by western motifs – for example, the legends of 'God's Arrow', 'The Castle on Duck's Legs' and 'The Tree of the World' – attest to the same sort of notion of a stratified heaven as the mythology of ancient Turkic inscriptions. Thus the Magyars not only possessed a political organization, concept of power and body of beliefs similar to those of other steppe peoples, but also, beyond this, there was for them an integral connection between these manifestations, an attitude towards the place of human life within the cosmic scheme, which is the most typical characteristic of peoples of this cultural complex.

The Magyar principality was just as much an institution in harmony with the cosmos, and thereby the guarantor of the people's prosperity and welfare, as the Hun empire or the Khazar and Turkic khaganates. Precisely for this reason, the Magyar ruler enjoyed essentially the same authority as the great monarchs of the steppes, his sway over his peoples displaying autocratic, or even despotic, features. As the Byzantine emperor Leo the Wise, who knew them from first-hand experience, wrote: 'Yet this people, which stands under the rule of a single head, is held in check by fear, not by love, and the chiefs subject transgressors to severe punishments.' During the raids in the West those who were not obedient to the orders of leaders were disciplined with the whip. It was an oriental despotism, a political formation which raised the leader to a dizzying height above ordinary mortals.

The tendency for dignities to become hereditary, which is a characteristic of the Turkic type of state organization, is also found amongst the Conquest-period Magyars, with the posts of tribal chieftain and judge remaining in the hands of the same families right up to the close of the pagan era. Just as the Turks had the concept of a ruler's charisma being transmitted to the dignitaries whom he appointed, the Magyars too had their seven princely personages 'of noble birth, mighty in war and unwavering in loyalty' alongside a leader who was 'more distinguished in the affairs of his race and mightier in war'. One group of Magyar clan names bore connotations of wild animals and birds, just like the *Turul* ('hawk') name of the princely clan, so we may suppose that behind these lay similar totemistic percepts and a sense of themselves as some sort of 'elect'. Several old Hungarian family names derive from Turkic titles of dignity; that of the Bő clan, for instance, is a derivative of the Turkish *beg* 'noble, chief'.

The advantages of this tier-like, stratified organization were seen primarily in war. Emperor Leo the Wise, in his *Taktiká*, differentiates those nomad peoples who were under the rule of a 'single head' from those 'lazy peoples under many heads'.

He included the Magyars among the former category and speaks with great admiration of their military discipline. The Conquest-period Magyars, like all nomadic peoples, were inherently warriors [...]

They owed their military successes primarily to the strictness of their political organization, but their equipment, their weaponry and, by no means least, the quality of their horse-stock played a major part. The principal weapon of the Magyars was the bow but hand-combat implements also had an important place. The products of the Norse armoury workshops in Russia found their way to them besides the typical curved sabre of the nomads.

Their marauding expeditions consisted of an unprecedented series of feats of equestrian daring in which the horse was the nomad Magyar's indispensible helpmate. Although they had kept a wide range of domestic animals since the era of Bulgar-Turkic influence, horse-breeding was to remain their chief occupation... According to the metrical data for horse skeletons uncovered from Conquest-period graves, the pedigree of their horses led back to the Tarpan, the purest-bred Eurasian wild horse indigenous to the western parts of the steppe zone, with some admixture from the Mongolian pony, the so-called Taki, through contact with Central Asian peoples. [pp. 52-57]

GYÖRGY GYÖRFFY
'A honfoglalás és megtelepedés'
[The conquest and settlement].
In: Magyarország története [History of Hungary], Vol. I/I, Budapest, 1984.

The Carpathian basin at the end of the 9th century: legend and reality

Around 1200, Anonymus attempted to answer the question as to whom the Magyars encountered when they entered the Carpathian basin. However, since he did not glean sufficient information from the written sources, whilst he scorned the traditions that the people passed down by word of mouth, he tried to give an answer based on a projection of his own age back into the distant past and on deliberate etymologization.

Anonymus' aim was to provide historical justification for the ancestral property rights held by certain aristocratic families. He learnt from these families whom they regarded as their ancestors in the Conquest era, and which counties they had occupied, but in order to create roles for these ancestors in heroic battles, he also needed opponents for the heroes to defeat. He was unable to find these, however, in the written sources available to him (Regino and the *Gesta Ungarorum*). Mainly to meet this requirement, therefore, Anonymus revived the pre-Conquest countries and leaders of the Carpathian basin, partly from the 'countries' of the tenth-century Magyar tribal chieftains who lived on in the tradition, partly from glosses that he attached to place-names.

According to Anonymus, the territory between the Danube and Tisza rivers, from Ungvár to Titel, was inhabited by the leader Salanus, a relative of the Bulgar-Slav khagan (czar). (This name was read by the poet Vörösmarty as Zalán, although Anonymus' orthography would only allow a reading of Salan or Chalan.) A county sherriff (*ispán*), Laborc, whom the Magyars had allegedly hanged at the place where the River Laborc flows into the Bodrog, vas made one of Salanus' subordinates. Marót, leader of the Khazar-populated duchy of Bihar, who bore the epithet 'Mén' (= 'Stallion') on account of his 'numerous mistresses', was turned into the leader of a region where the presence of two villages called Marót-laka (= Marót's abode) betrayed to Anonymus Marót's dwelling-place. In the Nyitra region, according to him, there ruled the Czech leader Zobor, who was hunted down by Huba and his companions and hanged by them on Mount Zobor. The Temes region, according to him, was inhabited by the leader Galád, ancestor of Ajtony (in the Middle Ages several places there went by the name of Galád, and a village of Gilád can still be found there today). In Transylvania the 'Blak' (= Vlach or Wallachian) leader Gyalu ruled; he was defeated by the ancestor of the Gyulas at the place where Gyula castle stands.

The collectors of living folk customs even these days still come across name-explicative legends of this kind according to which place-name X or Y derives from the fact that a person called X or Y died there. From this it is plain that in Anonymus' case we are dealing with folk etymologies associated with toponyms that were mostly from the Árpádian era. In some instances Anonymus was very wide of the mark indeed because the toponym which was made to masquerade as a leader's name did not even derive from a personal name. Thus, the name Zobor is the same word as modern Polish *sabor*, which originally meant 'convent, assembly of monks'. With Gyalu and Galád the geographical names do come from personal names; however, they do not preserve pre-Conquest names but those of tenth-century Magyar property-owners. The fictitious nature of Anonymus' 'Pannonian leaders' is nowhere better characterized than by the fact that contemporary sources mention approximately 20 rulers and major historical personages who played a part in the ninth-century history of the Carpathian basin. Not one of these names is acknowledged by Anonymus: his leading figures are found only in the corpus of Árpádian-age place-names whilst most of the peoples who have a role in his work only had a connection with the Carpathian basin around 1200." [pp. 584-87]

The Wars Prefacing the Conquest

Ever since wave after wave of migration had begun to threaten the Eastern Roman Empire, the shrewd diplomatic device of setting barbarian peoples against one another had become a stock weapon in the armory of the masters of Byzantium. After the collapse of the Avar empire there was no-one left to mobilize against a Bulgaria that was now reinforced with Avar warriors, and Byzantium was powerless in the face of Bulgar attacks. Only in 815, and at the price of great pecuniary sacrifices, did they succeed in establishing a thirty-year peace. After this had elapsed, the West too began to press Bulgaria hard to start the process of embracing Christianity (861-865). The Bulgar Khaganate, forced into peace on the condition that it converted to Greek Orthodoxy, once again became a dangerous adversary to Byzantium when the Byzantine-educated Symeon, son of the zealous Christian convert, Czar Boris, succeeded to the throne (893).

Graeco-Bulgarian hostility broke out in the wake of a restriction in trade that was damaging to Bulgaria. After Symeon's accession, two Greek merchants who enjoyed inordinate influence at the Byzantine court managed to induce Emperor Leo VI to ban Bulgarian traders from Byzantium, restrict their market to Salonika, and impose heavy duties on them. After ineffective protests, Czar Symeon declared war on the Emperor and in Macedonia he beat the Byzantine army that marched against him.

On this, the Emperor requested Magyar assistance against the Bulgars. He despatched the patrician Niketas Skleros by ship to the lower Danube to treat with the Magyar leaders. Laden with gifts, the aristocratic ambassador met with Árpád and Kursan and persuaded them to send an army against Symeon. After the warlord bearing the title of *gyula* and the less powerful senior king, or *kende*, had consented, the Emperor sent a fleet under the command of admiral Eustathios to transport the Magyar army across the Danube. Command of the army was entrusted to Árpád's son, Levente, who was leader of the Kavars, which indicates that only military auxiliaries took part in the raid-like action. Whilst the East Roman general, Nikephoros Phokas, attacked Bulgaria from the south, Levente's army successfully disembarked in the north and in several clashes inflicted defeats on the Bulgars that were severe enough to make it difficult for even Czar Symeon himself to find refuge in the castle of Durostorum (modern Silistra). Having taken many prisoners around Preslav and Madara, the raiding army set off home.

Via the Greek ships that were waiting for them on the lower Danube, they sent word to Emperor Leo that he should ransom the Bulgar prisoners. In response, the

Emperor sent representatives from the capital to Etelköz and complied with their request.

This expedition, which Byzantine sources recount as happening after the solar eclipse of 891 and the death of Patriarch Stephen (893), must be dated to 894 because after it, but still before the Pecheneg attack of 895, Emperor Leo and Czar Symeon took measures that required longer journeys by sea.

In 894, when an anti-Bulgar alliance between Byzantium and the Magyars had come into being to counter the joining of Bulgar and Frankish forces against Moravia, Svatopluk had only the Magyars to turn to as natural allies for help in breaking out of the blockade on trade that Arnulf had imposed against him from Germany to Bulgaria. The Moravian prince probably sent his ambassadors to Árpád and the *kende*, Kursan, in Spring 894 with a request to launch an offensive into the Carpathian basin and attack his enemies, above all in Pannonia. It is almost certainly the memory of this alliance that was preserved in the Legend of the White Horse. According to the more detailed Hungarian chronicles, Svatopluk, son of Prince Marót (= Moravian), made a pact with Álmos' son, Árpád, and Kündü's son, 'Kusid', who was recorded as having been an envoy. The legend has it that Kusid, on Árpád's behalf, presented Prince Svatopluk with a white horse, a saddle and a halter, and received in return a tuft of grass, a pitcher of water and a clump of soil. This latter gesture, which has been interpreted as a purchase of the country, was indeed a nomad rite for entering into a contract. The Bulgar khagan Omurtag concluded the 'Thirty Years' Peace' with Leo V in 815 in accordance with both Christian and Bulgar practice. The Bulgar ceremony comprised the tasting of blood from a dog that had been sundered in two, followed by the Emperor sprinkling a goblet of water on the ground, turning a saddle upside down, touching a halter, and then holding aloft a tuft of grass. The Magyars had the same procedure for concluding an agreement… [pp. 588-590]

Since the middle of the ninth century the princes of Moravia had tried to expand into Pannonia, which, aside from their attempts at conquest, was also connected with efforts directed at building up an independent Church (the only way that they could reach Rome whilst circumventing the Franks was through Pannonia). The means to this end was to be the extermination of the Bavarians in Pannonia, along with their Slav vassals and their colonies, and most likely the capture of the occasional earthwork fortress. If the battles between the Magyars and Moravians in Pannonia that are recorded in the Hungarian chronicles have any basis in tradition, then that preserves a memory of Magyar armies sweeping into Pannonia from the south and the east, on their return from Italy, and clashing with the warriors of Prince Mojmir, who had become the Magyars' enemies with the conclusion of the Frankish-Magyar pact and, having received news of Arnulf's death, themselves wanted to take Pannonia into their possession. According to the Hungarian Chronicle, the Magyars routed the Moravians near Bánhida.

The occupation of Pannonia was facilitated by the fact that the repeated Moravian ravages had sapped the Frankish-Bavarian property-owning class, along with their retainers and scanty settlers, and forced them to flight. At the same time, the capture of forts with earthwork defences, such as Zalavár, could hardly have presented much of a problem to the Magyars who only the previous year had taken Modena in Lombardy, despite its stone-wall defences, and had even made an attempt to seize Venice.

The depleted Slovene population of Pannonia did not flee the country; however, a radical change in their settlement pattern ensued. Most of the Slav names given to streams in the Balaton region, western Transdanubia and the Drava region survived, but all place-names fell into disuse and the ninth-century cemeteries were shut down. On the other hand, it is likely that the clan organization of the Slavones remained intact south of the River Drava.

The upshot of the Magyar-Moravian conflicts in Pannonia was that in 900 the Magyar armies, advancing north of the Danube, took over Moravia's possessions in the Nyitra region. That the Little Alföld, up to the border with Great Moravia in the Little Carpathians, came under Magyar rule during 900 at the latest is evident from the fact that in the autumn of that year a Magyar army set off against Bavaria from the northern bank of the Danube.

By the summer of 900 the whole of the Carpathian basin had fallen into the hands of the Magyars; the border territories had still to be secured and recognition in law obtained before the settlement process could be completed.

In the summer of 900, Árpád and Kursan sent envoys to Lewis III the Child, the Franks' new emperor, with an offer of peace. The Magyar leaders plainly wanted to gain recognition of their occupation of Pannonia and the Moravian marchlands. Since the Frankish court was unwilling to renounce this part of Charlemagne's conquests in favour of the 'new Avars' and repudiated the envoys, branding them as spies, two Magyar armies advanced on Bavaria out of the Little Alföld in the course of the autumn – the larger one on the left (northerly) bank of the Danube, the smaller one on the right bank. The southern army ransacked 'above the Enns', in Upper Austria, and returned home with much booty; the northern group, however, suffered a defeat from the army of the Margrave Luitpold and Richard, Bishop of Passau. The Bavarians then began hastily to construct the stone castle of Ennsburg.

The loss of the Bavarian and Moravian marchlands and the establishment of a new 'Avar' suzerainty brought deadly enemies together. In January 901 Moravian envoys appeared at Regensburg seeking peace. The Bavarian and Moravian leaders both there and in Moravia cemented the pact and the alliance on oath. The anti-Magyar alliance, preparing to counter-attack, did not remain inactive. There are isolated references in chronicles for the years 901-902 which apprise us of a Magyar defeat in the Frank-Moravian-Magyar borderlands; this prompted the Magyar princes to a decisive military campaign in the autumn of 902. As the entry for this year in the Swabian Annals – 'War with the Hungarians in Moravia, and the country was overcome' – betrays, the Magyars destroyed the Kingdom of Great Moravia in its own homeland. In 906 Regino was recounting as an event that was already in the past the fact that after Svatopluk's death (894) 'his sons held on to his country uneasily for a short while, and the Hungarians razed everything to the ground'... [pp. 602-603]

According to Anonymus, Árpád's summer quarters, from April to October, were on Csepel Island, and this was where he kept his horse-breeding stock. The site of his winter quarters is indicated by the village name Árpád, near the Roman city of Sopianae, the '*Quinque basilicae*' of the ninth century (modern Pécs). Consequently, Árpád would appear to have shuttled between Csepel and Pécs, on the right bank of the Danube; presumably leaving the Danube at the fording place of Szekcső (modern Dunaszekcső) which was visited by Mohamedan travellers; judging by the positions of his sons' quarters, however, he also owned the left bank of the Danube along this section.

Árpád's partner in the dual leadership, Kündü's son, Kursan, who inherited the rank of *kende*, is said by Anonymus to have chosen Óbuda, another ruined city of antiquity, as the site for his winter court. South of the military camp at Aquincum, one can still see today the large amphitheatre that in the Middle Ages, when its walls were still standing high, was called Kurszánvár ('Kursan's castle'). The Danube fording-place of Megyer that went with it was between Békásmegyer (Buda) and Káposztásmegyer (Pest); on its Buda bank lay a village of Slav pottery-makers whereas neighbouring Budakalász was originally a settlement of Muslims of Khwarizmian stock. A toponymic trace of Kursan's summer quarters also survived on one of the larger islands in the Danube, Korszán (1268) in the Danubian Lowland of the Csallóköz or Velky´ Ostrov Z˘itny´, and it is therefore likely that he owned the right bank of the Danube between Budapest and Győr. One can conjecture that after the overthrow of Moravia in 902 Kursan wanted to locate his summer quarters still further up the Danube, in the Viennese basin; it was to this area that the Bavarians sent a peace delegation to him in 904 and treacherously killed him at the welcoming banquet.

One of the big questions for early Hungarian history is the change in the style of leadership that ensued after 904.

DEZSŐ DÜMMERTH
Az Árpádok nyomában
[In the footsteps of the Árpáds],
4th ed., Budapest, 1987.

The Árpád who met Bishop Methodius likewise represents a special and remarkable type of personal development in a monarch. We still do not know as much about the life of Árpád and Álmos as we do about Attila, but it is characteristic that even Bulchu, the rival of Árpád's descendants, was unable to dispel the perception of Árpád as a 'Great Prince', which in this context points not simply to his authority in itself but also, from what we know of his character, to spiritual attributes. These attributes, which strike one as unusual in the barbarian era, may be conceived as further developments of a personality type. Attila, out of what is still some nebulous sense of dread, spares a Rome that was at his mercy. Árpád, however, is already a 'freethinker': he sees no offence against his ancestor's religion in also believing in the prayers of a faith that is alien to him but at a higher cultural level; indeed, he becomes absorbed in a lengthy discourse with a Christian bishop. All this definitely suggests a high degree of cultivation and sensitivity for the conditions of his era." [p. 114]

GYULA KRISTÓ
'Törzsek és törzsnévi helynevek'
[Tribes and tribal-name toponyms].
In: Magyar őstörténeti tanulmányok [Studies in Magyar prehistory], Budapest, pp. 222-223.

According to István Dénes 'the Magyar tribes... had already been brought together under a unified command in pre-Conquest times', whilst in the tenth century 'the leading role of the central authority was continually strengthened, despite the occasionally independent foreign relations and enterprises of individual tribes, and the preconditions for the creation of a state had evolved by the end of the century'. It cannot be our task here to give a historiographically complete account of all the viewpoints on this question that have been expressed in recent years in the specialist literature; at best it has only been possible, here and now, to point out the main trends.

The sort of risks that threaten the specialist literature, as it tries to steer a course between the Scylla and Charybdis of nation and tribal alliance, with the tribes themselves being relegated to the background, are shown not only by the contradictions that may be detected in various works but ultimately by the very facts of tenth-century Hungarian history. In 1958 György Györffy published an essay entitled 'From Magyar clan to county organization, from tribe to country' in the historical journal *Századok*. The third chapter of Antal Bartha's book on *Magyar Society in the Ninth and Tenth Centuries* was given the heading 'From tribal federation to state'. On this, Gusztáv Heckenast noted, in his review of Bartha's book, that 'the chapter bears the title 'From tribal federation to state' but in the end what is found there does not convince one that the political structure of the Conquest-period Magyars was merely a tribal federation'.

The contradictions and risks will not be eliminable until we again begin to accept that tribal arrangements played an extremely important part in the political and ethnic organization of the tenth-century Magyars.

Although there is not space to document the claim in detail, we can broadly outline the elements that prompt this final conclusion. It is not permissible to write the tribes out of tenth-century Hungarian history when: 1) Emperor Constantine, the main Byzantine source on the Conquest and the first half of the tenth century, does not mention any Magyar clans in contrast to the clans of e.g. the Pechenegs, but only writes about tribes; 2) the Byzantine ruler does not speak about Magyar tribes in a general sense, in the way that Leo the Wise – departing in some places from his source, Mavríkios – did, but he actually lists the tribes by name; 3) 'it reinforces the emperor's credibility... that the names of our tribes can be traced in Hungarian place-names'; 4) the one-time existence of the seven tribes mentioned by Constantine is decisively confirmed by Anonymus' information, independently of Constantine, about the *Hetumoger* (Seven Magyars); 5) granted the many onslaughts on the trustworthiness of the emperor's intelligence relating to the tribes, with remarks about the two different levels of his text and the precariousness of his chronology, it is nevertheless indisputable that in speaking about his own era, about conditions around the year 950, he refers to the eight clans of the Magyars (seven of them Magyar and one Kavar) as a political reality: 'These eight tribes of the Turks do not obey their own particular princes but have a joint agreement to fight together with all earnestness and zeal upon the rivers, wheresoever war breaks out'; 6) it similarly adverts to the existence and political reality of the Magyar tribes around 950 that the Byzantine emperor, in the mid-tenth century, should address his letters 'to the princes of the Turks (= Magyars)', unlike his use of the address 'to the khagans of Khazaria', yet according to Constantine's own information 'each tribe has a prince' alongside the dignitaries of the tribal confereration (a first chief, who came by succession from Árpád's family, and also the γυλας (Gylas) and the χαρχας (Karchas), to whom the above information that the eight tribes 'do not obey their own particular princes' must relate; 7) 'King Stephen himself, in order to secure absolute power, was obliged to clash with the lords of tribally partitioned territories: Koppány of the Somogy country, Gyula of Transylvania, and Ajtony of Marosvár, who held the Tisza-Maros region', all of whom – and here we might also add Vata of the Békés region – since we know the approximate extent of their settlement areas, were indeed probably more tribal chiefs than clan heads; 8) the outline that emerges from our earlier analysis was that once Géza and Stephen had crushed the tribal centres in their struggles against the rebellious leaders, the populations of free herdsmen and free peasants who broke away from the late tenth-century and eleventh-century tribal constraints could only have kept alive the idea of still belonging to a tribe whilst they moved around the country, and could only have established places bearing tribal names when they settled down on a strange territory, if the tribes whose memory they preserved had been a political reality, at least up to the turn of the tenth and eleventh centuries.

So to our fourth question, we can give the following answer: from our investigations it would seem that it is of prime importance for research into Magyar prehistory to ponder whether the most stable and strongest political institution and ethnic framework in tenth-century Hungary was not the tribe, as against those concepts which lay great stress on either the clan on the one hand, or the tribal confederation on the other, or both equally. And if the analysis here should hold its ground, the results of our investigation can hardly be without consequences for the more strictly defined area of Magyar prehistory in respect of the way that the tenth century, and possibly even earlier centuries, are judged.

On the question of place-names, I see as decisive one of the points made by Samu Szádeczky-Kardoss in his published paper 'A contribution to the question of the double Conquest', delivered to the Szeged Group of the Classical Studies Society (Szeged, 1971), namely, that we have nothing to go on for determining the dates when Hungarian place-names were bestowed after the fall of the Roman empire and before the practice of documentary recording began in Hungary in the eleventh century. To this we may add that it is only historical instinct which dictates a firm belief that all the early Hungarian-language place-names derive from Árpád's Magyars. According to the hypothesis of a double Conquest, a significant portion of these place-names are memorials to the Magyars of the first Conquest. [pp. 222-223]

P. VERES
'Les antécédants de la conquête du pays par les Hongrois'.
In: Les anciens hongrois et les ethnies voisines à l'Est, ed. I. Erdélyi, Budapest, 1977, p. 283-305.

The reasons for the Conquest

In the era of the Great Migrations, which coincided with a period of wetter climate, the Magyar tribes nomadized the steppes of West Siberia and Kazakhstan in the Black Sea region, in the Khazar Khaganate, which was more favourable to their semi-nomadic way of life. Adapting, little by little, to a sedentary mode of life, they came under inter-ethnic influences and borrowed Turkic loanwords of a Bulgar-Chuvash character which attest to the existence of agriculture. This symbiosis of plough-farming and nomadic animal breeding in the culture of the Magyar tribes is confirmed by linguistics as well as by Arabic sources of the period.

The temporary drought which commenced at the turn of the ninth and tenth centuries, and which destroyed the cultures and farming peoples that had flourished until then on the East European steppe (*inter alia* with the settlement of the nomads) also spelled ruin to the mixed farming economy of the Magyars in the Etelköz. Instead of adapting to the new environment of the dry steppe, the Magyars chose to move over the western perimeter of the steppe into the Carpathian basin, with its milder, less drought-susceptible climate.

Under the more favourable environmental conditions of the Danube basin, they were able to pursue their old mixed farming economy. The occupation of the final homeland in 896 was an economic necessity, a consequence, above all, of the environmental change and the economic difficulties in adapting that this change entailed. This conclusion is borne out by a great many facts, both direct and indirect. [p. 305]

The anthropology of Árpád's Magyars

PÁL LIPTÁK
A magyarság etnogenézisének paleoantropológiája [Palaeo-anthropology of the ethnogenesis of the Hungarian people].
Doctoral dissertation, Szeged, 1967.

a) Most characteristic of the ruling stratum are the Turanid, Uralic, Pamirian and other brachycranial racial elements.

b) The anthropological picture of the middle stratum differs markedly from that of the ruling stratum, even though the racial components that make up the middle stratum were also demonstrable, in smaller proportions, in the ruling stratum. The most essential components of this warrior caste were the Mediterranean, Nordoid (this might also be a tall, robust Mediterranean type) and Pamirian races. It is highly characteristic, and significant, that the Turanid and Uralic races are almost completely missing from this stratum.

c) The anthropological components of the common people can be characterized on the basis of large series of examples. If these are taken together, the Mediterranean and Nordoid components are the most notable, as with the middle stratum, but there is additionally a significant Cromagnoid contribution. In general the Cromagnoid-A race is found in a higher ratio: however, in some instances Cromagnoid-B components also have a considerable share in the population, and this – precisely because of its rarity – must be regarded as a characteristic feature. [pp. 9-10]

Culture and Settlement

A number of fairly brief quotations are presented to show how Hungarian researchers, following various approaches, have attempted to describe the culture and economy of the Árpádian Magyars.

ISTVÁN KNIEZSA
'Magyarország népei a XI.-ik században' [Peoples of Hungary in the ninth century].
In: Szent István Emlékkönyve [St Stephen memorial volume], Vol. II, Budapest, 1938.

The Magyars of the Conquest did not occupy the whole country all at once, but in stages. Whilst they had already settled in some regions by the early tenth century, they effectively took possession of other territories only in the eleventh, twelfth, and even the thirteenth or fourteenth centuries… In coming to our conclusions about the settlement areas of the Magyars in the tenth and eleventh centuries, three types of evidence have been utilized: 1) historical, 2) linguistic, and 3) archaeological.

1) Historical evidence: a) data relating to the settlement areas of the conquering tribes… b) data relating to the border defence of Hungary in the Árpádian age…

2) Linguistic evidence: a) place and personal names of Magyar origin that occur in sources deriving from the eleventh century or, at latest, from the beginning of the twelfth century; b) the Magyar names for the centres of the oldest 'royal counties'; c) place-names which were formed from the names of Conquest-period Magyar tribes; d) Hungarian places-names of Slavic origin in which the original Slavic nasalized vowels [õ] and [ẽ] were retained. […] In the north of Hungary, near the Slovakian territories, there is another phonetic peculiarity that is of value in dating, namely, the [g] > [h] change of Slovakian. g) Hungarian place-names in which Hungarian [g] corresponds to Slovakian [h] point to a somewhat earlier period.

3) Archaeological evidence. [p. 369]

We can compare the oldest borderline of the area of Magyar settlement which is verifiable using modern data with the contour of the beech and pine forests. Obviously, the Magyars, as a fishing and animal-breeding people, occupied only those territories which were suited to their accustomed lifestyle in every respect; dense beech and pine forests, however, since they lack a grassy undergrowth, were not suitable for this mode of life… Our map shows the correctness of this proposition quite well. From the ninth century onwards, however, the beech-line can no longer be considered an obstacle to encroachment by the Magyars… [p. 374]

… it is certain that fragments of the Avars nevertheless held on in many places, possibly in considerable numbers. We know that even in 875 the Avars of western Hungary were still living under their own khagans between Sabaria (Szombathely) and Lower Austrian Carnuntum (Deutsch-Altenburg), where Charlemagne had allowed them to settle in 804, at their own request. We may conjecture, however, that considerable numbers of Avars also remained in places beyond the reach of Frankish authority, especially on the great plain of the Alföld. [p. 434]

GYULA KRISTÓ
'Szempontok korai helyneveink történeti tipológiájához'
[Considerations for a historical typology of early Hungarian place-names],
Acta Universitatis Szegediensis, LV (1976).

In this article, Kristó sets out his concerns about the methods employed by István Kniezsa.

... the process of creating toponyms from tribal names cannot have ended in the early of middle eleventh century but carried on for centuries after that... Thus it is certainly necessary to relax the rigidity of a typological dating which, regardless of circumstances, has place-names that derive from (or are homomorphic with) tribal names as being minted solely and exclusively in the tenth century (or possibly into the first half of the eleventh century)... Through the place-names of tribal origin he gives a picture of only a relatively small number of the tribal fragments which ended up in the environs of foreign tribes. To be sure, he gives information on the direction and countless sites of the dispersion (forced settlement, as the specialist literature wrongly calls it) for barely a handful. [pp. 42-43]

But a new concept of dating was already gaining currency by the late 1940s. László Makkay listed place-names that were derived from purely ethnic names together with those derived from tribal names, in other words, restricting their dating to the tenth century... These ethnic names [Kazár = Khazar, Káliz = Khwarizmian, Székely, Varsány] have unjustifiably been placed in the same group as the tribal names. [p. 58]

With regard to the service peoples: Yet in what way does Györffy explain how his supposition of the very existence of a system of (barbarian) service-peoples was possible at all – or justified – among the Magyars of the tenth century? By reference to the Mongol analogy. On this extremely important point it is again necessary to cite Györffy's own words: 'The pattern of settlement of the Conquest-period Magyar leaders was so similar to that of the Golden Horde's first leaders that we may also postulate similar arrangements in respect of service peoples'. In other words: because in an earlier study Györffy considered that the movements of thirteenth-century Mongol aristocrats up and down river banks were also applicable to tenth-century Magyar notables – quite groundlessly in view of climatic conditions in the Carpathian basin – this now becomes the basis of, and evidence for, a hasty, unwarranted and arbitrary analogy for the existence and nature of a Magyar utilization of service-peoples... Thus the quite arbitrary Mongol analogy leads, without any kind of evidence being given, to the avowal of an advanced and, from a class view-point, stratified tenth-century Magyar society. [p. 70]

ISTVÁN SZABÓ
A falurendszer kialakulása Magyarországon (X-XV. század)
[Evolution of the village system in Hungary (10th to 15th centuries)],
Budapest, 1966.

Before settling in the Carpathian basin, the Magyar people had lived for a long period on the great Eurasian steppe. That was what had nourished them, nurtured them, formed them. The contemporary sources – mainly Arabic, Persian and Greek – whose writers, in the ninth and tenth centuries, were the first to take notice of the Magyars living in the lands of Lebedia and the Etelköz, recorded for us the characteristic features of nomad peoples of the great steppe... [p. 7]

... during the 1-1½ centuries that they spent in the region between the Danube and Tisza rivers the Magyars in general became village-dwellers and house-builders. [p. 10]

The Magyar people, in the 1-2 centuries after their arrival from the steppe into their new homeland, which in many respects can be regarded as the most westerly extension of the Eurasian steppe... showed a very rapid development of permanent settlement into villages... It cannot be left out of the reckoning that the Slavic population encountered by the Magyars during their occupation of Hungary's territory, principally in the western half of Transdanubia and the northwestern districts, were by then already living in permanent village settlements, and that their dwellings, mean though they might have been, were fixed structures. [p. ll]

Hitherto it has already been acknowledged by Hungarian researchers that the formation of the first stratum of the Magyar village system was synonymous with the transformation of the nomadic winter quarters into permanent villages. [p. 14]

The quarters were always on the banks of a lake or stream: this was indispensible for the watering of their animals. [p. 17]

GUSZTÁV HECKENAST
Fejedelmi (királyi) szolgálónépek a korai Árpád-korban
[Princely (royal) 'service' peoples in the early Árpádian era],
Budapest, 1970.

Depending on the nature of their occupations, the service peoples were able to meet the obligations placed on them in two ways: either they could work a certain amount of time for their master, or they could supply a certain agreed amount of goods... The preparation of valuable, not readily available raw materials could not be entrusted to craftsmen working in their own dwellings. Thus the smiths at Pannonhalma monastery, of whom 23 who lived at Nyalka, six at Keresztur, two each at Varsány and Alsók, and four at Tepeje, travelled to work in the allodial forge-shops... Nor were peasant dwellings the places where spinning and weaving were carried out for landowners but a *gynaeceum* or *pysalia* specially built for the purpose. Accordingly, the great majority of service peoples merely kept house in their own hamlets whereas the services that they rendered – which tended to provide the name for their dwelling-places – were not carried out there but at some manorial centre. [pp. 77-78]

FERENCE MAKSAY
A magyar falu középkori településrendje
[The settlement pattern of the medieval
Hungarian village],
Budapest, 1971.

It may be taken for granted that the winter quarters of the loosely conglomerated peoples of the ninth to tenth centuries quite soon – as early as the beginning of the tenth century – began to fragment into their component parts with the advent of more secure times. Some of the better-defended herdsmen's settlements, which survived somewhat longer, may have fallen victim to the reorganizing and regrouping operations which commenced during the reign of Prince Géza: they were crushed as the refuges of the old order.

Typical of the period beginning in the mid-tenth century were hamlets that lay a good few kilometres apart and gave space, certainly at first, to a few clans, then, with the ever-increasing fragmentation of the clan-structure, to an average of 30-40 family households. Subsequently these tended to cast off further settlement-groups rather than grow in size. This was necessitated, not just by the custom of summer-quartering, but also by the spread of agriculture, for ploughlands had to be close to the dwelling-places. Archaeological researches have demonstrated the establishment and increasing fixedness of these settlements – a few thousand in number – by unearthing traces of many cemeteries and settlements that were in continuous use for at least one to two hundred years after the Coquest. Within a short time they covered practically all the land that was suitable for settlement, smaller populations in much of the Alföld and larger ones in more developed Transdanubia. In the Csongrád area the settlements were arranged 1.5-3 km apart, and the distance was equally small in Békés and the Bodrogköz: within a 7 km radius around Téglás, in the northern part of the Tiszántúl region, traces have been found of 13 pre-Mongol Conquest settlements. Only tracts of land that were completely unserviceable for agricultural purposes at the time (e.g. the Hánság and Rétköz) remained uninhabited, being fringed by villages with extensive lands.

The majority of the Conquest-period and tenth-century hamlets that we have been dealing with up to now continued to be 'winter quarters'; in other words, quite apart from any change in site that might have occurred with the passage of time, during the milder part of the year some or all of their inhabitants sought pastures for their animals, and summer quarters for themselves, in the surrounding countryside. However, the area within which this seasonal migration could take place shrank continuously, just as did the numbers of families and family members engaged in open-range herding that would set out each year. This was the result of the smaller size of the new country compared with the old, then the spread in use of the plough and the slow acceptance by local populations and settled captives of a more sedentary way of life. Some temporary herdsmen's (and fishing) settlements encroached quite closely on winter quarters, or even became directly attached to them; in some places they occupied two or three times the space of the settlement's core territory, as the diggings at Doboz and Kardoskút have shown. Other summer quarters were kept out in the open on distant islands or meadows, as is suspected, for example, in the Bodrogköz. Life was little different whether the people lived close to or remote from settlements: copious quantities of the characteristic relics of the material culture of these semi-nomads, who sheltered in tents or makeshift 'seasonal' huts and prepared their meals, steppe-style, in stewpots over open fires, will still be being found in Hungary – but apart from here, only on the steppe-lands that lie to the east – for centuries to come.

IVÁN BALASSA
'A néprajztudomány és a magyar őstörténet'
[Anthropology and Magyar prehistory].
In: Az Őshazától a Kárpátokig [From ancient homeland
to the Carpathians], ed. V. Szombathy, Budapest, 1985, pp. 72-107.

Right up to the era of land drainage, the water chestnut (*Trapa natans*) – Hungarian *sulyom*, or *suly* in the Transdanubian dialect – was of great significance as a dietary supplement. It used to be cultivated in great quantities, and to some extent still is grown, in shallow-watered, muddy-bottomed marshes. An annual plant, it has a cylindrical stem up to two metres long; its rhomboid leaves appear at the water surface only in June. The fruit, which usually has five spines, begins to ripen in August and September: its taste and nutritional value rival those of the sweet chestnut. The Hungarian name of the water chestnut is probably of Finno-Ugrian derivation, being the back-vowel counterpart of the *sül* – or *sün* – in the word for 'hedgehog' – a parallel which supports the idea that both plant and animal were named for their spiny appearance…

The floating sweet-grass or manna-grass (*Glyceria fluitans*) is one of the most important marsh plants, thriving on water margins. Growing to one meter or more in height and slow to ripen, so that it readily drops its seeds, it is known both in Europe and in Asia. It was generally harvested by women, who would hold a sieve below its spikes to catch the grain as it was knocked loose from the plant. The dried manna-seeds were boiled in milk or as a gruel or might be made into a mush. The possibility has been raised that 'manna-grass' may have be the earliest connotation of the Hungarian word *köles* (now meaning 'millet'), which in the Ugric language had the sense of 'flour, gruel'. That *köles* may once have had the connotation 'Glyceria fluitans' has been deduced from the fact that, starting in the twelfth century, the geographical name Köleser is commonly encountered, though it was not customary to name rivers after cereals.

Among many other edible marsh plants with a long history, mention should also made of the *gyékény* 'reedmace' (*Typha latifolia* and *T. angustifolia*; the Hungarian word is of pre-Conquest Old Turkic origin), which is an extraordinarily rich source of starch, as well as the *elecset* 'flowering rush' (*Butomus umbellatus*), which resembles the *káka* 'bulrush' and hence is sometimes called 'flowering bulrush' in Hungarian. In the past, the rhizomes of both the reedmace and flowering rush were a common staple food, later on a standby in leaner times, being used to make a mush or porridge, sometimes a type of scone or griddle-cake. It is known that these plants were not only familiar to the peoples of North-eastern Europe and Asia but also used by them for food.

The above few pieces of information may serve to convince us that the gathering and utilization of edible marsh-growing plants have a history going far back into the past. The Magyars of the Conquest brought this knowledge with them, as is corroborated, among other things, by the Finno-Ugrian, Ugric or Old Turkic origin of their names Elements of similar antiquity have likewise been preserved until recent times by bee-keeping, which right up to the middle of the last century was carried out in a manner which had changed little, or not at all, over centuries or millennia. It is well known that the Hungarian words *méh* 'bee' and *méz* 'honey' belong to the most ancient stratum of the Finno-Ugrian language, but to this it has been possible more recently to add the words *odú* and *ereszt*, originally meaning 'beehive' and 'swarm', respectively. The element *fedemes* which frequently occurs in geographical names may have meant 'beehive, apiary' and was bestowed primarily on villages that supplied honey to the landowner. Votyak *podam* 'beehive fashioned from a tree hollow' is a morphological equivalent. Hungarian *lép* 'honeycomb', also of Finno-Ugrian derivation, is connected with the above. Another Hungarian word that fits into this series is the originailly Old Turkic *köpü* 'beehive', and this completes the picture of a coherent beekeeping vocabulary which without any doubt has a significance extending beyond mere scavenging for honey The importance of apiculture is further emphasized by the presence of a good many bee-keepers amongst the service peoples of the eleventh century. This is hinted at by geographical names: however, that fact alone is not sufficient so one may add the further potential evidence provided by the 'rock hives' that can be found mainly in North-eastern Hungary. These are regular cavities of variable size that were hollowed out of rocks and used in the eleventh and twelfth centuries: in the view of experts, they may have been suitable for beekeeping. Although counterparts to them are also seen in the Balkans, the links would seem to point more in the direction of Saltovo-Mayatsk culture or the Crimea and Caucasus regions. Detailed investigation of this remains a task for the future, but there is no doubt that the keeping, and some handling, of bees in straw 'skeps', wooden hives or even rock cavities demanded of bee-keepers a settled mode of life.

I have already made reference to the major role that water played in the life of the early Magyars. We have yet to mention fishing – both passive and active methods – in this connection. It is commonly thought that fishing is the best researched area of Hungarian ethnography. I would like to modify this if only to say that it was the area where work commenced the earliest and where the prehistorical implications of the findings were the first to be explored. The classical work of Ottó Herman, though soon due to celebrate the centenary of its publication, remains the foundation of all research into fishing. Several years after its appearance, Bernát Munkácsi undertook an etymological study of the Hungarian vocabulary of fishing, and this was followed by János Jankó's investigation of the origins and affinities of Hungarian fishing in which, ahead of his time, he drew on the huge Russian literature and significant field-work to examine the subject. He showed that a major part of the implements and methods of Hungarian fishing originated from pre-Conquest times, thereby demonstrating that even then fishing already played an important role in the life of the Magyars.

More than eight decades later, the time is certainly ripe for a close scrutiny of the fruits of Jankó's epochal work. The available Hungarian material, both ethnographic and historical, has grown many times over. Sadly, however, we have yet to find a researcher with a sufficient grasp of the subject, particularly in its wider East European context, to venture a new synthesis.

Some partial results of minor note have emerged, it is true, but nobody has summarized this important branch of activity, which again called for a lifestyle that was to some degree sedentary.

I cannot undertake here to set out the pre-Conquest elements of Hungarian fishing as this would be a task for a separate volume in itself.

All I can do is state in general terms that they include numerous larger and smaller implements and procedures whose appellations, forms, history and affinities are proof that their provenance must be sought before the Conquest. It suffices for me to mention fish-weirs or garths (Hu. *vejsze*), that is, labyrinths constructed from reeds, or possibly cane, from which a fish, once it had entered, is unable to escape. The Hungarian word *para* 'cork float for net' – indeed, the word *háló* 'net' itself – can be traced back to the Finno-Ugrian era, as can *hajó* 'ship', which is still used in dialect with its original meaning 'canoe'.

Contacts with the fishing practices of the early Turkic peoples are indicated by the adoption of their word *gyalom* for larger-sized trawl nets and *káta* for the bag end of the net, which also go back to the distant past. A gang of men was needed to handle these huge nets, which could be several hundred metres' long... [pp. 78-81]

KÁROLY MESTERHÁZY
Nemzetiségi szervezet és az osztályviszonyok kialakulása a honfoglaló magyarságnál
[Clan organization and the emergence of class relations among Magyars of the Conquest period].
Thesis for Candidate's degree, Budapest, 1976.

We are able to make deductions about the way of life of the Conquest-period Magyars from the density and nature of tenth-century settlements. What are, for us, the best-known Árpádian-era settlements and cemeteries, at the more thoroughly explored archaeological sites in the present-day counties of Hajdú and Bihar, especially in the Biharkeresztes district, indicate a settlement pattern that already in the tenth century was of a density that the written sources would lead us to suppose was only reached by the late eleventh century. The distances of settlements, both large and small, from one another was in places no more than 1.5-2 km... The density of settlements which has emerged from archaeological surveys is at odds with a shifting nomadic economy and even a semi-nomadic style of life. The character of the tenth-century settlements likewise speaks for a sedentary lifestyle. [p. l]

We can trace the remains of two large groups of Conquest-period Magyars back towards the east in two directions. Relics of the leadership and middle strata are found mainly in Bashkiria and to its south (Tankeyevka, Bolshiye Tarkhani, Bolshiye Tigani, Tyetyushi), whilst finds typical of the Magyar common people have come to light chiefly in the region of the former province of Poltava, the Chernigov area, and along the Oka river. [p. 3]

GYULA LÁSZLÓ
'A magyar őstörténet régészete'
[The archaeology of Magyar prehistory].
In: A magyarság őstörténete [Prehistory of the Magyars], ed. L. Ligeti, Budapest, 1943 [Reprinted 1986], pp. 191-207.

Burial everywhere is regulated by strict laws; there can be no question that this phenomenon [the regular placing of sword, bow and arrows on the opposite side of the body to where they were worn in life] was the result of carelessness. Burial in this fashion is still the custom to the present day amongst most of the Altaic peoples; moreover, the reason given is that they conceive of the other world as a continuation – albeit a mirror picture – of this life. In the life beyond the left hand becomes the right hand, and what was on the right side ends up on the left side. The fact that the same explanation and the same method of interment are encountered equally amongst Christian, Buddhist or Islamic peoples indicates a provenance from the times before the great world religions. In this way, then, we can trace the custom up to roughly the era of the Magyar Conquest, so there is no methodological objection to the comparison and there is no danger of our falling into the trap, well known to ethnography, of reading the sense of some secondary explanation into the Conquest-period Magyars' belief in an afterlife.

The exchange of left for right and burial with a skinned horse are no longer regular unities amongst the Conquest-era Magyars. I have already noted that one observes great variation in the placing of the horse bones. We may guess that individualization of the former culture, the beginnings of its disintegration, must be at the back of this. Thus we see reflected in the graves the same symptoms as can be observed in post-Conquest political behaviour. After a prolonged internal development of their culture, the Magyars stood on the brink of cultural change as the bearers of an exhausted hyperculture. That was why it was able to assimilate so rapidly the Christian civilization of North-west Europe. I see behind this cultural change an amalgamation of the distinct cultures of the equestrian nomad and the peasant and the emergence of modern Hungarian man. However, we are not yet in a position to see clearly the exuberance of the process at that time; a great deal of detailed work will be needed to sort out clearly the specific questions that ought to be addressed and obtain a final answer to the question of the origin of the culture outlined above. We may, perhaps, never be able to study the subsequent course of the process because with Christianization the diversity of burial customs was replaced by the strictly prescribed rules of the Church.

The mere fact that Magyar burial customs, and the ideology which lay behind them, can be found today amongst the peoples of Central Asia does not imply a Central Asian provenance of the Magyars. As we have seen, these burial customs were at that time, and even earlier, just as widespread in southern Russia as in the Central Asian territories to which Scythian culture diffused. On the European side of the Urals this corpus of practices died out early in the wake of Christianity's advance, but it has survived down to the present day in parts further to the east that were cut off from the new European developments. Not long ago, I pointed out that a few memories of the ancient method of burial still lurk amongst the folk burial customs of Hungary today.

If we now look more closely at the territory that was the setting for Magyar prehistory, we cannot fail to notice that the region was at that time in much closer contact with Europe than in the period after St Stephen. The facts show that the land and culture of southern Russia were integral components of Europe. The culture of our part of the world is a fusion of three civilizations of equal rank but different character: Mediterranean Classical, North German, and South Russian steppe culture. [pp. 200-201]

MÁRIA KRESZ
'A magyar szűcsmunka történeti rétegei'
[Historical strata of fur-making in Hungary],
Ethnographia, (1978).

The long history of fur-making and fur decoration permits one to conjecture that Conquest-era Magyars wore sheepskin jerkins (*ködmön*) and bodices with appliqué decorations, as well as trimming their leather purses with appliqué-work, and that these perished in the ground. Nevertheless several elements of this art have been preserved in the remote mining districts of Transylvania, in Transylvanian villages of the 'Mezőség' region to the north of modern Cluj, and even at scattered places on the Hungarian Alföld. [p. 340]

ANTAL BARTHA
A IX-X. századi magyar társadalom
[Magyar society in the ninth and tenth centuries],
Budapest, 1968.

The weight of a sabre is 0.5 kg per metre length, its blade 0.8 metre long. A double-edged broadsword weighs 1.0 kg per metre length, its blade is 0.9 metre long. We may take the total weight of a sabre to be 0.5 kg since that amount of iron was certainly needed to make a blade 0.8 m long.

According to Arabic sources, the Magyar tribes were able to muster 20,000 mounted warriors, so if every warrior had a sabre then that would have required a total of 10,000 kg (nearly 10 Imperial tons) of finely wrought iron. However, a warrior's equipment did not consist merely of a sabre; a pair of stirrups, a bit and arrowheads were also indispensible items of his equipment. Pairs of stirrups have been measured as weighing 0.30, 0.36, 0.40 and 0.48 kg, and bits 0.12, 0.17 and 0.52 kg. Thus for 20,000 horsemen a 0.30 kg pair of stirrups would mean 6,000 kg, and a 0.36 kg pair 7,200 kg of iron; similarly a 0.17 kg bit would mean 3,400 kg of worked iron... It follows that the minimum quantity of iron required for a ninth-century Magyar army of the size mentioned by the Arabic sources... must have been between 19,400 and 20,000 kg... A society which was able to produce amounts of iron of this order for its fighting men could not have been at a low level of development. [p. 106]

[István Erős made similar calculations in the early 1940s but did not publish his conclusions.]

GÉZA FEHÉR
A bolgár-törökök szerepe és műveltsége
[The place and culture of the Bulgar Turks],
Budapest, 1940.

Certainly, just as the Hungarian language and the material of Hungarian ethnography, ethnology and archaeology are important sources for understanding the language and culture of the Bulgar Turks, so too the valuable material relating to the Bulgar Turks that is available to us is important for understanding the primitive culture of the Magyars. But it is equally true that in many cases the data can only be interpreted by studying both together. [p. ...]

For it is certain that in the ninth century the Bulgars began to re-open the salt mines of the River Mures region of Transylvania that had fallen into disuse since Roman times... Bulgarian-Turkic and Bulgarian-Slavonic geographical names are found around the salt-mining centres. [p. 17]

... What we see is that in eastern Hungary can be found Bulgarian-Turkic and Bulgarian-Slavonic place-names originating from the ninth century. Pest, which is incontrovertibly a Bulgarian-Slavonic name, completely fits into this sequence. In the tenth century the Bulgar city-founders were joined by Mohammedan Bulgar settlers... [p. 19]

In his diplomatic report Liutprand complains that at a dinner in the court the Emperor Nikephoros nade him sit opposite a Bulgarian ambassador, cropped in the Magyar fashion. [p. 99]

One item from his book on ceremonial at the Byzantine court: the camp steward was obliged to take along with him, for the emperor's use, a Magyar – that is, Scythian – basin, his woollen 'blanket', together with a leather bath-tub. [p. 100]

... One thing is sure: the evolution of East European culture is not comprehensible without a knowledge of the cultural influence of the Bulgar Turks and Conquest-period Magyars. [p. 110]

Controversy over the "Double Conquest"

ISTVÁN FODOR
Verecke híres útján...
[On Verecke's renowned road...],
Budapest, 1975.

I share the views of those who are unable to accept the hypothesis of a 'double Conquest' due the serious arguments which speak against it. The chief difficulties, as I see them, are as follows: 1) The genesis of the Avars who arrived on Hungarian soil around 670 A.D. in no way took place on territory that, in the light of current knowledge, was at any time inhabited by Finno-Ugrian peoples, therefore the Avars could hardly have spoken a Finno-Ugrian – or more specifically, Hungarian – language.
2) It does not seem likely either that a Magyar ethnic group of any great size joined up, somewhere in East Europe, with Avars advancing westwards out of Asia...
3) Archaeological finds in Hungary categorically conflict with the supposition that the Avars lived on in appreciable numbers to see the Magyar Conquest... The basis for the subsequent ethnogenesis of the Magyars... was the population which moved into Hungary in 895. 4)

The overwhelming majority of the Árpádian conquerors was Magyar... 5) Lastly, not one contemporary source suggests that Magyars lived in Hungary prior to 895... [p. 239]

GYULA KRISTÓ
'A kettős honfoglalás elméletéről'
[The hypothesis of a double Conquest],
História, (1983)

For according to Gyula László 'the late Avar and the 895-96 Conquest-era cemeteries complement one another in disclosing to us the linguistic boundary of Hungarian in the eleventh century'! Yet in writing this, László collates two things which are at least two millennia apart, since Kniezsa's map, which depicts the ethnic situation that – with strong reservations – pertained by the end of the eleventh century,... is inappropriate to provide any decisive evidence with regard to the ethnic classification of late Avar graves. It is inappropriate because the Magyars who held Transdanubia from the beginning of the tenth century had two centuries in which to establish the Hungarian place-names whose late eleventh century status is reflected in Kniezsa's map.

According to Gyula László, the southeren, eastern and western parts of Transdanubia are crowded with late Avar burial grounds, whereas cemeteries of the Árpádian Magyars are absent. However, since Kniezsa's map classifies the basic population of this area as Magyar, László deduces that the region's almost purely Hungarian place-names must have been bestowed by the late Avars, that is, the Magyars of the first Conquest. It is not as if there were a compelling need, there is no reason at all to justify why one should – or could attribute the Hungarian place-names of Transdanubia to a Magyar population which arrived there before the Árpádian Magyars. Gyula László does not take into account the possibility that burials of the Árpádian Magyars do not have to be sought solely in those graves which are furnished with partial horse burials, sabres and belt decorations (at all events, with rich grave goods), but that the Magyars of the 895 Conquest might have a part (even if not an exclusive part) in the closely packed, poorly furnished rows of graves that traditionally have been classed as belonging to Bjelo Brdo culture. This radically alters the picture of the settlement history of Transdanubia; the presence of Árpádian Magyars in Transdanubia from the start of the tenth century onwards now becomes archaeologically demonstrable, and we can in turn, through them, readily account for the late eleventh-century corpus of Hungarian place-names. [pp. 26-27]

GYULA LÁSZLÓ
'Baráti vita Kristó Gyulával'
[A friendly dispute with Gyula Kristó],
História, (1983).

First of all... I am delighted to see that my archaeological inference that a new people appeared in large numbers in the Carpathian basin around 670, and that this new people was On ogur, is already taken for granted as 'indisputable fact' by Kristó (and, indeed, recently by György Györffy as well). However, in doing so they have also accepted, willy-nilly, the basic premise of the 'double Conquest' hypothesis.

Yet it is not that which Gyula Kristó takes issue with but with the suggestion that the mass of this new people spoke Hungarian.

It can be shown, both archaeologically and anthropologically, that large numbers of a people with belts bearing griffin-and-tendril decorations – the Onogurs – survived to the time of the Árpádian Conquest and the establishment of a Hungarian kingdom, as it is in their late cemeteries that we see the appearance of the temporal rings, which cannot be dated to any earlier than the mid-tenth century. In the light of this, I would pose a question...: Is there any trace in Hungary's early place-names – for there certainly should be – of the assimilation of a large mass of people? There is none, beause the bulk of our early place-names are Hungarian; in the border zones and at scattered places elsewhere they are Slavonic, and in some areas Turkic relics are also demonstrable... [p. 27]

PÉTER KIRÁLY
'Ungarus, Hungarius, Onger',
Élet és Tudomány, 31 October 1986,
1382-1383 (excerpts).

I noticed that hitherto, in their studies of the Latin-language sources that relate to the Magyar Conquest, our historians had paid attention only to the ethnic name in the plural forms *Ungri*, *Ungari* or *Hungary* but never to the singular forms *Ungarus*, *Hungarius*, *Hunger*, *Onger* or *Wanger*. Yet the latter can be traced – as personal names from as early as 731 and 736 onwards.

For a long time the thought nagged me that someone should (re-)examine the various monastery rolls, necrologies (death-rolls) and other surviving documents to check whether they too might conceal Hungarian personal names. That was how I came to make a study of the Latin sources from Germany, and it is the results of these researches – which were based primarily on the rolls of monasteries belonging to the confraternity (monastic settlement) of Reichenau (*Augia Dives*) by Lake Constance and documentary material at St Gall in Switzerland – that I would like to present here.

I have managed to uncover a great many personal names which had previously gone unremarked but which fall within our sphere of interest. The earliest personal names discovered include: *Ungarus* (731, Glatt-St Gall),

Hungaer (761, Liptingen-St Gall), *Hunger* (8th-9th century, Salzburg-Moosburg), *Hungarius* (797-809, Wiessenburg), *Wanger* (812, Hoffs-St Gall), *Unger* (9th-10th century, Brescia), and *Onger* (9th-l0th century, Kempten). In all, I was able to find some sixty items of similar data from the eighth and ninth centuries, most of them from Germany (Frankish, Alaman, Bavarian), France and Italy...

Sources of this type are extremely laconic, recording merely the personal name and in some cases, at best, an occupation (e.g. witness, landowner, monk, church elder, steward, bishop)... I did not find any early Hungarian name of Finno-Ugrian character amongst the several tens of thousands of personal names that were scanned. Here too, however, an acceptable explanation offers itself for the equation *Ungarus* = Magyar, and it runs as follows. Attempts to derive the names *Hungar, Hunger,* etc. from German common words are by no means convincing, partly because they cannot account for the formation of all the name variants, partly beause some German experts themselves also believe it possible to make the identification with 'Magyar'. I too, therefore, find it more acceptable to derive the personal names *Ungarus, Hungarius, Onger* and *Wanger* from the ethnic name *Onogur*, or possibly from *Unogor* or *Hunogor*, on the supposition that they were either direct (German) borrowings or transmitted via Slavonic... The personal names *Ungarus, Hungaricus,* etc. are authentic, fixed as to time and place, and the correctness of their reading is beyond doubt. It is merely in their interpretation that further study is called for: do they connote 'Onogur' or 'Magyar'?... The existence of a reference to a *Via Ungarorum*, or Hungarians' Road, recorded at Sesto, North Italy, in the year 760, is food for thought in this respect. [pp. 1382-83]

DEZSŐ CSALLÁNY
'Avar törzsszervezet'
[Avar tribal organization].
Jósa András Múzeum Évkönyve, VIII-IX (1965-68), Budapest, 1967.

Thus the Avars did not die out, they were not slaughtered, nor did they become Slavonized, but they continued to hold on to their original settlement areas and kept their own Finno-Ugrian tongue – the language spoken by modern Hungarians – down to the present day. [p. 50]
Thus there were two Conquests of Hungary:

1) The conquest of 568: The khagan Bayan and his Finno-Ugrian people along with retinues of Turks and Bulgar-Turks whose Finno-Ugrianization (Avarization) I am unable to fix in time because the bilingualism of the 950s applied both to the Avars and Bulgars, and to the Avars and Turks.

2) The second Conquest: this occurred in 896 with the entry of numerous Turkic and Iranian-speaking peoples, tribes, etc. who subsequently lost their Turkic and Iranian languages in the same way as the Bulgar-Turks had been assimilated. This process was later to be repeated with the Pechenegs and Cumans as well.

The second Conquest did not introduce the Finno-Ugrian language, it merely supplied the Avar tribal confederation with a new ruling dynasty, a new rallying force, and provided a new homeland for the newcomers. The relationship of the Avar tribes and the peoples of the second Conquest to one another has not been clarified. We have yet to find out how the Turks took possession of land within the tribal confederation, whether in dispersed groups or in larger blocks as in the Upper Tisza region. [p. 53]

Peoples of Hungary in the Conquest Period

LÁSZLÓ RÁSONYI
Hidak a Dunán
[Bridges over the Danube],
Budapest, 1981.

Rásonyi considers that the 'Vlachs', or Wallachians, who are mentioned by Anonymus, were a Qarluk-Turkish people.

... The '*terra Blacorum*' (land of the Vlachs, or 'Wallachia') initially belonged to the marches under Bulgar rule. Later on, however, with the retreat of Bulgar authority, both this region and the '*silva Blacorum et Bissenorum*' (forest of the Vlachs and Pechenegs) of the Persani hills in the northen Harghita region may have been part of the inner borderline of Transylvania. The part of central Transylvania that lies along the Tirnava and Somes (Számos) valleys was still the Vlachs' land, and possibly the core of their settlement area, before the Székely entered Transylvania. [p. 68]

On the Pecheneg attack: The Magyar Conquest of Hungary would have taken place even without this event as, in the course of history up till then, all the peoples who had lived on the eastern approaches to the Carpathian Mountains sooner or later made a determined effort to penetrate further within the Carpathian ring. The Magyars put a stop to this process by gaining a firm and permanent foothold in the Carpathian basin. The significance of the Pecheneg attack was that it precipitated the Magyar Conquest much more quickly than would otherwise have been the case. [p. 82]

ERIK MOLNÁR
A magyar társadalom története
az őskortól az Árpád-korig
[Magyar social history from prehistoric times
to the Árpádian age],
2nd ed., Budapest, 1949.

The Slavonic society of Moravia and western Hungary had more advanced forces of production at its disposal than did the Magyars of the Conquest era. This is shown by the dominant role that tillage with the wheeled plough played in their agriculture, their implementation of a regular crop-rotation system, their already partial adoption of stabling for animal husbandry and their systematic growing of fodder-crops, their mining and iron-smelting industries, and their level of technology in general… their social organization was on a higher level than the Magyars' pastoral nomadic society. [p. 110]

The fortresses which the central leadership of the Slavs had made their headquarters now became headquarters of the principal Magyar chieftains… In the castle-district (county) that remained in his grasp, a leader had at his disposal a whole string of Slav bailiffs (ispán) and the fortress garrisons of freemen… [p. 110]

The Slav castle-districts were perpetuated along with their officials, from bailiffs down through captains and sergeants to the gaolers, their cavalry retinues, dungeons and other institutions. [p. 122-23]

Parts of the Slav population of Hungary already in the ninth century reached a level of productive forces which the pure-blooded Magyars were generally only to achieve at the end of the twelfth century… Thus, during the tenth to the twelfth centuries the pure-blooded Magyars were to advance from the middle to the upper level of barbarianism, becoming a 'cultured' people in the original sense of a farming people, with its implication of agriculture as the basis of all cultural development. [p. 167]

Archaeology and the Conquest

This selection covers a number of questions that are constantly being raised by archaeologists and which have already been touched on in other sections of this Reader. Such "overlaps" are inevitable but will, I believe, increase the reader's appreciation of the multifaceted nature of the problems rather than add to the confusion.

Due to the limitations of space here, as in other sections, it has been necessary to omit mention of many excellent pieces of work. For references to these the reader should consult the comprehensive bibliography prepared by J. Banner and I. Jakabffy (*A Közép-Duna-medence régészeti bibliográfiája – Archäologische Bibliographie des Mitteldonaubeckens – Bibliographie archéologique du bassin du Danube moyen*, 4 vols., Budapest, 1954, 1961, 1968 and 1981).

BÉLA SZŐKE
A honfoglaló és kora Árpád-kori magyarság régészeti emlékei
[**Archaeological relics of the Conquest-era and early Árpádian-age Magyars**],
Budapest, 1962.

Stratification of wealth had already begun to appear in an explicit form amongst the Magyars during the ninth century. The society could be divided into basically three strata – a wealthy ruling class, a middle stratum, and the common people. In the archaeological record it is extremely difficult to draw a line between the heritages of the ruling and middle strata since the latter made every effort to assimilate itself to the wealthier and more powerful ruling class. For that reason, no attempt will be made to discuss the archaeological heritages of the two strata separately; however, we shall try, wherever possible, to outline within a single chapter those aspects where they can be differentiated. Among the Conquest-era Magyars, the boundary between the archaeological heritages of these two strata and the common people can be drawn very sharply. The difference is so striking that, up to now, the relics that have been preserved in the commoners' cemeteries were thought to be non-Magyar. [p. 11]

… The European and Hungarian specialist literature attributed the large, row-ordered, 10th- and 11th-century burial grounds of the Carpathian basin to the Slavs, whilst the material culture of these cemeteries was called Bjelo Brdo culture after one of the Slavonic burial grounds in Yugoslavia. The basis for this stance was that researchers were only able to envisage the Conquest-era Magyars as a ruling people which imposed its settlement on the indigenous Slav population of the Carpathian basin and forced it into slavery. It is a viewpoint that was captured in Hungarian art of the last century by the monumental canvases depicting the Conquest that were painted by Mihály Munkácsy and Árpád Feszty.

Archaeologist-historians, including the most eminent among them – the likes of J. Hampel, J. Niederle and J. Eisner – simply disregarded the fact that the relics of a simple, much poorer culture appeared in the Carpathian basin at one and the same time as the rich and often splendid material remains of the Conquest-era Magyars. This culture represented the mass of the people, the commoners: it had evolved on the wooded steppe terrain of South Russia and emerged in the Carpathian basin as a closed culture of a completely new complexion. The anthropological remains of the bearers of this culture likewise represent a new population in the Danube-Tisza region. As we have already stated, these cemeteries conceal the Magyar common people of the Conquest… The common people were not nomadic animal-breeders. [p. 101]

ISTVÁN DIENES
A honfoglaló magyarok
[**Magyars of the Conquest era**],
Budapest, 1973.

As the weather became milder daily life moved out of cramped, dark and smoke-filled huts into more spacious, well ventilated tents. Not infrequently the two types of dwelling were also geographically separated, and we may speculate that the poor of a settlement, with their huts of assorted sizes, some of them no more than wretched hovels, drew increasingly apart from the ditch-ringed yurts that served as permanent abodes for the wealthier. The outlines of complex systems of ramparts and ditches can be traced in early villages. In the traces of ditch system lying outside the group of huts – near to the line of earthworks, punctuated by gates, which enclosed the whole settlement – it is possible to see the remains of walls and ditches that protected pens for the animals kept in the settlement, as well as hayfields and gardens.

The visitor to the encampments of dignitaries was confronted with a quite different picture. He might glimpse from a distance or, turning into the fortress, might suddenly be struck by the gleaming whiteness of their felt tents, bleached with bone-meal lime, with the tented pavilion of the leader standing out from the rest in its size and central position. Gaily coloured appliqué decor covered the outer rim of the smoke-hole in the ridge of the tent, the lower borders of the dome-like roofing, and the felt door-flaps over the entrance. Brocades and rugs lined the interior walls, whilst finely worked leather and furs upholstered their ornately carved couches and stools. When an eminent guest was being received, services of gold and silver jugs and goblets, brimming with drinks, were set up on benches by the door. Aromatic herbs were sprinkled on the fire, glowing in the centre of the tent, to make its smoke more fragrant. Among the household items was toiletry equipment, including a raised, water-filled leather sack, with a tap, under which the traveller could wash off the grime of his journey. The Magyars called this a csorgó; its name was recorded for us as tserga by Constantine Porphyrogenitus in his De Caerimoniis, as the Byzantine emperor ordered that when he was away campaigning the bathing facilities that the Magyar nobility enjoyed were to be arranged for him in camp. Regular sentries were posted on the outskirts of the encampment, and strangers were obliged to dismount on reaching the outermost of these lookouts. If his intentions were honourable, a traveller would voluntarily surrender his weapons here, his clothes and packs would be searched, and, having handed over his still fully harnessed horse to the guards' safekeeping, he would make the rest of his way to the leader's tent on foot, between the tents, he may have caught sight of a row of treasure-wagons, laden with fabrics, furs, precious metals and jewels, the emblem of the camp's commander attached to a pole and the standards that were set up around the central tent, the number of which designated his rank up to the seven standards of a khan.

Workshops and Market-places in Town Centres

A good number of the simpler articles used in the more humble households were made by the family themselves. The preparation and finishing of leather and furs and the carving of wooden articles was the men's work; spinning, weaving and sewing were the women's lot. Women also had the tiring job of producing the felt fabric that was used for tent-coverings and linings, for overcoats and saddle-cloths. This was usually performed on a share-cropping basis for the more well-to-do, whose huge flocks of sheep they would shear for the great quantities of fleeces that were needed. The awning of just one yurt required felt made with some 130-160 kg of fleece. Since the felt had to be mended and replaced at frequent intervals, because of its short useful life of only 5-7 years, the prospect of poorer people being able to afford their own yurt was beyond their reach. The most skilful members of the village communities would also undertake certain crafts on a cottage-industry scale as diggings at settlements have uncovered spinning sheds, iron-beating workshops and pottery kilns. In this manner all the most necessary handicraft articles could be obtained by barter within every settlement. This is also deducible from the fact that the earliest laws of Hungary strictly prohibited – as non-taxable transactions – all barter that was conducted outside the market-place – in other words, at the domestic level. The poorer people would also turn up at the markets with their craft produce as they could only offer the added value of their own labour to compete with the bulk-produced raw materials of the wealthy, and this was their only means of obtaining goods that they were unable to produce for themselves. By collecting goods from others in a settlement, more resourceful individuals might sell these on for a profit at the market. The law referred to such individuals as poor traders.

Notables were considerably more demanding in their standards of clothing, equipment and housekeeping, hence they endeavoured to bring in skilled craftsmen to settle around their quarters and work to the orders of their family and the upper ranks of their retinue. Hungarian craft names of pre-Conquest Turkic origin, such as ács 'carpenter' and szűcs 'furrier', as well as those derived from Finno-Ugrian words, such as vasverő 'smith', fazekas 'potter', fonó 'spinner' and others, attest to the fact that the separation of certain craft activities from agriculture had already occurred long before. The uniformity of the Conquest-era heritage, extending to the entire population, the conventional forms of certain types of articles, the concordance of units of measure and of often highly complex structural elements, and the similarity of decorative principles make it obvious that all this could only have evolved and perpetuated after many centuries of practice in their workshops. Innumerable finds convince one that the Magyars had access to highly trained blacksmiths, armourers, saddlers, bow-makers, silversmiths and harness-makers who possessed great craftsmanship and long experience. [pp. 32-33]

BÉLA KÜRTI
'Honfoglaláskori magyar temető Szeged-Algyőn'
[A Conquest-period Magyar cemetery at Szeged-Algyő],
Móra Ferenc Múzeum Évkönyve, (1978-79).

On the 83 graves in the cemetery: Judged from its size and structure, the Algyő cemetery represents a unit larger than a clan, yet it has a smaller number of bodies and is richer than the commoners' burial grounds. Presumably it was a cemetery for middle-stratum families that were unrelated to one another but belonged to a single community (village). Many burial customs argue for a subdivision into groups within the cemetery, which means that at the same time we must map out different groups, each with their own tradition, within the community... [p. 343]

PÉTER TOMKA
'Avarkori régészetünk orientalisztikai vonatkozásairól'
[Orientalistic aspects of Avar-period archaeology in Hungary].
In: Kelet-kutatás, Budapest, 1974.

It is certain that here in Hungary the Árpádian conquerors came across other ethnic groups (and languages), apart from the Slavs; and if these were not Magyar, they could only have been Bulgar-Turks. This, therefore, offers us the real possibility of being able to derive a part – perhaps a major part – of the Bulgar-Turkic (Chuvash and even Mongol) loanwords in the Hungarian language from the post-Conquest period in the Carpathian basin, rather than from the Kuban or Don regions and the uncertain period of dependency on the Khazars. This hypothesis is supported by the socio-economic identity that can be seen from the Hungarian language loanwords and from the late Avar cemeteries (a more exact identity than that which Antal Bartha conjures up with the Saltovo-Mayatskoye culture). It is also supported by the fact that neighbouring peoples called the Magyars 'Onogurs' (Ungar, Venger) so unambiguously that the expression *Marka Ungarorum* was already in currency before the Conquest. The same hypothesis has also been arrived at by Imre Boba (paper read to the International Archaeological Conference at Szeged in 1971). The hypothesis likewise explains a circumstance which, alongside Gyula László's conjecture, seems to present a cogent argument, namely, that the Hungarian tongue was able to survive amidst a welter of neighbouring Indo-European languages and did not share the fate of the Danube Bulgars' Turkic tongue. For it would have been able to call on the Bulgar Turks who were already in Hungary for rapidly assimilating aid, and in this sense the linguistic influence of the Bulgar Turks in the country may have preceded that of the Slavs. Furthermore, the coincidence of 'Magyar' place-names and late Avar archaeological sites, the problem of the late Avar-period antecedents of 'Magyar' villages, and the absence of any 'Avar' place-names are also rendered explicable... [p. 343]

KATALIN KŐHALMI
'A honfoglaló magyarság fegyverzetének nomád háttere'
[The nomad background of the weaponry used by the Conquest-era Magyars].
In: Keletkutatás, Budapest, 1974.

Two of the five features that Miss Kőhalmi identifies as common features of weaponry between nomads and the Magyar conquerors are summed up as follows:

1. First of all, the appearance and disappearance of certain types of weapons amongst the steppe nomads is a consequence not of capricious 'fashion', but of a general principle – that new weaponry gives rise to effective defensive counter-measures, and these measures in turn provoke the development of even more effective weaponry, and so on – which applies to steppe weaponry too.

2. Secondly, wherever our ancestors may have dwelt, whether on the steppe or in territories that bordered the steppe, they had to attain the prevailing standard of weaponry otherwise they would not have survived. [p. 155]

PÉTER NÉMETH
'A szabolcsi földvár kutatásának hét éve'
[Seven years' research on the earthwork fortress at Szabolcs].
In: Régészeti barangolások Magyarországon [Archaeological excursions in Hungary], ed. V. Szombathy, Budapest, 1975.

Our historians have read the foundation of the Hungarian state into the process of adopting a foreign institution, the county organization, and extending it to the whole area of the Carpathian basin, but here I shall pick out just one essential aspect of the topic. Researchers have been in disagreement only over the question of who originally created the 'castle-district' system – the Franks, who pushed the boundaries of their empire out as far as the Danube during Charlemagne's reign, or the Slavs, whose presence is attested by many Hungarian place-names, including the appellations of several of our counties (Borsova = 'belonging to Borš', Csongrád = 'Black Castle', Visegrád = 'Upper Castle'). Considering that in the vocabulary of state and county administration, and the early Hungarian Church which was connected with it, we find many words of Slavonic origin or transmission (e.g. *király* 'king', *ispán* 'castlebailiff', *püspök* 'bishop', *esperes* 'archdeacon', *plébános* 'parson', *pap* 'priest', *szent* 'saint'), the majority of historians have championed a Slav provenance. György Györffy can claim to have first raised the possibility that Hungary's county system was of Magyar origin, the result of transforming – by concession or by force – the clan organization of territorial division that developed after the Conquest into a royal county system; he also backed this up with data from historical geography, linguistics, ethnography, etc. Its roots, therefore, go back only to the Conquest, and not earlier, even if there are some places, such as Sopron or Győr, where the county seats or centres were planted on Roman ruins. The written sources have little to say about all this so that we must turn to archaeology for assistance in supplying decisive evidence from exploration of the institutions of any Árpádian-age county seats which may still be traceable.

It was with thoughts roughly like those in mind that, on 1 July 1969, the day on which sondage of the earthworks of Szabolcs fortress began. I turned up at the site, with my team of helpers from the village of Kék. I had already worked closely with this group for two years by then: together we had excavated a ninth-century burial ground at Kék (that was how the ten-member team had come to be recruited), the foundations of an Árpádian-era church at Hene, and the earthwork fortress and monastery at Beszerec. During this period they had become used to many oddities and had long got over their initial reluctance about opening graves, but even they were set to wondering by the sight of the Szabolcs earth fort and the vast scale of the work that was to be undertaken.

Szabolcs fort is one of the largest and most picturesque of Hungary's earth-and-timber fortifications. Of triangular ground plan, it lies in the western part of the community's centre. In olden times the ramparts on the north and south-west sides ran along the left bank of the Tisza, but all that can be seen of that nowadays, since the regulation of the river, is a shallow ox-bow that only rarely fills with water. Measured as the shortest distance between the high points at each angle, the rampart on the north-west side is 272.5 metres long, that on the south-west side 194 metres, and that on the east side 322.5 metres. Measured along its external faces, the fort is enclosed by ramparts of 337, 235 and 387 metres' length and covers an area of more than 33,000 square metres [8 acres]. The ramparts stand 1320.5 metres above the present level of the flood plain and 6-11 metres above that of the fort's interior. [pp. 236-37]

LÁSZLÓ KOVÁCS
'A honfoglaló magyar lándzsás sír jelölés és néprajzi megfelelői'
[The use of spears to mark the graves of Conquest-era Magyars and its ethnographic counterparts].
In: Előmunkálatok a Magyarság Néprajzához [Preparatory work towards an Ethnography of the Hungarians], Vol. 10, Budapest, 1982.

...A description of two of the three authenticated grave finds has passed down to us. In the one at Szob, found lying besides the River Felka, the tip of a pinnate iron spearhead extended beyond the skull of an elderly man; in other words, the spear fitted into the grave with its shaft still intact... In the Tiszabezdéd grave, the iron spearhead was found between the thigh bones of an old man, lying parallel with them and about 10-12 cm higher, with its tip pointing towards the pelvis. Thus in this case the shaft of the spear must have been broken in two before the burial...

It is evident, therefore, that if it was prescribed by their burial rites, our Conquest-era ancestors found ways of placing a spear in the grave. [p.]

In the light of the foregoing, we can scarcely doubt that spears were in use, if only to a limited extent, and accordingly we must suppose that our forebears for some reason deliberately avoided burying this weapon in their graves. Is there any way of discovering this reason?... We have no evidence of... the survival of this presumed Conquest-era practice of using the spear as a grave-marker. The report from 1474 of a funerary banner being attached to a spear therefore either represents a completely independent phenomenon or might be a relic of the practice that can no longer be established. [p. 81]

GYULA LÁSZLÓ
'A zempléni honfoglaláskori vezérsírról'
[The Conquest-period chieftain's grave at Zemplén]
Archaeologiai Értesítő, (1976): 79-85.

A brief comment on one of the ideas about the grave find at Zemplin that are propounded at length by Voitech Budinský-Kričˇka and Nándor Fettich (*Das altungarische Fürstengrab von Zemplin. Bratislava*, 1973).

... Fettich explains the positioning of the sword by suggesting that the body, with the weapon belt strapped on, was lifted and turned over on its stomach... Most surprising of all is his deduction that when the body was turned over the head no longer fitted into the coffin and so was cut off... [p. 80]

Anthropology of the Conquest-era Magyars

Certain anthropological findings have already been included in earlier sections of this Reader. Here work by three of Lajos Bartucz's most talented pupils is highlighted.

JÁNOS NEMESKÉRI
'Az embertan és a magyar őstörténet'
[Anthropology and Magyar prehistory].
In: A magyarság őstörténete [Prehistory of the Magyars], ed. L. Ligeti, Budapest, 1943 [Reprinted 1986], pp. 223-39.

Anthropological material from the Conquest era is very scanty, yet the validity of the racial composition gained from its study is corroborated to an astonishing degree by the racial composition of the modern Hungarian population. All the studies that have been carried out to date on the living population have identified as major racial elements the East Baltic and Turanid types which are found with Magyars of the Conquest era.

According to studies completed up to now, the racial components of the present-day population of
Hungary are as follows:

1. East Baltic		25%
2. Turanid		25%
3. Dinaric		20%
4. Alpine		10%
5. Taurid		8%
6. Mongoloid		4%
7. Nordic		7%
8. Mediterranean and other		1%

The ancient, and also major, elements that have been preserved in the modern Hungarian population can be distinguished through certain combinations of features... [p. 230]

From the prehistorical point of view, two important elements in the racial composition of Conquest-era Magyars – the East Baltic (Sibirid) and the Turano-Taurid (Tungid) – require further analysis by anthropological investigation of the Finno-Ugrian and Turkic peoples. Here we are in a much more favourable situation in terms of what is known from anthropological study of the Finno-Ugrians than is the case for the Turkic ethnikon.

We can approach the questions of the anthropological origin and subsequent ethnogenesis of the Finno-Ugrians by drawing on the joint efforts of palaeo-archaeology and physical anthropology. From the palaeo-archaeological findings it can be shown that with the passing of the Old Stone Age a primitive fishing-hunting culture emerged over a vast, continuous area in the primeval forests of northern Eurasia. By the end of the Neolithic and the beginning of the Copper Age this culture was already associated with a long-headed (to mesocephalic) type which appeared in the area of interface between the ranges of the proto-Europid and Mongoloid races. Consistent with this contiguity of the two ranges, the proto-Europid type acquired Mongoloid features and vice versa. The effects of this change and the intensive racial intermixing that it triggered were only later to be manifested to their full extent. The former can be identified as a primitive East Baltic type, the latter as a proto-Europid-Mongoloid type. From the presence of intermixing and the intensity of traits, the area of interface between the two racial types – i. e. the ancient homeland of the East Baltic type – can be localized in large part to the western side of the Urals and in smaller part to the eastern slopes. From there the fishing-hunting culture of the East Baltic and Sibirid races diffused, or rather evolved, westwards and eastwards across northern Eurasia. The traits of the East Baltic type that are known to us today, therefore, were established in an area between the Urals and the upper reaches of the Volga which also includes the former ancient homeland of the Finno-Ugrian peoples. [p. 232-33]

PÁL LIPTÁK
'A magyar őstörténet kérdései az antropológiai kutatások alapján'
[The problems of Magyar prehistory based on anthropological researches].
In: Magyar őstörténeti tanulmányok [Studies in Magyar prehistory], Budapest, 1977.

The Hungarian population of the tenth to the thirteenth centuries, otherwise known as 'Árpád's Magyars' or the Magyars of the Conquest era, on the evidence of its tribal names (only two of which – Megyer and Nyék – are of Ugrian origin), must have included a certain number of clans that spoke a Turkic language (Onogur or Turkic) as well as Hungarian-speaking tribes and clans... [p. 238]

... The anthropological features of the different social strata were divergent.

a) For the ruling stratum Turanid (t), Uralic (u), Pamirian (p) and other brachycranial racial components (e.g. pre-Asiatic) are the most characteristic. The series [of skeletal finds] formed by ruling-class Magyars of the Conquest era from the Danube-Tisza interfluvial area confirms the Turkic character of this stratum. This view finds support in the anthropological material from the eighth- to ninth-century Volga Bulgar cemetery near Bolshiye Tarkhani that was studied, as previously mentioned, by Akimova. I have had an opportunity to analyse this material taxonomically at first hand (it is held in the collection of the Anthropological Museum, Lomonosov University, Moscow), Round-headed Europid types (with more or less Pamirian features), Turanids and a long-headed racial component are characteristic of both series.

b) The anthropological picture of the middle stratum differs strikingly from that of the ruling class, even though its racial components are also found in smaller proportions in the latter stratum. The most important constituents of this warrior caste are a gracile Mediterranean (m) and a Nordoid (n) or narrow-faced, dolichomorphic type (this latter might also represent a tall, robust Mediterranean (am) type). Lastly, the Pamirian {p) race is a significant component. A specific and distinctive finding is the virtual absence of Turanid and Uralic races from this stratum.

c) The anthropological components of the common people may be characterized on the basis of those series that date from the Árpádian age. Taking these overall, the most notable constituents, as with the middle stratum, are Nordoid (31%) and Mediterranean (28%) but there is in addition a significant Cromagnoid quota (22%). In general, the Cromagnoid-A (crA) type can be demonstrated in higher ratio but in some instances there is also a considerable Cromagnoid-B (crB) component in certain Árpádian-era populations, and this – precisely because of its rare occurrence must be regarded as characteristic. Round-headed elements play a much smaller part (13%) than in the Avar period... [pp. 238-40]

Finally, something should be said about scientific collaboration between linguist-philologists, archaeologists, physical anthropologists and ethnographers in researching the prehistory, or ethnogenesis, of the Magyars... Let us answer the question as to what anthropology can contribute to the above social sciences. To begin with the most important, the continuity of a population in a given area can be stated with much greater confidence, and in relation to a much longer period, from a study of skeletal material obtained from well documented excavations. Thus, the population stock of an area may have remained the same despite changes in dress or burial rite that took place over time. Under these circumstances, the archaeologist can only say that the continuity cannot be shown from the archaeological record; the anthropologist can choose to maintain his (contrary) opinion, if the material that he has studied suggests this. In such cases, however, it is usual for archaeologists and historians to ignore the historical anthropologist's findings. In the Avar period there were very significant anthropological differences between the various populations. It is also possible, however, to place a one-sided reliance on statistical procedures. If differences that have been established by others, using other methods, are obscured by this, then that is undoubtedly due to a fault in the procedure. On the basis of, let us say, a mere 10 quantitatively measured data, and by paying no attention at all to qualitative morphological features, it is possible to pronounce any series 'similar' to any other. If, on top of that, the specialist carries out a statistical comparison but neglects the taxonomic differentiating value of the anthropological features, the end result will be completely misleading. [p. 241]

KINGA ÉRY
'Regionális különbségek a magyarság X. századi embertani anyagában'
[Regional differences in the tenth-century Hungarian anthropological material],
Anthropologiai Közlemények, 22 (1978).

In the course of the metric and taxonomic comparison it became apparent that finds of similar character were not occurring sporadically throughout the country but were concentrated in certain areas. On this basis we were able to distinguish four regional groups.

The most striking feature of Group A was that Europids made up no more than 33% of the total, whilst Europo-Mongoloids accounted for 67%. Furthermore, amongst the latter the frequency of Turanids was extremely high (82%). The centre for finds of this group was between the Danube and Tisza rivers... In Group B, Europids constituted 64% of the total, Europo-Mongoloids 36%, and Uralic, rather than Turanid, elements were most common amongst the latter... The sites for these finds were located within a 70 km radius on either side of the Tisza in the Bodrogköz region, but especially on the left bank. The chief characteristic of Group C is the 95% dominance of Europids, which means that Europo-Mongoloid individuals were found only exceptionally in this group... it had the largest distribution area. Belonging to this group were not only all known finds from Transdanubia, but also all finds originating from the hill country between Gödöllő and Ceglédbercel as well as the Cserhát and Mátra Hills to the north. Group D comprises six sites lying within a short distance of one another in Békés County... Europids make up 67% and the 33% Europo-Mongoloid contribution was all Turanid... For quite large areas of the country we still do not have any Magyar anthropological finds dating to the tenth century so that it remains a task for further reasearch to clarify the true number of their regional groups and their exact distribution areas.

Ancient Beliefs

VILMOS DIÓSZEGI
A pogány magyarok hitvilága
[Belief-world of the pagan Magyars],
Budapest, 1967.

Shamanistic notions may have formed the backbone of the pagan Magyars' cosmology. However, such a concept of the world, it should be emphasized, can hardly have been uniform for the pagan Magyar population was not homogeneous either. Apart from the tribes of Finno-Ugrian tongue, the Nyék and Megyer, the remainder were all Turkic speakers; it is difficult to believe that the belief-worlds of tribes of such diverse origins would have been precisely identical. We can be almost equally sure that the beliefs of tribes that spoke the same language would likewise have differed to a greater or lesser degree. It must also be pointed out that the pagan Magyars probably came into contact with organized religions even before the Conquest. They may have become acquainted with Judaism during the time when they were still a part of the Khazar empire... and it is not impossible that they also encountered Christianity before the Conquest. [pp. 8-9]

... As a result of investigation from many different angles, it has become apparent that a whole series of features of the Magyar belief-world go back to Conquest era.

The pagan Magyar cosmology was characterized by the Tree-that-Reached-the-Sky and its associated sun and moon, the country of snakes, lizards and frogs, the spirits around the Tree-of-the-World, and a belief in life-spirits and free souls, or multiple souls. The selection of *táltos*-designates by marks of illness, their claims to gain knowledge through prolonged sleeps and dismemberment of their bodies, and their initiation by climbing the Tree-that-Reached-the-Sky, both in their individual details and in their entirety, project before us notions that the Conquest-era Magyars built up about the táltos-designate. The táltos, holding a single-headed frame-drum with rattles as his stead, his head-dress of owl-feathers and antlers, the notched or ladder-like 'táltos-tree' – these are the items of equipment of the pagan Magyar táltoses, whilst manifestations of ancient táltos activities can be seen in the contest that takes place in animal form during their trances and the summoning up of spirits by the use of interjections... The clusters of notions that are associated with the pagan Magyar cosmology and the shamanism of kindred peoples mesh together like two perfectly matched cogwheels that have neither superfluous nor missing teeth. [pp. 134-135]

From all of this it would appear that the folk culture of modern Hungary has an ancient stratum which derives from shamanism, and that this was the belief-world of the pagan Magyars.

ISTVÁN DIENES
'A sámánok társadalmi szerepe a nomád államban'
[The social function of shamans in the nomad state].
In: Az Őshazától a Kárpátokig [From ancient homeland
to the Carpathians], ed. V. Szombathy, Budapest, 1985, pp. 375-387.

One cannot regard peoples who lived under the conditions of a pre-feudal, barbarian society simply as believers in shamanism, even if it is clear that shamans of the traditional type did pursue their activities among lower-ranking strata. The shamans had no decisive role in the religious life of these empires; at most their presence is an indication that the given period was in process of transformation and fermentation, giving further vitality to some elements that were characteristic of earlier stages of development. The shaman, picked out for the task and initiated into the mysteries of his craft by celestial and underworld forces, remained an irreplaceable personality in the religious life of smaller communities. For them the shaman was a person invested with magical powers who, without causing injury, was able to expel from his body at exactly the right moment the trance-soul that represented his own personality and, by virtue of being an initiate, take on the particular form that characterized the free soul in order to seek out any nook or corner of the Universe and so fulfil his clients' wishes. Thus he was able to seek out the lost soul of a sick person and guide it back to its proper place; to accompany to the other world the souls of the dead that might haunt this world, and prevent their returning again; to ensure that the soul of a sacrificial animal reached the appropriate deity; to find people or animals who were out of sight, etc.

For understandable reasons, it is only the memories of the one-time traditional magician-priest figure of the táltos, of humble rank and representing no threat to the Christian-feudal system, that have survived in the folk beliefs of Hungary. We can concentrate first of all on the use of magic for healing purposes as, until very recently, this was the shamans' most important function. In illnesses where there was loss of consciousness they were able to conjure up the lost free soul and induce it to return into the skull. Evidence of the existence of a shaman aristocracy, under the direction of a chief shaman and in the service of the ruling dynasty and leadership, being distributed amongst their courts, is only indirect and is drawn from parallel phenomena and the sources previously mentioned. Even without this knowledge, we would have to suspect that the prestige of the shamans authenticated the narratives of bards, minstrels and similar itinerant story-tellers which shaped the public consciousness. We have only to recall here the corpus of Hungarian legends (e.g. the Legend of the Wondrous Stag, which by its testimony of a 'community of blood relationship', served to foster a sense of common origin and group identity in an ethnically heterogeneous, socially stratified population, or the Turul legend, with its hints of the celestial provenance of the Árpádian house and its profession of the sacral,

charismatic underpinning of the dynasty's rule), or the epic songs (glimpses of which are obtained from the chronicles and fragmentary folk legends and tales) which promoted a cult of the leadership, a uniform system of common law, identical moral norms, and a uniformity of mythology, dress, weaponry and *objets d'art* which is so well attested from archaeological sources. Each of these bears witness to a strong central rule and a current of thought that served the needs of this centralization.

Obviously the shaman-aristocrats of the court were the instigators and propogators of a quasi-religious system of beliefs – resembling the early Greek, Roman and German mythologies that replaced the shamanism of prehistoric Europe – which represented a higher order of spiritual conviction than shamanism itself. States depending on feudal relationships were welded together not just by the weapons of the military retinues which attended the overlord, but equally by psychological factors sanctified by the court shamans. [pp. 386-387]

GYULA MORAVCSIK
Byzantinische Mission im Kreize der Türkvölker an der Nordküste des Schwarzen Meeres,
Oxford, 1966.

Newly converted peoples were allowed to use their own mother-tongue in church rituals and in the liturgy, and it was entrusted to the missionaries to translate the Holy Scriptures into all the various languages. St John Chrysostom speaks of translating the Bible into barbarian tongues. From St Jerome's information that the Huns were learning psalms it can be deduced that they were translated into the Hun language. According to trustworthy sources a Hunnic-language translation was produced for the Huns (= Sabirs) who lived to the north of the Caucasus. In his dispute with the Roman priests, Constantine (Cyril) lists among the peoples who were able to praise God in their own tongue, for example, the Avars, Turks and Khazars. [p. 14]

ISTVÁN DIENES
'A honfoglaló magyarok lélekhiedelmei'
[Spiritual beliefs of the Conquest-era Magyars].
In: Régészeti barangolások Magyarországon
[Archaeological excursions in Hungary],
ed. V. Szombathy. Budapest,1978.

By way of introduction, let it be said straight away that the notion of a 'shadow-soul', or free soul as scholars call it, is a far from primitive concept; it lies much closer in its essence to belief in an abstract soul than one might think. Whilst the medieval Christian view of the world might be said to be 'naive', because it still proclaimed the classical Earth-centred, Ptolemaic cosmology, one would not go so far as to call the great philosophers of the Classical and Middle Ages 'primitive' simply because in those more remote times they did not have the appropriate instrumentation to discover certain regularities of the natural sciences. It should come as no surprise, then, if our pagan forefathers, too, thought of the world as a flat disk, or spoke about three levels of the Universe (i.e. an upper domain of the gods, glittering with gold, our own Earth in the centre, and a dark, forbidding underworld), and believed that the heavens were held up by a column at the centre of the world, etc. All these things pertain to their beliefs in just the same way as the faith they invested in a supreme being, the celestial God. It may well be that the idea of a 'shadow-soul' was rooted somewhere amongst shamanistic notions which stretch back to a common Finno-Ugrian past, but this does not mean that it necessarily disappeared from the ancient pagan religion, much more advanced though it may have been than the prehistoric shamanism, for there were still many things that they would only have been able to comprehend in the traditional ways. Furthermore, this distinctive concept of souls forms part of a coherent system of beliefs by which man's purpose in life could be rationalized. The notion of a shadow-soul and its 'soulbird', which took to flight from the east at dawn, was in those days used to explain man's birth on this Earth. Arriving from afar, from his clan's Tree-of-Life or the spirits of the ancestors, the soul dwelt in his body throughout his life; loss of the soul was the cause of his illnesses and, eventually, his death. According to this faith, however, mortal beings did not pass away once and for all, since it was precisely a belief in the soul's departure from the lifeless body, and its migration to an otherworld that lay far to the west, which fostered hope of an existence in the afterlife. As we can see, therefore, one should not read 'ancient' as implying a primitive concept. In those days, man was not able to interpret the Universe, and his own place within it, in any better or more convincing way, so that these highly rational and plausible articles of faith would have been able to endure and, even if they changed somewhat in the course of time, become an integral part of the ancient Magyar religion. [pp. 174-175]

I end this section with two examples from the work of the types of writer that one might term "enthusiasts" or "Romantics".

ŐSI GYÖKÉR
[Ancient Roots], ed. Ferenc Jós Badiny, May-June 1978 issue, Buenos Aires.

Indeed, according to the founder of the Hungarian state, **our Priest-King Árpád the Great** and his **Celestial Emissary, the Turul**, the eagle on the silver disk from Rakamaz is acknowledged to be an ancient depiction of our **Turul Legend**. I think it probable that Our Lord Jesus regarded **Árpád** – the **Celestial Emissary** of the Árpádian Magyar People, the followers and preservers of the true and pure faith in Jesus – as his Celestially Called successor, and **Árpád** (Ar-Bad) was also the name of Jesus which his believers used in their prayers. [p. 72]

The article was published under the pseudonym "Patesi" and thus was written by the journal's editor.

ALBERT FEJÉR (ed.)
Arvisurák
[The Arvisuras],
King City, 1980.

Under the rubric "The rune of Arvisura, Nagybodor and Galga: the Kavar Conquest":

Kavar warriors arriving from the apple-blossom festival raised a complaint against Álmos and demanded that the laws of the Arvisura be enforced against him. The grand duke thereupon resigned from all his offices. Since Gyula could not bring an action against his own father in the Council of Elders, Álmos was executed at daybreak on the basis of the law of the Kavars from Lóbérc. Three days later he was taken by relays of horses to the land of the Kavars and, in denunciation of his crimes, they placed the grand duke belly-downwards in his coffin lest any complaint should be raised against them by the powers above. The site of the grave was pointed out to Duke Verecke, but he declared a burial mound (kurgan) of the shaman Zemplén at Abaújvár as the shrine, though he built a penitents' shrine on the grave... Árpád mentioned in his report to Duke Tárkány that the more stockily built Kavar horses made the journey without any losses. [p. 169]

The Magyar "Raids" in the West

One of the most significant new contributions to this controversial area of Hungarian history is that of Szabolcs Vajay (see page ...).

GYÖRGY GYÖRFFY
'A kalandozások kora.
1. Zsákmányoló és adóztató hadjáratok'
[The age of the raids,
1. Expeditions of plunder and tribute].
In: Magyarország Története [History of Hungary], Vol. I/I, ed. A. Bartha, Budapest, 1984, pp. 651-679.

Equally prejudiced, but in the opposite way, is the view of the Magyars as a more primitive people and as destroyers of civilization, which sees in these expeditions nothing other than opportunistic pillage and devastation, involving all nomad menfolk, whereas similar campaigns by other, more advanced peoples, since they were not barbarians, are judged by different criteria. However, tenth-century Europe was less tempted to make distinctions between one kind of destruction and another. Thus Ruotger, commenting in the middle of the century on Henry the Fowler's accession to the throne, writes: 'Whilst here there was the wild Danish people, ruling dry land and seas, there from a hundred sides rose the gnashing of teeth of the barbarian Slavs in their fury, and, not least, the ruthlessness of the vengeful Magyars, violating the borders of the Moravians whose empire they had not long before expropriated with savage intemperance, putting the length and breadth of the territory to fire and the sword.' However, Ruotger here overlooked the fact that the Moravians themselves had earlier ravaged neighbouring provinces just as their Frankish enemies had done in Moravia, or Christian powers, using Magyar mercenaries, had done in other countries. The chief difference between the raids of the Magyars and those of other peoples lay in the fact that the Magyars had a much larger cavalry than others, and their horsemen were able to mount surprise attacks over ten times the distance that their allies could cover, so it was precisely this surplus that made them as feared as Attila's Huns or the Viking and Arab sea-raiders.

It is also questionable to what degree it is permissible to read a Finno-Ugrian-Magyar military involvement into the wars of the heterogeneous Magyar tribal confederation. Bearing in mind that it was precisely in the warrior strata that Turkic and Iranian elements were more prominently represented, and that there are extant references to Slav brothers-in-arms alongside them, it is plainly not possible to look on the raiders and judge them by modern linguistic notions of national identity.

Finally, we must also deal with the historical-economic approach which explained the raids as resulting from a crisis in pastoral society. In this view, the Magyars' nomadic pastoral society was confined within a smaller territory after the Conquest: consequently the free herdsmen who were displaced from farming turned to pillaging raids as a means of creating a livelihood for themselves, primarily by putting prisoners to work on their lands as serfs. This explanation lost its rationale, however, when it became clear that the commoner stratum of the Conquest-era

Magyars were semi-nomads who also tilled the soil, whilst the bulk of the warriors, who would be absent on raids during the growing season, were drawn from the middle stratum. Also conflicting with the 'crisis' theory are the facts that raiding expeditions had also taken place before the Conquest, whilst the Norse and the Russians had unleashed similar actions against Khazar, Volga Bulgar and Byzantine centres. At the same time, observation of living nomadic peoples teaches us that nomads who lose their pasture-lands and animals sink to the bottom of society, becoming peasants on the estates of the wealthy, whilst only a part of the warriors become soldiers in the retinue of the new master. The extent to which prisoners became workers on the land, or servants and artisans at the courts of the leaders, or were sold off as slaves is something that archaeological and anthropological researches of the future may be able to clarify. One thing that is known, however, is that from the 920s onwards warriors who took part in the raids preferred to exchange prisoners for other valuables whilst they were still outside Hungary, rather than bring them back home.

If historical and archaeological investigations have led to the conclusion that it was primarily the middle stratum which took part in the raids, whilst an important contribution can also be demonstrated from Kavars led by Magyar dukes, then a change in the mode of production of the middle stratum could not have been directly related to an increase or cessation of raiding activity. The sources which throw accurate light on the circumstances of the incursions show, if anything, that as great a role in precipitating such actions as any combative disposition on the part of the Magyar warriors was played by the initiatives of various European powers, who were willing to exploit Magyar light cavalry against their enemies in the same way as the Byzantines used their Scythian neighbours in the same way throughout their thousand-year history.

After the Conquest had taken place there was merely a slight change from the older pattern in the profile of the allies who sought to use the Magyars. Just as the Magyars had formerly 'fought together with the Khazars' in all their wars, and just as requests for campaigns up until 900 had come from Bulgars, Byzantines, Moravians and Franks, now, after they had settled into their new surroundings, similar proposals came more commonly from Italy, the Carolingian faction in France, the Bavarians, western Slavs, Russians and Bulgars as well as the Byzantines. [pp. 652-653]

ERIK MOLNÁR
A magyar társadalom története az őskortól az Árpád-korig
[Magyar social history from prehistoric times to the Árpádian era],
2nd ed., Budapest, 1949.

Even if we put the Magyar population who took part in the Conquest at only 160,000... the 30,000 square kilometres of land which passed into clan ownership would not have been able to provide a decent livelihood for 120,000 pastoral nomads. [p. 117-118]

An improvement in productive forces – the switch to plough-farming as a means of production, or at least a significant expansion of agriculture would have been able to lead the Magyar people out of the crisis. However, the herdsman, used as he is to the easy work of extensive animal husbandry, does not make the changeover to the heavy toil of tilling the land as long as there are other possibilities. [p. 116]

The plundering campaigns of a nomadic people do not call for closer explanation... The raid for booty is one of the standard stratagems in the lives of pastoral societies... But raiding wars were unable to overcome the crisis.

EMMA LEDERER
'A feudális viszonyok fejlődése
(A honfoglalástól az államalapításig)'
[The emergence of feudal relations
(From the Conquest to the foundation of the state)].
In: Magyarország története. I. Az őskortól 1526-ig
[History of Hungary. I. From prehistorical times to 1526], eds. L. Elekes,
E. Lederer & Gy. Székely, Budapest, 1961, pp. 39-67.

Under the heading of 'Crisis in pastoral society': ... the occupied territories proved to be extremely confined, especially when we recall that a large part of the land had already been put to the plough by Slav peasants... Middle-ranking Magyar herders thus saw raiding wars as a way out of their crisis. These wars hastened the complete breakdown of the clan society and the emergence of class relations... [p. 48]

In describing the 'raids' we must take as our starting point the already-mentioned Engelsian thesis [*The Origin of the Family, Private Property and the State*] of a society in which 'War... was carried on for the sake of pure pillage'. [p. 50]

The Magyars at the head of the raids were not army commanders in any 'national' sense but the leaders of booty-seeking campaigns that served their own interests. [p. 52]

In peacetime, with no raiding wars, the masters still endeavoured to keep their permanent military retinues and to perpetuate their existence as guarantees of their power... Posts in the military retinues were taken up by free herdsmen who were no longer productive and whose only chance of a livelihood was the security that a lord could provide. [p. 55]

SZABOLCS DE VAJAY
Der Eintritt des ungarischen Stämmebundes
in die europäische Geschichte (862-933),
Mainz, 1968.

It can now be taken as proven that the Hungarian raids were not just 'incursions by barbarian hordes'. Initially, they were strategic operations, often of a defensive nature, but later on they became military ventures with *European* implications. The Hungarian troops were not only well organized and equipped but were also superbly disciplined: they never devastated territories of their allies and they took care at all times to comply with the obligations of their treaties.

The second and third periods in the history of the Hungarian raids present, by and large, a similar picture, even if from 940 onwards military discipline became increasingly lax, leading ultimately to the decisive defeat at Lechfeld in 955... [p. 81]

... the military ventures of the Hungarians were not arbitrary expeditions of looting and pillage but previously well thought-out strategic operations that were often of European significance and of great moment...

The formal diplomatic relations which existed between the Hungarians and some German princes, the kings of Italy, and the tribes of the Dalmatians and Bohemians have long been known... The author believes that... the existence of such diplomatic relations can also be demonstrated with supporters of the Caroligians, in their struggle against the rebellious Robertines.

The central political line followed by the Hungarians in all their alliances always reveals a logical plan. In all their agreements they strove to secure peace in one direction in order to leave themselves with a free hand on another side... To corroborate this, it is enough to draw attention to the Hungarians' first western alliance with the Moravian Princes Ratislav and Svatopluk (862-863, 880-889), the treaty with the East Roman Emperor, Leo VI (894-895), the alliance with Emperor Arnulf (892-899), the agreement on peace and aid with Berengar of Italy (902-924), the alliance with Arnulf of Bavaria (913-921), the alliance with the Carolingian Franks (917-926), and the truce with the German king (926-933), which was soon extended, with the annexation of Swabia (926) and Bavaria (927), into an imperial treaty. [pp. 82-83]

KORNÉL BAKAY
A magyar államalapítás
[The foundation of the Hungarian state],
Budapest, 1978.

Over seven decades from the end of the ninth century, the Magyars conducted more than 40 campaigns against the countries of Central, West and South Europe. In the course of these raids they took away untold amounts of booty. In this respect it is not unwarranted, within limits, to call these forays marauding ventures. Italy, Bavaria, Moravia, Saxony, the Frankish Empire, Thuringia, Bulgaria and Byzantium were held to ransom; as Simon Kézai relates in his chronicle, 'The Hungarians... right up to the time of Duke Géza menaced and held the world to ransom, first here, then there'. [p. 27]

No other people, apart from the Arabs and Vikings, carried out military operations on such a vast scale... The thought that these were not uncoordinated, chance forays did present itself in bourgeois history-writing. The same conclusion has been reached more recently after extremely careful analysis of the sources. I also tend to the view that the raiding campaigns should be seen as having had a definite purpose. Once the data have been arranged into an overall picture, it truly does appear that, almost without exception, the Magyars only made raids on West Europe at the request of western rulers or potentates who were striving for domination. Thus, directly or indirectly, they had a hand in the fact that no strong central authority emerged during the first half of the tenth century in Italy, France or the the German Kingdom. At that time the Magyar principality would in no way have been able to withstand a strong, militarily united power. The proof of this can be seen in the defeats suffered at Merseburg in 933 and at Augsburg in 955. [pp. 30-31]

LAJOS TARDY
Kis magyar történetek
[Short stories about the Magyars], Budapest, 1986.

… The Magyar population which took up its abode in Pannonia was depleted not only by continual battle losses but also by those who fell captive to soldiers of the peoples and towns that were attacked in these wars, or those who broke their ties for any other reason. In accordance with the practice of the time, sanctified by age-old custom (one could almost say unwritten law), starting as serfs, then, in their son's or grandson's generation, becoming freemen, they were gradually assimilated into the population of the lands through which they had originally marched with far from peaceful intentions or where they had fallen into captivity.

Researchers into demographic trends among the Magyars have not devoted much attention to this phenomenon, although the outlines of the problem do emerge in one of Károly Czeglédy's studies, where he acquaints his readers with a contemporary account of Abu-Marvan ibn Haijan, one of the famous personages of tenth-century Moorish historical writing. According to this source, prior to their attack on northern Spain in 942, the Magyars passed through Lombardy. 'An envoy sent from Zaragoza by Muhammed ibn Hassim, the lord of the city, arrived with Magyar prisoners, who were led before the caliph. The caliph looked them over, the Magyars were then converted to Islam and ended up in the caliph's guard '… The forced conscription of Magyar raiders who were taken prisoner must have been fairly widespread… for instance, a contingent of Magyars who were captured in the 934 campaign were sent by Emperor Romanos to Lombardy for military service… [p. 5]

Folk Memories and Poetry

ZSIGMOND SZENDREY
'Történeti népmondák'
[Historical folk legends].
Ethnographia, XXI (1923), 46-47.

l. Milota (Szabolcs-Szatmár County). When the Magyars arrived in Poland, the king there was Terebes. Árpád's son was called Béla, whilst Terebes' daughter was called Milota. The two youngsters began to think of marriage as soon as they saw one another. But they could not be together for the time being because the country [Hungary] had to be occupied first of all, and so they parted from one another. When the Magyars reached Hungary, Béla stayed here to maintain law and order whilst Árpád moved on with the army. Béla had a great deal of trouble with the leader of the Slovaks, who harboured a grudge against him because, amongst other things, he too wanted to have Milota as his wife. Once, when Béla had set off to see his lover again, the Slovak leader attacked him with a large company of troops and captured him. The Magyars tried in vain to set Béla free but they were unable to discover where he was concealed. The leader of the Slovaks sent them a message that he would release Béla if Milota would marry him; otherwise he would rather kill the prince and himself too. What else could Milota do but become the wife of the Slovak leader? But the wily Slovak still did not let the prince go because he was fearful of his vengeance. But both Milota and the Magyars kept on seraching until they hit upon his hiding-place. The warriors freed Béla and he straight away took up his sword in order to seek his revenge. At that very moment Milota, who had disguised herself as a Slovak soldier to set her lover free, came up to him. But Béla did not recognize her in the soldier's uniform and before she could utter a word he ran her through with his sword. Only now did the prince recognize the girl from her voice, but it was already too late to help matters. He buried her on the spot where she had died and he himself settled down to live there. A community sprang up around the prince's dwelling and that is how the village of Milota came into being.

2. Borchalom (Olcsvaapáti, Szabolcs-Szatmár County). Whenever Árpád captured a large piece of land, he himself would continue to press on with the army whilst leaving behind a few thousand men and one of his chiefs to keep law and order among the population. In this region it was a certain Borc who was made the chief. Now Borc had no liking at all for peace and quiet because he wanted to be away fighting along with the other chiefs. But Árpád had decided upon this because he was tired of listening to the old man's moaning and groaning. Borc was always saying that they should never have left their old homeland because that was against God's will, as He had not given them the land for them to abandon it. He said that the better things went for the Magyars, the greater would be the price they would have to pay one of these days; so whenever he heard about the successes of the Magyars, he would just shake his head. Now when they brought Borc the news that the whole of the country was now Árpád's, he became extremely sad and troubled at heart. He sensed that something extremely unpleasant would have to happen and, as he did not want to stay around to see this, he had himself buried by his faithful retainers in a hill. This is why, to this day, the hill is called Borchalom ['Borc's mound']. But Borc will not stay there forever because he will reappear when the fate of the Magyars changes permanently for the better. And that is why all will not be well with the world until the side of Borchalom opens up.

3. Hadad (= modern Hodod, Romania; former Szilágy County, Transylvania). When the Magyars came into Hungary, Árpád picked his bravest men and sent them with his wiliest chiefs to the fortress of Bihar. In this castle there lived a Saracen king who was such a doughty warrior and well-tested man that not one opponent had ever succeeded in defeating him up till then. The hand-

picked company started on its way and when they arrived in the area they pitched their camp next to a great marsh. One of the officers advised their commander that he should not take his family and the other womenfolk with them right up to the walls of Bihar because there was no knowing how things would turn out with the cunning Saracen king. So the commander asked what he should do with them. '*Hadd ott*! Leave them there!' said the officer, pointing to the marsh. And that was what he did. Then, when they had captured Bihar, the commander had a fortress built in the marshes and moved into it. That is how this community got the name Hadad.

4. Ad, Balla, Mocsolya (former Szilágy County, Transylvania). Od, Balla and Mocsolya were among the valiant warriors who were highly valued by Árpád. When they were dividing up the country and all the leaders were being given their own properties, these three also went up to Árpád to ask him for land. Their request was granted and the land around here was given to them. But at that time the lord of this region was a very powerful king, and however valiantly they fought, there was no way they could be a match for the king's great number of soldiers, what were they to do? They learned that the king had three beautiful daughters so, since there were three of them, they asked for the hands of the three daughters in marriage. Since the king did not have any objection, because he was allowed to remain the lord until he died, and the daughters were not averse to the three celebrated heroes, they were soon able to reach agreement.

5. Kokodvár (Parasznya, Szatmár County; now Borsod-Abaúj-Zemplén County). Our old people were told by the oldsters of their day that a company of pagan Magyar troops is sleeping in this hill. They did not want to accept the new religion and preferred to be buried alive there and wait until the life of the Magyars once again becomes free. Then they will awaken and come out from the hill, but until then they continue to slumber there. [pp. 46-47]

DÁNIEL BERZSENYI
To the Hungarians

… Raise up your dormant national spirit!
Let hurricane howl, a thousand dangers come:
I fear not. The horn's clarion-call,
The prancing flight of whinnying horses,

Bravely will I watch. No hosts needed, only
Spirit, and free peoples can do wondrous deeds.
That is what made Rome lord of all the world,
And Marathon and Buda's castle famous.

FERENC KÖLCSEY
National Anthem

(excerpt)

Peaks of high Carpathian hills
Thou didst give our sires;
Sons of Bedeguz receiv'd
Thus their fair hearth-fires;
Where the waves of Tisza glide,
Where the Danube rages,
Valiant seed of Árpád grew,
Flourish'd through the ages.

[trans W. Kirkconnell, *The Magyar Muse*,
Winnipeg, 1933]

MIHÁLY VÖRÖSMARTY
The Flight of Zalán

(excerpt from the Prologue)

Ancient glory of ours, where are you lost in the mist of night
Centuries have gone by, and you, with slowly expiring light
Deep beneath them, walk alone. Over you dense clouds
                              drift on
And the unwreathed form of melancholy forgetfulness.
Where is he who, loosening his bold lips to the martial
                              song,
Shall rouse with his words the clarion call of the
                              abyssmal depths,

And after the centuries' delay shall conjure up for us
Leopard-skinned Árpád, the might of his people, slayers
                              of armies?
Where is he? Oh! In thousands they turn away silent:
                              a dream
Butchers their hearts, and with them aslumber the
                              ancient glory.

....

I feel a certainty of strength; swelling within my breast
Fantasies that display the sight of Ügek in his triumph,
And of the graceful hero Álmos, and Álmos' lordly son,
Árpád of the leopard-skin …

SÁNDOR PETŐFI
Lehel …

…He the hero, and this his horn!… This hero's
Death provoked the very skies to commote.
Nine hundred years gone, and the rumbling now
Finds its echo in the song of my lute.
You Jászians and you Cumans, listen to this
Because, I believe, he will interest thee
Most vitally, he, and his horn-blowing feats,
Lehel, the shiverer of countries he.

JÁNOS ARANY
The Death of King Buda

(excerpt from Canto 5)

Meanwhile the minstrel's lute sounds sweet and long,
Bringing, for memory's sake, an ancient story:
Of Hunor and of Magyar speaks the song,
Forebears whom Hun and Magyar claim with glory.

    How from old Asia, their far home (it sings)
    They set out, through a miracle of Heaven,
    Chasing a hind, and in their wanderings
    Coming to Scythia, two tribes' rich leaven.

(excerpt from Canto 6)

    The bird flies on from bough to bough;
    The song is pass'd from lip to lip;
    Green grass grows o'er old heroes now,
    But song revives their fellowship.

    Forth to hunt they ride again,
    The brave sons that fair Enéh bore,
    Hunor and Magyar, champions twain,
    Ménrót's twin sons in days of yore.

[trans. W. Kirkconnell, *The Death of King Buda*,
Cleveland, 1936]

ENDRE ADY
I am the Son of Gog and Magog

Son of Gog and Magog – that's me.
In vain I hammer on doors and walls
And yet I would still ask of you:
Is it right to cry beneath Carpathian hills?

By Verecke's historic route I came,
In my ear ancient Magyar songs still blaze,
Am I free to break through at Dévény
With modern songs fit for modern days?

Into my ear pour boiling hot lead
So I can be the new, singing Vazul,
And so I don't have to hear life's new songs,
Trample me down roughly, evilly.

Yet till then, crying, in pain, waiting nothing,
On new wings the song nevertheless soars
And if it receives a hundred curses,
It's still triumphant, still new and Magyar.

PÉTER VERES
Bölcs és balgatag őseink
[Our wise and foolish ancestors]
Budapest, 1968.

"… Knowing how the herdsman's mind works, there was no sense in going on any further than Hungary. Indeed, even within the country there was no sense in wandering about here and there onto distant lands, because there was enough for the livestock to eat even during the summer. Pastoral peoples became used to being continually on the move only because their livestock took them. And livestock are driven on in their search for better pastures, or even just for fresher, greener grass, by their stomachs, the insatiable rumens of grazing animals.

They did not have to be always on the move because Mediterranean cyclones arrived here from the south and south-west, and Atlantic rain-clouds from the west, to continually renew meadows that had withered and run to seed, dried-out or been grazed to the ground after each spring's sprouting. And even if now and then, once or twice in ten years, there was a drought during the summer, livestock still managed to survive on the parched areas around rivers and streams, and livestock still managed to survive on the sour grasses of discharges, inland waters and undrained lakes. And sour grasslands like this could be found even on the harder, more alkaline soils of the Tiszántúl or the sands of Szabolcs and the interfluvial region between the Danube and Tisza. It was not so good to eat, and the livestock could not be fattened or give milk as they could with sweet grass or flowery meadows, but they did not perish from starvation and did not even lose condition in the way that they had done over there, on the parched and rainless Eurasian steppes.

The winters, too, were milder and shorter here; livestock that had been reared for the rigours of the climate over there must have thought themselves in paradise here, as one can detect from the texts and tone of the Hungarian chronicles and even from our legends ('grass, water'). The conquerors must have thought, first and foremost, in the way that herdsmen think, though the Magyars were not just made up of herders. They also had their lords, soldiers, craftsmen and farmers, but as the chronicles attest, and as the herdsmen's logic and the traditions that they brought with them, and even the laws of the first kings (payment in young bullocks), show, that was the dominant point of view at the beginning." [pp. 27-28]

ÁRPÁD TÓTH
In a Tavern at Aquincum

Barman, old Swabian! Bring me a glass of heady wine,
Cool as evening breeze outside, from sorrow dun-yellow.
Bring brimming beakers to the table, old fellow,
Let me sit out this lonely, lordly feast in silence.

Sit down and let's clink glasses, let the cunning blue,
Deep in those beady Germanic eyes, dwindle away,
Ancestral brother, dreamy Swabe – Don't you feel it, say?
One has to cry. See how Aquincum's stones bury us, too!

Raise your glass, drink! To whom? – A toast to that dead
                                                    lass,
Long ago now, who floated here in heated bath-house,
Lapped by gentle wavelets, whilst on her flaxen tresses
The mournful sunlight of declining Rome sank fast.

Oh, is there any other place where the idle
Golden sun can expire and glory decline this way?
The happy, brash forebears of how many peoples, say,
Were sombrely embraced by Aquincum's crepuscule?

Let's raise glasses to one, a bronzed, subdued horseman.
He stopped by the river at dusk, gazed at trees that bled,
He knew not why. His heart with mourning infiltrated,
Like twilight's dew on breastplate of gleaming iron.

Around here, on these pavements, tent-domes did
                                                    sprout like
Big, clumsy bubbles in the tide of the migrations.
They have long since exploded without trace or issue.
But that dark horseman may have been a forebear of mine.

Your glass, old Swabian! Aquincum's evening sparkles.
A declining folk's son watches as the sun falls. Drink!
This was ever the game, comedy eternal,
Let fresher races search out the cheerful fires of a new dawn.

Your glass!… We can still drain with ease the mournful cup,
Drink to that alien girl to come, in distant future,
Who will lie down here for her nuptials, and on the tombs
Of mad, orphaned peoples conceive her care-free brood…

GYULA ILLYÉS
Árpád

A people that had scarce seen even a knoll,
Yet here before them peaks steeple to the sky!
First rain and now – October's end – a snowy mire;
Icy ground slips under hooves of startled horses.

No path to follow, only the white drifts
Piled up in mountain pass; no beaten track, nor step,
Wheels, not made for rocky river-beds, break up,
Draught oxen, used to gentle plains, slide and slip.

But no time to think: move on, whate'er the fate!
A troop of Pechenegs and vengeful Bulgars
Just yesterday picked up the trail not far.
Onward! Up! Get across, whatever waits!

Barely a woman, hardly any chatter;
Vengeance does not fuss who it accosts.
No old ones either. Everything was lost
That once united: judge, soothsayer, priest, altar.

Old widowers and orphans in straggling line:
Are these enough for the Magyars to survive?
These wept for their mothers, those for their wives
As the bedraggled host reached the first incline.

Only now did their predicament hit home.
No prospect, but one step wrong and – dark abyss.
Fog around, a future of hopelessness.
Their dead left where they fell, naked earth their tomb,

For even here they could not stop and rest.
What of the nation? Best, perhaps, scatter to the winds,
Let each one take wretched fate in his own hands.
Ukkó might drive his Pechenegs with less zest

If he could not strike one blow at the whole tribe.
"Let the last of King Attila's kith and kin
Fly where they can, like tree struck by lightning"
Was the thought to which hearts and minds subscribed.

And their leader, too. Why so stern and speechless?
For Árpád let no word pass as, reining back
His pony mount, his feet almost touching ground,
He wheeled away from the precipice.

For him the burden of planning had begun.
What were his thoughts as alone he rode,
His wild-cat's eyes veiled as the effort showed
Of focussing his mind on what should be done?

If 'what-will-be-will-be' were not a disaster,
Perhaps they could return to the land they had left.
But there – perpetual bondage they could expect,
For there's none so cruel as brother-turned-master.

But if they pressed on and crossed this pass,
What would become of these widows and orphans
Faced with a world of total strangers? A generation
That would look back on itself as aliens.

New homes and new wives for survivors, it's true.
Yet good as the wives might be to the men,
The children they bore would have alien features;
Half-castes at first, but that would not continue.

The slant of their lynx-eyes would soon smooth away,
Their skin slowly lose its yellow-gold lustre,
As Latin and Slav and Germanic mothers
Showered love on their infants in tenderest play.

The better the stock of the brides-to-be,
The deeper the graves that their wombs would present;
For, make no mistake, the beaming content
Of Mongol glee, the eye-fire of Huns would flee,

And all the other traits, heart-warming signs,
With which each infant would always call to mind
The memory of your honoured dead father
As he swore eternal life for his tribe!

But to live with heart stripped bare, what then?
Abandoning body and soul – because
The old God likewise looks after his own.
What, then, is left? What do we get in return?

These are the things that gave cause to ponder,
Though he left them unsaid in the depths of his shame,
Till Árpád grasped that life still had an aim,
Even were body and soul the price of surrender.

'Whatever it takes,' was the still unsaid thought,
'We shall be free' – and this a sentiment
More of the heart than clear in his head
As he spurred his pony to a gallop.

Then, mounting a rock by the straggling throng,
He waved them on. Hurry! With eyes flickering over
Familiar faces, like a shepherd with his ewes,
As into Europe his people pushed on.

GYULA JUHÁSZ
Emese's Dream

In the depths of an Asian tent
On a night of Asian nights,
Under a falling meteor's light
By waters of the Don she dreamt.

Our fair mother, mother of fates,
She dreamt in fevered restlessness,
Shuddering from an evil spell
That a dark Asian night mediated.

Near to her heart, what was to come;
Deep in her soul, primal forest,
Stretching to the far occident,
And never infertile its womb.

She dreamt and she saw with great zest,
From her loins, flowing far and wide,
Gushed an overpowering tide,
Which sped to melancholy West.

Proud armies its flood cannot withstand,
Are swept away triumphantly;
Old Turul hovers patiently,
Its wings stretched in guardian span.

Ever deeper, deeper the sleep,
More frightful and dark the dream,
Bloody gore swells the ancient stream;
In it sky-high dams of slaves are heaped.

Dream, Oh! dream, Oh! fecund dream,
On that far-away Asian land,
When will you find your happy end,
Oh! mother-dream of Emese?

Printed in Hungary, 1999
Dürer Printing House, Gyula